Prehistory in Peril

Artist's conception of a Basketmaker II habitation such as once existed in the Falls
Creek rock shelters.

PREHISTORY IN PERIL

The Worst and Best
of Durango Archaeology

by

FLORENCE C. LISTER

UNIVERSITY PRESS OF COLORADO

Copyright © 1997 by the University Press of Colorado

Published by the University Press of Colorado
P.O. Box 849
Niwot, Colorado 80544
(303) 530-5337

The University Press of Colorado is a cooperative publishing enterprise supported, in part, by Adams State College, Colorado State University, Fort Lewis College, Mesa State College, Metropolitan State College of Denver, University of Colorado, University of Northern Colorado, University of Southern Colorado, and Western State College of Colorado.

The paper used in this publication meets the minimum requirements of the American National Standard for Information Sciences–Permanence of Paper for Printed Library Materials. ANSI Z39.48-1984.

Library of Congress Cataloging-in-Publication Data

Lister, Florence Cline.
    Prehistory in peril: the worst and the best of Durango archaeology / Florence C. Lister.
        p.   cm.
    Includes bibliographical references and index.
    ISBN 0-87081-443-5 (cloth: alk. paper). – ISBN 0-87081-448-6 (pbk.: alk. paper)
    1. Pueblo Indians – Antiquities.   2. Excavations (Archaeology) – Colorado – Durango Region – History.   3. Archaeology – Southwest, New – History.   4. Durango Region (Colo.) – Antiquities.   I. Title.
    E99.P9L519   1997
    978.8'2901 – dc21   96-53288
                                                                     CIP

        10   9   8   7   6   5   4   3   2   1

Contents

Figures and Maps

FIGURES

MAPS

Acknowledgments

The archivists and archaeologists who so generously provided time and advice on this project are too many to name individually. Each has been sincerely thanked personally. However, particular acknowledgments are due Karen Adams, David Breternitz, Charles Brockway, William Buckles, Nancy and Laurens Hammack, Gary Matlock, Shirley Powell, William Robinson, John Sanders, and R. Gwinn Vivian for loan of background materials. Line drawings were executed by Nancy B. Lamm, and some photographs were provided by Ernest Cotton and Garth Buchanan. The staff of the University of Colorado Museum kindly selected a corn sample from their collections of Falls Creek rock shelter materials for dating, the results of which are significant in studies of the adoption of agriculture by the early peoples in the northern periphery of the ancestral Pueblo world. Funding by the Colorado Historical Society through the Friends of the Falls Creek Rock Shelters and by the San Juan–Rio Grande National Forest is gratefully acknowledged. A very special thanks is extended to Ian "Sandy" Thompson and William Lipe for critiquing the draft manuscript. Their help and encouragement were invaluable.

Introduction

This book has two focuses. One is the history of the archaeological discoveries in the upper Animas River district of southern Colorado, the center of which is the modern city of Durango. Of special interest are two alcoves in a cliff just north of town where particularly important finds were made. The other subject is the prehistoric cultural pattern revealed in the area. The history mirrors an important formative period in the discipline of Southwestern archaeology that in this instance took bizarre turns. The prehistory is that of an early variant culture distinctive in some respects from known contemporary expressions that now, a half century after its original verification, merits reconsideration.

The years between the two world wars represented the adolescence of Southwestern archaeology. As in human pubescence, the era was characterized by exuberance, turmoil, and lack of self-discipline. Collecting frenzy, casual or no documentation, personality clashes, and a headlong rush to unfounded conclusions were its growing pains. Such was the archaeology of the upper Animas district in the 1930s and 1940s, whose repercussions would be felt for decades.

It was in the early period of Southwestern archaeology that a few men with means but no formal, applicable training embarked on prehistorical research and subsidized publication of their personal ideas. These were also the glory days of pot-hunting, when others without academic credentials—but with strong backs, a sense of curiosity, and sometimes the prospect of turning a profit—tackled ancient ruins with shovels and trowels all across the 100,000-square-mile Colorado Plateau of Colorado, Utah, Arizona, and New Mexico. Because professional archaeologists actively working in the Southwest were still relatively few, both the dilettante-patron and the amateur digger often proved valuable allies in unraveling the past. All three interested groups came together in the upper Animas district, where an adversarial climate sometimes pitted professionals and nonprofessionals against each other. No other branch of science had to cope with the threat of so many interested but unqualified enthusiasts.

In the Durango region an ingredient that added to the volatile mix of amateurism and professionalism was a small-town press eager to recount local prehistory–and the activities of those involved–but frequently uncritical in doing so. Unwittingly, these reporters contributed to the breakdown of the investigative alliance into a seemingly endless saga of misunderstanding, acrimony, complicity, and outright ridiculousness that to some extent overshadowed the important research results.

It took twenty-five years for the decades of divisiveness and destruction described here to give way to more rational perspectives. In the interim, the ranks of both professionals and nonprofessionals burgeoned and their participation in the science was more sharply defined. Both fieldwork and analysis fell into the hands of individuals academically and technically well versed in an array of sophisticated techniques. There remained no room for the amateur digger unless he or she operated in consultation with a professional, followed set standard procedures, and published the results of the inquiry.

At present there is recognition among archaeologists that public education about the goals of archaeology is vital in obtaining support for preservation of our national patrimony and that, through taxation, the general public indirectly foots the bill for most of the work. Scientists give generously of their time in presenting their research through lectures and nontechnical articles and books, serving in advisory capacities for related endeavors, and leading excursions to interpret sites of interest. They aim to alert citizens to the value of preservation and to the Archaeological Resources Protection Act of 1979, with its stiff penalties for vandalism and looting of sites.

Another change taking place in the study of prehistory is being wrought by a component of the cultural mosaic that all too frequently has been ignored: the natives whose ancestral heritage constitutes the bedrock of American archaeology. Activists in this group rightfully point out that for the century that white men and women have intruded into their old world, the treatment of the Indian dead has been disrespectful. The period upon which this book primarily focuses exemplified the cavalier, even racist, attitudes of diggers toward the burials they purposefully sought out or encountered by chance. For the amateurs, the admitted attraction of burials was the complete objects they often contained; the human bones were merely extra baggage to cart away and eventually discard. For the archaeologists, one hopes that the cultural evidence and physical anthropological information found in graves were of primary importance. Nevertheless, burial goods sometimes ended up in personal collections, and unstudied skeletons were warehoused in museums.

The basic problem was the white excavators' lack of understanding of the worldview of the Native Americans, which gave special meaning to the spirits of their departed. In the eyes of many non-Indian diggers, because prehistoric graves were unmarked and often in the midst of household rubbish, they lacked sanctity. Moreover, the prevailing view of the white majority was that the modern Indians were about to disappear into the American melting pot, taking their culture with them, so there was no need to hesitate about robbing graves of which they probably were unaware.

The introduction of modern archaeology to the Durango area during the 1970s coincided with the growing civil rights movement, one aspect of which was a strengthening of Indian identity. That political empowerment gave Native American groups a voice to protest what they saw as Anglo insensitivity toward their dead and certain sacred objects and places. Scientists were put on notice that much of the activity that once took place in the Durango district in the name of archaeology—for example, the exhumation and display of human remains or burial offerings—would no longer be countenanced. Ultimately, in 1990 this undercurrent of resentment culminated in congressional enactment of the Native American Graves Protection and Repatriation Act (NAGPRA), which regulated the excavation of Indian burial sites on federal and tribal lands. One result of this legislation was that regional museums have been required to inventory their collections and must be prepared to relinquish them to whoever can prove cultural affiliation.

Introduction

Those who do not make the pursuit of antiquity a vocation and thus prefer to be called avocational archaeologists have formed the San Juan Basin Archaeological Society, actually the third such organization in the town's history. Membership is open to anyone interested and requires the acceptance of a code of ethics formulated by the state archaeological society that prohibits illegal collecting or sale of artifacts or desecration of burial sites. The overall goal is to learn about the region's long, fascinating past and to enjoy it through taking classes conducted by the state archaeologist in basic survey and laboratory techniques, attending various presentations, and becoming acquainted with the natural and cultural attractions of this special sector of the Southwest.

The San Juan National Forest, within which the Falls Creek rock shelters described in this book are situated, now has staff archaeologists whose tasks include protecting cultural resources from depredation. The rock shelters were added to the National Register of Historic Places in 1985. Through the Trust for Public Lands and the effort of members of the San Juan Basin Archaeological Society, 530 acres of a private ranch were added in 1993 to the San Juan–National Forest holdings to create the Falls Creek Archaeological Area. In addition to affording security for all prehistoric sites in the valley, it also seeks to preserve the scenic riparian setting and the abundant wildlife. Avocational archaeologists assisted in surveys of the cultural resources of this acquisition. Local citizens also have formed a group called Friends of the Falls Creek Rock Shelters to monitor the area and provide guides for weekly tours of the cliffside sites.

To protect, preserve, and enhance the archaeological remains within its jurisdiction, the city of Durango belatedly has enacted its own policing policy. It makes illegal the removal or disturbance of any such materials within the city limits unless proper authorization has been secured in accordance with federal and state laws. Full-time researchers, members of the local archaeological society who have completed training, and archaeology students from Fort Lewis College, where there is now a strong undergraduate Department of Anthropology, are eligible for such permits. Documentation of work and deposit of all retrieved specimens in a reputable museum are required.

Despite these positive efforts, mishaps still occur. Laws and peer pressure do not modify some kinds of human behavior. In a perfect world there would be no professional archaeologists exuding intellectual snobbery, no ruin owners bristling with suspicion about academics who make a living groveling into old rubble, and no rapacious suppliers or collectors flaunting ethical standards by severing gossamer filaments that mesh human cultures into spatial and temporal packages.

The centerpiece prehistory of this region is that of the Basketmakers of the Animas district, who were among the area's earliest inhabitants. During several episodes extending over many centuries, they adapted to a breathtakingly beautiful but demanding environment and then ultimately withdrew. What was once considered the vanguard of these ancient peoples and their material accomplishments was studied by Earl H. Morris in the late 1930s. His report, co-authored with Robert F. Burgh, published in 1954 and long out of print, stands as a landmark piece of scholarship for the times. However, more recent studies both in the immediate area and elsewhere in the Southwest now provide opportunity for reappraisal or broadened interpretation.

Further, during the past several decades considerable archaeological contract work has been done south of Durango that has bearing upon the regional story. Most of the results of these endeavors appear in technical reports presented to the governmental agencies involved and are not readily available for public perusal. A cursory review of this research is therefore appropriate.

Personally, a disconcerting aspect of delivering an unbiased account of seminal Durango area archaeology has been how to present Isaiah Ford "Zeke" Flora, a local amateur who found himself at the heart of a maelstrom. His vitriolic, often irrational, and contradictory pronouncements, manuscripts, and correspondence seemed indicative of emotional and mental disintegration. Although he would have seen it that way, my recounting of the outrageous notions conjured in his tormented mind is not malicious or derisive. Rather, it is partially an indictment against the scholarly few who might have stopped a personal and scientific tragedy had there been greater educational opportunity for amateurs such as Flora. Flora's actions, both positive and negative, were very much a part of the early record of the archaeology of the high country Basketmakers, so we will begin there.

Prehistory in Peril

PART I
Confrontational Archaeology

First Interest

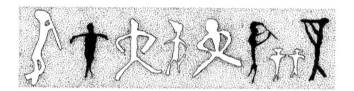

From the time she made her first public appearance, Esther was a sensation. Both those with genuine scientific interest and those with morbid curiosity flocked to the side of this two-thousand-year-old Basketmaker maiden to view her shriveled, earthly remains. The glass box in which she reposed at the Mesa Verde National Park museum was smudged daily with fingerprints of viewers who pressed too close. There were snickers, there were gasps, and for some, there was deeply felt reverence in looking into the unflinching, fleshed face of someone who had lived, labored, and died so long ago. According to some, they could sense her spirit.

Numerous news releases proclaimed her modern name and described her uniqueness. Life-size glossy posters and vividly colored postcards of her bony nakedness and facial grimace filled the racks of local curio shops. To many, she was for thirty years the symbol of regional antiquity. However, as with other more youthful and per-haps less worthy celebrities, fame was fleeting for Esther. When she finally was retired to permanent storage after protests from Native American groups, she quickly was forgotten by a fickle public. Never, however, was she forsaken by Zeke Flora, the man who lifted her from her trashy grave and forever claimed her as his own.

Isaiah Ford "Zeke" Flora, an unemployed machinist-welder, moved from Burgoon, Ohio, to Durango, Colorado, in the summer

of 1933. Quite by chance one of the first persons he met was Method-
ist minister Homer E. Root, whose hobby was scouting the country-
side in search of Indian relics. During a three-year period from 1932
through 1934, Root and his wife spent many hours probing trash
mounds associated with archaeological sites on Blue Mesa and
nearby terraces along both sides of the Animas River south of town.
They also investigated mounds on the ranches of three friends in the
lower La Plata Valley toward Farmington, New Mexico, and the
Montezuma Valley near Cortez, Colorado. They pot-hunted in a
very literal sense after learning that ancient burials made in these
deposits generally were accompanied by earthenware vessels. They
did little digging in house remains but concentrated instead on grave
robbing. Their activities produced large assortments of pottery dating
from the eighth-century beginning efforts of local Anasazi artisans to
the culmination of the regional craft some six hundred years later.

Reverend Root exercised his artistic talents by painstakingly
piecing together shattered pots and on occasion expertly filling in
missing portions of design. Such total restoration was common
among both collectors and scientists at the time, but the practice fortunately has been discontinued because inevitably the integrity of the
object is compromised. Root also followed another vogue, mounting
his arrow point collection in star, circular, or other geometric patterns, believing that such presentation enhanced their appeal. He
kept carefully hand-lettered ledgers of the general source of his finds,
but descriptions of the sites or the artifacts they yielded lack sufficient
specificity to be useful to contemporary archaeologists. Although the
Root home was decorated with displays of some of the reclaimed
Anasazi handiwork, large collections were sold to at least four institutions.[1] Those transactions encouraged further vandalism of archaeological resources.

Having been interested in Mound Builder lore as a youth, Flora
was intrigued anew through his contact with Root. Although he did
not then realize it, he had come to a land of plenty where the plunder
of prehistory was an entrenched fact of life.

Southwestern Colorado and adjacent parts of New Mexico, Arizona, and Utah were ripe with ancient ruins within the deep shadows

of their craggy canyons and across their rouged mesas. Explorations of these antiquities began almost on the heels of the first influx of whites following the tumult of the Civil War. It was then that prospectors looking for precious metals, government surveyors cataloging natural and cultural wonders, and settlers clearing land and chasing stray cattle came upon what seemed a countless number of abandoned and collapsed shelters and scatters of telltale human debris.

Although the great houses of Chaco Canyon and Aztec, New Mexico, south of Durango had been visited and mapped periodically from the time the United States took control in the mid-nineteenth century, it was the chance sightings in the 1870s and 1880s of the Mesa Verde cliff dwellings to the west that stirred the blood. Their improbable, seemingly inaccessible locations high on stony cliff faces, laced by nearby stands of evergreens and embraced in deafening silence rent only by the trill of an occasional canyon wren, had universal appeal. When interlopers, such as the Wetherill brothers from the farming community of Mancos at the foot of the Mesa Verde, learned they also contained hundreds of aboriginal objects, the rush to the Indian lodestone was on. Conservation of cultural resources was not a frontier ethic.

Although a few men with academic credentials confined their efforts to descriptive mapping and recording of sites—Gustaf Nordenskiöld being an outstanding example at Mesa Verde—others with less education collected portable specimens for fun and profit. Their names are larded through the early history of Southwestern archaeology because of their exploits and fabulous finds. They climbed into previously unknown houses and granaries decaying along gorge ledges. They gathered up and took away pottery vessels bearing lustrous black designs against a white background; soft twined bags made of woven fibers dyed in contrasting golden, red, and black hues; and large, stout, tapered burden baskets meant to be outfitted with a forehead tumpline and carried on the back. Other finds were yucca fiber sandals to protect feet from bruising trespass over sand, rocks, and cactus; long necklaces of finely shaped and drilled shell and colored stone; and robes made of a woven yucca fiber base wrapped with strips of rabbit fur or turkey feathers. Additional recoveries were wooden cradleboards with cross-withes bound in cushioning animal hides to comfort and protect infants; ground stone axes and mauls, some with original wooden handles still attached by rawhide thongs; wooden digging sticks and stone hoes to till the stubborn soil; bows and arrow shafts for the hunt; and even the remains of the humans themselves who made and used this every-day hardware.

Everything seemed primitive yet so ingenious for a people who apparently lived on a Stone Age level without the benefit of metal tools, mechanical devices, or beasts of burden. It was exhilarating–and potentially marketable–booty. The few voices raised in protest over the incoming tidal wave of vandalism went unheeded. Hard currency was much needed because the worst financial depression of the nineteenth century had closed many Colorado mines, smelters, and businesses.[2]

In the small town of Durango, while treasure hunters staked their claims, a new breed of armchair archaeologists vicariously shared their adventures and tried to learn something of the mysterious past of this borderland to which they recently had moved. In 1893 both groups came together to form the Durango Historical and Archaeological Society.[3] Charles McLoyd, Howard Graham, and D. W. Ayres, present at the first meeting, between them already had made ten arduous pack trips into many alcoves weathered into the broken lands of southeast Utah. There they found numerous ruins from which they took panniers full of goods discarded by the ancients. They publicly exhibited some of their trophies in Durango, including a naturally desiccated human body, a mummy in the Southwestern sense, which they seated on the driver's seat of a wagon in a local parade. Sales were made to both private individuals and institutions.[4]

It is of some interest that two of the ten charter members of the society were ministers in Durango. They were Reverends G. W. Pollock and Clayton Grinnel. A third, Reverend C. H. Green, bought an artifact collection amassed in 1890-1891 in Grand Gulch, Utah, by McLoyd and Graham and the next season went back with McLoyd and Ayres on a second expedition, for which he paid.[5] Perhaps these men of the cloth had the benefit of time and money to indulge themselves in a new hobby, or perhaps their educations promoted an interest in human ancestry.

Although a few professionals protested this indiscriminate ransacking or counseled application of scientific procedures; other academics and their backers were not blameless in the rampant despoliation. Had they been more responsive when initially contacted, some irreparable damage to sites and dispersal of their contents might not have occurred. But they either were disinterested in the potentially significant area of inquiry presented by the antiquities of the Colorado Plateau, lacked funds for fieldwork, or were not ready to endure the certain hardships. They found it easier to buy collections or hire searchers for specimens. Research was not a priority.

In little more than a decade the easy pickings were over. That did not mean an end to pot-hunting, as the activity was now called, because earthenwares were the usual findings. Many accessible cliff dwellings had been thoroughly searched. House mounds in the open had been pot-holed or plowed into oblivion. In 1906 a belated national Antiquities Act made it illegal to dig in or take artifacts from archaeological sites on public lands without proper authorization. Shortly, ruins in Chaco Canyon and Mesa Verde became federal preserves through lobbying efforts mounted by regional scholars and a few concerned citizens who feared the loss of the nation's patrimony. The law curbed but did not end random disturbance of sites. The country was too vast, too remote, too alluring in its rich trove of relics to be controlled merely by a piece of legislation.

It was not just cowboys, traders, and adventure seekers who continued digging in out-of-the-way places to add to private holdings; some federal employees and scientists of varied backgrounds did their share of vacuuming up artifacts. Moreover, respected institutions of learning bought collections without verification of sources or subsidized diggers to unearth specimens that often later were stowed away in museum vaults, never to be seen by the public or analyzed by students. All had voracious appetites for tatters of the past. It was as if a young, drifting society such as embraced the West instinctively needed roots, even those that were neither genetically nor culturally relevant.

It was common practice among settlers to eradicate or reuse old living areas if they interfered with development of the land. Farmers converted suitable ancient structures into root cellars or barns. Cows and sheep bedded down amid aboriginal rubbish. Excavators took over intact shelters as storerooms, kitchens, blacksmith shops, and even privies.[6] Stones shaped by Indian mauls went into new walls, and aged wooden beams and lintels went into campfires.

Because Durango was situated equidistant from Mesa Verde, where before World War I major ruins were being cleared and repaired, and Aztec Ruins, New Mexico, where in 1916 formal excavations commenced, local businesses profited from a swelling volume of visitors drawn to these prehistoric magnets.[7] It was obvious that money was to be made in various ways from the area's unique features. Nevertheless, despite such encouragement, for many the thrill of discovery and clandestine collecting slowly faded. The Durango Historical and Archaeological Society quietly disbanded.

For a growing number of scholars, however, the tempo of serious research into the region's past accelerated as sites in different ecological settings and of seemingly various ages were explored. Piece by piece the basic building blocks for future interpretations were being laid. The decade of the 1920s was particularly fruitful.

First, with discoveries made in 1927 at Folsom in northeastern New Mexico of stone spear points embedded between vertebrae of extinct bison, skeptics became convinced that humans had indeed been in the Southwest thousands of years earlier than formerly believed. However tantalizing that idea was, between Early Man, as the bison hunters were then called, and the ancestors of modern Pueblo Indians thought to be represented in the Colorado Plateau remains there were an unknown number of centuries of silence.

Second, a meeting that same year of some forty persons engaged in regional studies convened at Pecos Pueblo in New Mexico to pool information and ideas for a generalized chronology of the cultural evolution of the northern Southwest. Having begun with the earliest and latest identifiable expressions—both recognized in the southeastern Utah caves—of what appeared to be a continuum, professional field-workers had unearthed enough intervening artifacts so that conference participants could confidently suggest a sequence of seven distinct stages. Known as the Pecos Classification, it provided a useful framework through which a chaotic mass of data could be ordered.

Earliest in the proposed chronology were Basketmaker II and Basketmaker III. The apparently overlooked Basketmaker I stage was a hypothesized part of that great preliminary unknown when big-game hunters were replaced by peoples whose subsistence depended on smaller, modern species of animals and a panoply of native plants and whose social structure and array of material goods must have expanded. A major contribution of the 1890s collecting expeditions into southeast Utah, especially those led by Richard Wetherill, was the initial recognition of the Basketmaker II stage, later to be verified in northeastern Arizona by two Harvard archaeologists, A. V. Kidder and Samuel Guernsey. Evidence for Basketmaker III came from excavations in Chaco Canyon and Canyon de Chelly, both south of the San Juan River, and in the La Plata drainage southwest of Durango.[8]

Following the Basketmaker periods, the Pecos meeting outlined five successive stages of Pueblo development that ended with the contemporary Native American communities along the Rio Grande Valley in New Mexico and at Acoma, Laguna, and Zuni Pueblos and the Hopi villages. Colorado Plateau remains in the Four Corners area pertained to the first three Pueblo periods, after which there seems to have been a mass relocation elsewhere. In a few years the early Pueblo and the Basketmaker periods would be combined under a single name, Anasazi, to underscore a gradual cultural evolution through time.

The third development of the 1920s was the invaluable contribution of a time scale provided by the growth rings of certain evergreen trees used in prehistoric construction. Building episodes could be dated with a remarkably discrete precision unknown elsewhere in the world. The proposed Pecos Classification therefore could be supported by actual calendric dates.

Thus, by 1930 there was an almost euphoric feeling of excitement and anticipation surrounding the pursuit of Southwestern archaeology. The discipline had organized itself, and new discoveries and ideas were certain to be just over the horizon. Diggers for pay and also those who sought specimens for sale or personal satisfaction were eager to move ahead. Once again an economic depression played into their hands. On the positive side, in order to provide jobs, various government work programs, such as the Public Works Administration and the Civilian Conservation Corps, erected museums and visitor facilities, built roads and trails, and repaired ancient Indian structures in the area's national parks and monuments during this economic downturn. These endeavors greatly increased public awareness and appreciation of the many antiquities in the general vicinity. However, long-standing attitudes toward these antiquities as exploitable resources flourished. Pothunter attention focused on the verdant valley and hillsides surrounding Durango (Map 1.1).

Until this time, the many traces of aboriginal peoples to be found on the benches and in the bottomlands of the upper reaches of the Animas River had been largely ignored. This was because they were not the highly visible, hulking, cobblestone mounds left by slumped walls, or the jagged remnants of multiroomed, multistoried houses tucked into cliff openings such as were encountered in neighboring sectors. As described in a later account, "Prehistoric sites in our vicinity can be recognized by the circular depression or pit of the subterranean room that has not completely filled up to this day. Surrounding this pit are the remains of the man-made ridge that supported the smaller rooms. Scattered over the whole mounds are the broken fragments of pottery."[9]

It was not a scene to inspire any immediate action until suddenly a dozen enthusiastic weekend diggers, including the Roots, began prowling the territory for promising places to put their shovels down. They were stimulated by the churning up of Indian artifacts as Durango stretched beyond its original limits and by the creation of farmsteads on previously undeveloped, surrounding lands by migrant families fleeing the Dust Bowl.[10] It became increasingly obvious that this modern mountain town unknowingly had been founded in the core area of an extensive prehistoric occupation.

First Interest

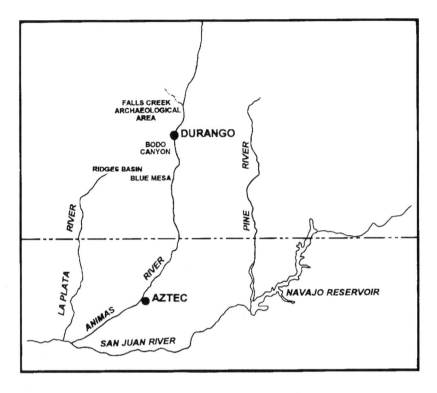

Map 1.1. Durango area of southwestern Colorado.

The new hobbyists came from many occupational backgrounds, none of which included training in acceptable archaeological field techniques. With the exception of Reverend Root, these enthusiasts did not amass large salable collections as did the first generation of diggers. Nevertheless, all lusted after Indian artifacts. To be fair, many earnestly desired to learn about the early peoples and undertook good-faith efforts to repair and understand salvaged materials. However, their activities were bound to engender conflicts with the emerging archaeological profession.

The second Durango archaeological society sprang up in the early 1930s, bringing together those interested in the past and present of the region's Native American populations. One participant was a member of the Graham family, which had participated in the earliest archaeological scouting expeditions to the western canyonlands forty years earlier.[11] The meetings gave members the opportunity to compare, exchange, or sell items retrieved during field explorations, to share experiences, and to listen to brief talks on related topics. It was a seemingly harmless intellectual, social, and sometimes profitable outlet in economically trying times. Zeke Flora, at age forty-five, quickly became a member (Fig. 1.1).

Arriving in Durango, as he later recounted, with twenty-three cents in his pocket and unable to find work in his trade, Flora took on a number of stopgap jobs. One was building trails to mining shafts and doing a bit of prospecting on the side. It was while engaged in cutting trees, moving boulders, and leveling paths that he became aware of unmistakable signs of some unknown predecessors who once may have lived or camped thereabouts.[12] On the day in 1934 when he turned the earth at one of these mountainside depressions to encounter a human skeleton accompanied by several earthenware bowls, he was gripped by a lifelong passion. Quite coincidentally, his father was a minister, and Flora, without realizing it, may have been conditioned as a youth to a quest for humankind's beginnings.

At first, Flora regarded the articles he reclaimed as manna from heaven. Like many other relic seekers, he may have falsely equated presumed antiquity with exaggerated monetary worth, but in the throes of the depression this was a compelling reason to proceed. Outside of scholarly ranks, there was no particular ethical stigma against such activity, and enforcement of the federal law was lax. There was no formal prohibition against digging on state or private land. So throughout the months following his first finds, Flora, with machinelike precision, wielded first a shovel and then his favorite hunting knife to open old dwellings, associated refuse heaps, and graves in the valley, both north and south of town. Ranchers gave him permission to explore sites on their property, but it is probable that Flora did not confine his excavations within those boundaries. Much of the area around Durango is federal land. Perhaps to counter legal troubles, he later claimed to have dug only on private property.

By the spring of 1934, Flora had amassed a collection of almost five hundred pottery vessels. In the process, he acquired necessary soil-reading skills. J. O. Brew, Harvard archaeologist, later commented

Fig. 1.1. Isaiah F. "Zeke" Flora with his digging tools and some recovered Basket-maker III pottery. "PIT AG" at lower left refers to an unknown site. *Courtesy Laboratory of Tree-Ring Research, University of Arizona, Tucson, Arizona.*

that this man could walk across a meadow in the dark and feel a pit-house underfoot. Flora himself liked to brag that he could stand in the middle of one of the ruin depressions, take a number of steps in a southerly direction, and know that he was in a burial plot where there were apt to be pots as well as human bones.[13] It was to his advantage that these ancients followed a somewhat standardized arrangement of living spaces so that soon one site looked much like another.

Without any relevant academic background, Flora did not then realize the value of recording the exact locations or characteristics of the places he exposed, nor did he note the proveniences of the specimens he recovered within them. He merely recorded the general locality and whether recovered pots were whole or broken. Pictures of his work reveal ragged pits, dangling plant roots, and a flexed skeleton in the hard earth, accompanied by one or more pottery vessels. Despite such damaging evidence, Flora was not a mindless looter. He engaged in what he described as "back trailing," that is, trying to interpret the past through recovered artifacts. He became a careful observer, and he gradually built up a fund of information about the minutiae of local antiquities that would help other collectors and, in time, trained scientists. Notwithstanding, because the retrieved pottery represented a marketable commodity to Flora, his most pressing interest was locating a buyer. That is when he introduced himself to Earl Morris.

Earl H. Morris, a trained archaeologist, was a product of the early-twentieth-century New Mexico outposts to the south of Durango that abutted the immense and barren Navajo Reservation. He had been an avid digger since boyhood, and by the 1930s his more legitimate archaeological exploits across the San Juan country (as well as in Guatemala and the Yucatán of Mexico) were legendary. Without question, he had more hands-on field experience in northern Southwestern prehistory than any other individual.[14] Aztec Ruins and Canyon de Chelly National Monuments were created to preserve antiquities he explored, but, in addition, he excavated scores of sites across the sweep of plateaus and canyons south of the San Juan River, within the mesa alcoves south of Mesa Verde, and along the La Plata drainage north of Farmington, New Mexico. In 1934, with

Public Works Administration funds, he was directing the reconstruction of the Great Kiva at Aztec Ruins, which thirteen years previously he had cleared on behalf of the American Museum of Natural History. That project, extensive repair efforts at the associated twelfth-century house compound, museum construction, and beautification of the monument grounds provided badly needed employment for crews of men drawn from the surrounding communities and consequently were the subject of a steady flow of local news releases.[15] Flora learned of Morris through these articles and hoped he had found a buyer for his pots.

Upon inspection, Morris judged the Flora pottery collection to be Basketmaker III, the period, according to the Pecos Classification, when pottery first appeared in the San Juan Basin. Tree-ring dating pegged the interval generally between A.D. 500 and A.D. 700, at which time a growing adherence to a sedentary lifeway made pottery useful rather than burdensome. Vessels were dirty gray, rough-surfaced, and shaped into small jars and deep bowls. Bowl interiors bore casually applied black decorations that Flora believed to be hieroglyphics with symbolic meanings.[16]

Unlike Root, Flora did not confine his explorations to possible burial grounds. He opened domestic structures that he described as small, circular pits a few feet below ground level, with reddened floor-level hearths, lateral passageways for entry or ventilation, and posthole depressions for roof supports. These pits were accompanied by foundations for a few flimsy surface rooms. To the south of these pits there generally was a pile of castoff goods embedded in drifted soil. Out beyond, there was an occasional row of post stubs that may have formed a stockade. Burials frequently were in thin refuse scattered about these areas. Flora's descriptions confirmed for Morris his designation of the pottery as Basketmaker III. If that were correct, apparently the Durango vicinity experienced a previously unrecognized but sizable occupation some fourteen hundred years ago. Flora deserved credit for bringing it to scientific attention.

Morris did not purchase the pottery because it was all of one cultural phase. Instead, he put Flora in touch with Harold S. Gladwin. One of several men from varied walks of life who came to Arizona in the late 1920s aiming to use private resources to explore the area's human past, Gladwin was the most flamboyant and controversial.[17] He had been a member of the New York Stock Exchange and was used to thinking big. In this case, big meant raising a multiroomed Pueblo-style research facility over the derelict foundations of a thirteenth-century Salado-culture houseblock on the outskirts of Globe. He called it Gila Pueblo. He began acquiring a representative collection of artifacts to study with the help of an anticipated staff of two archaeologists. Rumor had it that he was not particular about whether specimens had been taken from public or private lands or whether, beyond general areal location, specific site provenience data were provided. Of all the goods produced or used by the old Southwesterners, Gladwin considered pottery the most critical in delineating regional differences and interactions through time. Eventually, five rooms of the compound were devoted to processing and housing a display of some ten thousand ceramic vessels and dozens of boards upon which fragments were mounted to illustrate evolving styles.

With this Gila Pueblo acquisition initiative in full swing, Morris ultimately arranged a sale to Gladwin of 152 pots, a few projectile points, bone awls, grinding slabs, and tubular earthenware pipes that Flora had removed from more than sixty burials then considered to be Basketmaker III. Most of the excavations were on Blue Mesa, about five miles south of Durango (Map 1.2). Meanwhile, Root, who also dug on Blue Mesa, sold Gladwin his assortment of 182 pots.[18]

Through these two acquisitions from unidentified or vaguely described sources, the Durango potters were well represented at Gila Pueblo, but Gladwin wanted some field information to further delineate them. He saw in Flora a way to acquire it. Thus, two outsiders to the professional mainstream—one a blue-collar and one a blue blood—teamed up to undertake the first serious explorations in the Durango district.

On behalf of Gila Pueblo, for several field seasons Flora tramped the Animas Valley and uplands to note some fifteen hundred sites to which he assigned Gladwin's numerical designations. Later he adopted his own numbering system, thus confusing the record to the point that it is now impossible to pinpoint most of the sites. Flora's estimate of the number of sites might well have been exaggerated,

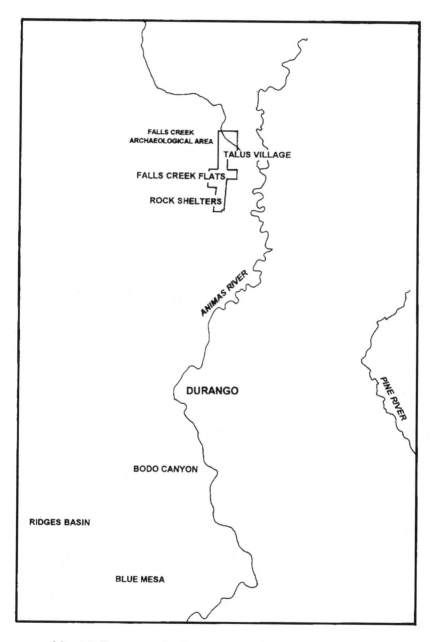

FALLS CREEK
ARCHAEOLOGICAL AREA

TALUS VILLAGE

FALLS CREEK FLATS

ROCK SHELTERS

ANIMAS RIVER

PINE RIVER

DURANGO

BODO CANYON

RIDGES BASIN

BLUE MESA

Map 1.2. Durango and primary associated archaeological zones.

but it was obvious that ancient dwellings were chockablock in the Animas drainage.

In 1936 Gladwin joined Flora in partially clearing the main Blue Mesa site that had produced many of the pieces of pottery in the purchased collection. His interest doubtless was stimulated by Morris, who wrote him, "The Blue Mesa site represents the largest uncontaminated BM III settlement that I have seen anywhere."[19] The village proved to consist of a grouping of pithouses separated by four rows of surface rooms. Gladwin estimated that several hundred units were present. No comprehensive report was written. Morris's evaluation of the site's age likely was based upon the kind of pottery fragments he observed on the surface, but nowadays it probably would be considered more closely allied to a later Pueblo I horizon.

Flora went on to excavate parts of similar hamlets, finding them to be fairly homogeneous complexes of pit structures and rows of surface chambers.[20] Gladwin later described one of them (Ign 12:27) as a typical "earth lodge."[21] It was a large oval room dug about five feet into the ground, with a central hearth, an encircling earthen bench, a vertical ventilator shaft at one side, and a probable truncated pole-and-earth roof supported by four spaced, vertical poles. Recovered specimens, mostly of types already familiar to Flora through his previous diggings, and whatever sketchy notes he made went to Gila Pueblo. An inventory includes a cradleboard, a stone ball, stone projectile points, bone gaming pieces, matting and basket fragments, clay pipes, cordage, lignite pendants, bone tools and awls, corncobs, a twined bag, grinding stones and slabs, stone axes, and bone tubes. Some of the listed 174 jars, 152 bowls, twenty-eight seed jars, and five miniatures may have been part of the Flora pottery collection that Gladwin purchased.[22]

Both Flora and Gladwin believed an important early horizon was represented in these excavations, one in which pottery and architecture already were present.[23] They agreed with Morris's assessment that it was Basketmaker III. In their jointly proposed cultural reconstruction, Basketmaker III people merged with a so-called X-Culture that they believed came from the Mississippi or Arkansas Valleys to initiate the Pueblo I stage and the long flow of culture that followed.

The next generation of archaeologists would consider the site to be Pueblo I.

Some time during his association with Gladwin, Flora also exposed parts of at least three sites that appeared to be earlier. The locations of two are uncertain, listed as Ign 17:3 and Ign 7:15, the former presumably southeast of town and the latter northeast of Animas City Mountain. The third, Ign 7:101, became known as Talus Village. Flora found circular earth-packed floors just slightly below the ground surface. They were not the remains of pithouses. The floors were thrust back into hillsides, rather like the Midwestern root cellars of Flora's youth. He noted in an unpublished review of Durango prehistory written in February 1938 that there were no fire-pits on those floors, but slabs of cists did protrude. Stone chips abounded. Pottery was absent. He believed the sites to represent a "pre-pottery" horizon, as he called it, preceding the Basketmaker III sites he had worked, but at the time he did not realize the significance of his discovery. Flora, who had no knowledge of wall or roof construction, had encountered the first known floors of Basketmaker II dwellings. It was an important addition to the growing Basketmaker data bank for which he never received credit.

Prior to these explorations, during a visit to Gila Pueblo in 1935, Flora met staff archaeologist Emil Haury. Haury showed him how the growth rings evident in cross sections of timbers or lumps of charcoal could be correlated with master charts to determine the wood's age. This was Flora's introduction to the new science of dendrochronology, dendrology being the study of trees and woody plants, and chronology the measuring of time by regular divisions.[24] Soon collecting wood samples from archaeological zones became as important to him as collecting pots.

Haury was well equipped to instruct Flora because he had studied the tree-ring dating process with its developer, astronomer A. E. Douglass. He went on to work in Douglass's laboratory at the University of Arizona and was present at the momentous discovery in the north central part of the state of a beam section exhibiting a growth pattern through which a series of dated modern rings could be connected to what formerly had been a floating prehistoric chronology.

With that linkage and the honing of techniques during the next few years, the readable wood timetable was extended backward from the present to the eras when the ancient people on the Colorado Plateau seemed to have first erected domestic structures. Flora was so fascinated by this new information and its application that he returned home determined to learn to decipher tree-rings himself.

Eagerly, Flora revisited his old diggings and sites he had not yet touched to gather wood samples. For the first time, in the early fall of 1935 he clambered up to the alcove above the intermittent stream in Falls Creek Valley that became known as the South Shelter to take a log protruding from trash strewn across the cave's floor. He sent V-cuts from it to Haury and to the Laboratory of Tree-Ring Research in Tucson, where researchers read dates of A.D. 649 and A.D. 650, well within the presumed span of the Basketmaker III.[25] At the time, no one knew there was an extensive earlier utilization of this particular place.

Stimulated by this tree-ring information, Flora on his own worked out what he thought was an acceptable date on a chunk of charcoal recovered from a Durango pithouse. Haury confirmed his finding. This was a remarkable feat on Flora's part, of which he was justifiably proud. He rapidly then dated ten beams from a site on Griffiths Heights (Ign 12:1), where a new housing project was underway, at A.D. 616. None represented a positive cutting date. When Haury co-authored a brief article placing the Durango materials in the A.D. 500–600 range, Flora felt he had gained archaeological respectability.[26] Soon he was made a Fellow of the Tree-Ring Society, a body with only fifteen members.[27] With this honor and perhaps some flattery, Flora went from a nobody to a somebody in regional studies and became almost suffocatingly self-important.

The adjectives driven, energetic, intelligent, and imaginative often are used to describe Harold Gladwin. Harvard anthropologist E. A. Hooton called him untrammeled and incorrigible.[28] Over a twenty-year period the contributions to Southwestern archaeology made through his foundation and his own prodigious efforts were considerable. However, to the dismay of colleagues, Gladwin sometimes demanded data but did not feel bound by them.[29] At other times he jumped right into the brew without the life preserver of fact. In retrospect, one wonders if it were not his influence on Flora, at the beginning of the novice's involvement in regional prehistory, that accounted for the demoralizing attitudes that were to come forth later. Certainly the tendency toward self-destruction through free fall from archaeological orthodoxy, the unreasonable prejudice against academia, and the lack of respect for the cultural integrity of archaeological sites were shared qualities. It was the discipline's loss and fault that Flora, an ambitious, engrossed, observant amateur, did not receive more constructive tutoring. Many unfortunate events would not then have transpired.

At the same time that the Gila Pueblo survey was going on, the National Youth Administration (NYA) opened an office in Durango to provide summer jobs for young people who had dropped out of school or needed employment training. Helen Sloan Daniels, wife of a local dentist and granddaughter of a pioneer San Juan area settler, was put in charge of its operation. Working with her were James G. Allen and Kenneth I. Ross, both associated with the Division of Education and Recreation in the Works Progress Administration. Motivated by the recent destruction of an archaeological site on Folsom Mesa by Civilian Conservation Corps crews chewing at a gravel pit, Daniels decided the NYA team could serve a useful civic purpose by monitoring further activities of this sort, perhaps even undertaking some actual excavations and preparing recovered specimens for an exhibit at the Durango Public Library, of which she was a trustee. Flora agreed to serve as a volunteer supervisor. Neither viewed such projects as improper.

From May 1936 through September 1939, favorable weather saw the NYA workers engaged in a number of related efforts. At least four sites near town were explored, and midden, pithouse, and post-and-mud surface structures were exposed. These included sites Ign 12:23 north of City Park on Reservoir Hill, Ign 12:18 east of the Animas River on Folsom Mesa, Ign 7:12 near Trimble Springs, and Ign 17A:3 southeast of town.

The most important excavation was at site Ign 12:1 in the Griffiths Heights (now Crestview) housing development west of town, where Flora had earlier gathered tree-ring samples. Daniels wanted to study the excavated dwelling in preparation for a diorama of a typical local Basketmaker III house that she envisioned for the library's Indian room.[30] After much of the original structure was cleaned out by the NYA diggers, some of the opened features were destroyed by vandals. Undaunted, Daniels persuaded the Forest Service to donate use of a truck and discarded timber so that her "boys" could erect a roof over what was left. With a roof in place, she reasoned, the site could be opened for public viewing. Before the roof was erected, however, the property was sold for taxes, and because the new owners did not want to contend with sightseers, the excavations were backfilled and essentially forgotten. However, in the 1930s, NYA team member Frank Lee wrote the first formal description of a Durango pithouse. Lee later found two other pithouses in the same neighborhood (Ign 12:58 and Ign 12:59), but little is known about them.[31]

Through her work with the NYA, Daniels herself became intrigued with the Indian past of the region. Her college work was not in this field, but she was intelligent and inquiring. She soon joined the growing ranks of local residents sharing similar interests.

Generally, Daniels accompanied the young men on the digs that Flora led and was present when some skulls were unearthed at the pre-pottery hillside sites. In comparing them with skulls removed from local pithouse burials, Flora pointed out features he considered distinctive. Daniels was captivated by the possibility of a major human discovery and promptly sought professional help. In a letter dated March 8, 1937, to the Field Museum of Natural History in Chicago, she relayed Flora's observations. "We have found a group of skulls from pre-pottery sites which are quite different from the Basket Maker III. Heavy brow ridges, low cranial arch, deep upper lip and thick jaw indicate that they are very early. . . . He is close to the Neanderthal style of beauty." She enclosed a photograph to prove the point.

In due time the Daniels letter was turned over to Paul S. Martin, curator of North American archaeology at the museum. Martin was engaged in a long-term research project in the vicinity of Lowry

Ruin, one hundred miles west of Durango, and was aware of the excavations going on in the Animas district. Because he heartily disapproved of them, he refused to examine the seemingly unusual skulls.[32] This rebuff made the local amateur group aware for the first time that their work, even when undertaken for the most honorable of reasons, was frowned upon in some scientific circles.

Although most regional collectors had human remains in their assortments of artifacts because of their association with desirable grave goods, there generally was only casual interest in them. Indian bones were simply part of the loot. Flora was unique in that he kept retrieved skulls and long bones carefully stored in boxes in a shed on his property. From time to time he lined the skulls up on a table in the yard so that he could photograph them from various angles to illustrate their perceived differences. Daniels just kept hers in a deep dresser drawer.[33]

Knowing of her keen interest in such matters, a friend told Daniels that a cave in the Animas area contained what seemed to be ancient paintings on a cliff face. Naturally, she wanted to investigate. At a meeting of the archaeological society, she asked Flora about it. Yes, he told her, he did know of that place because beginning in October 1935 and again at the very time of their conversation a year later, he was trenching there, searching for datable wood. During these explorations, he said he had unearthed the burial of an infant with a long skull and later sent five associated bone awls, some corncobs, a basketry fragment, braided cordage, a bit of a twined bag, and chipped stone implements to Gila Pueblo.[34] He considered the materials to be of the pre-pottery phase, but later work showed he had actually shoveled into a Basketmaker III level.

A few days later Daniels and her NYA group were guided to the pictograph site by Flora. They scrambled up a steep slope through a tangle of undergrowth and huge sandstone blocks to reach a lofty amphitheater beneath a shadowed overhang on the west side of Falls Creek Valley (Figs. 1.2, 1.3). Cool moist air welcomed them. The sandstone roof of the alcove was dark and splotchy. Thin reddish stone tablets had scaled from the back wall and drifted like a dune down across the floor. High above this loose deposit at the juncture

Fig. 1.2. View of Falls Creek Valley, looking northwest. Two rock shelters with aboriginal deposits are located at the base of the prominent white stratum. *Courtesy San Juan–Rio Grande National Forest.*

of geologic strata was a series of moist spots indicating tiny seeps. These may have been exploited by the ancient inhabitants to provide drinking water.

The Daniels party was more interested in some drawings on the stained ceiling near the north end of the shelter. At that place the floor level rose so that there was little more than head room between it and the overriding roof. In order to sketch the small, crudely painted images of humans, animals, and a flute player executed in white, black, and dark yellow, the observers had to assume awkward supine positions in the dirt and crane their necks.[35]

A freshly opened pit near the front of the alcove had been left by Charles M. Drager, La Plata County agent, who confessed to being on the prowl for specimens. In his digging at this site, he found a cache of six one-hand and two-hand grinding stones, the bleached bones of an infant, and a slab of wood that he thought might have

Fig. 1.3. Opening to South Shelter, Falls Creek Valley. *Courtesy San Juan–Rio Grande National Forest.*

been part of a hard cradleboard.[36] Daniels retrieved a few pinyon shells, a kernel of corn, and some small colored rocks from the loosened dirt.

To entertain a visiting artist friend during August 1937, Daniels returned to Falls Creek Valley. This time she and several companions made their way to a narrow recess north of the one seen earlier. There they were excited to observe a mass of tiny indistinct drawings in red, green, yellow, black, and white sprinkled along the vertical face of the back wall of the long opening. They laboriously copied many of them. Daniels decided that some day she would reproduce the pictographs as a wall mural for a future Durango museum. At the time, knowing of Flora's interest in tree-ring dating, Daniels and her friends retrieved some pieces of charcoal lying about the surface and put them in their knapsacks. Shortly, Daniels delivered the charcoal to Flora and showed him a snapshot of the overhang. According to her recollection, she pointed to a spot on the picture, saying, "That is the place to dig." And within a few days, dig Flora did.[37]

Making his way up an embankment thickly overgrown with scrub oak, poison ivy, and brush, Flora accompanied by Daniels, stuck his shovel into an earth-packed cleft at the south end of the pictograph alcove to make a thrilling discovery, one that would bring him immense personal gratification and, ultimately, great unhappiness. Moreover, it would change his life. Artifacts came tumbling out of the loosely consolidated fill of a roomlike space formed between fallen slabs of rock. Above a foot-deep layer of decayed plant material and pack-rat dung there was a trash deposit containing oddments of daily life amid dust, dried excrement, leaves, stone chips, and animal bones. Some articles were relatively complete, but most were fragmentary or badly worn. Included were bits of animal hides; robes made of rabbit fur strips on a fiber backing; fiber matting; an atlatl (dart thrower) fragment; a cradleboard; tattered baskets and splints; cordage; one yucca sandal and one of hide; bundles of cornhusks; hundreds of loose assorted seed, stone, shell, and berry beads; several complete necklaces; and twined bags. This find was especially exhilarating to Flora because perishables of this sort—particularly in such fine condition——were not present in the open sites he was accustomed to exploring.

His excitement intensified when he ascertained that nineteen people of both sexes and all ages were buried amid the refuse. Two more were crammed into a smaller crevice around a fallen block of stone. What remained of most were their bleached skeletons, skulls, or stray bones that had been disarticulated by rodents or successive interments. However, two nearly intact bodies were naturally desiccated by the aridity of the burial space. Portions of several others still retained bits of skin tissue and hair.

The most perfectly preserved specimen was a young female. Flora found her lying on her back on a bedding of cedar bark strips, with her legs and feet turned up under her body and tied in place with a buckskin thong, a yucca leaf, and a short rope woven of human hair.[38] Perhaps she was trussed in this way to accommodate the available space. Her arms were crossed over her abdomen and tied together with a piece of yucca cord. She wore a yucca girdle and loincloth and was covered by a rabbit fur robe.

Another body was that of a juvenile male who was wrapped in a tanned hide and placed on a cedar bark mat. He wore the scraps of a skimpy loincloth. His dark reddish hair was roughly cropped, which Flora surmised was done after death to secure weaving material. Two baskets were placed upside down over his head and one was laid beside the body as offerings.

Additional burials were of special interest. One was that of a gray-haired old lady. She wore only a yucca girdle. At her side was a small basket, inside of which was a buckskin pouch containing a stone pipe, an unusual possession for a woman. Was she perhaps a medicine woman, or did she simply enjoy an occasional smoke?

Another notable burial was that of the Bead Girl, a young girl—obviously dearly loved—who was interred with the family jewels: a string of beautifully polished red and black stone beads wrapped around her knees, and a long necklace and pendant of olivella shells from the far Pacific hung around her neck.

Because no earthenwares were present in the crevice deposit, Flora judged the humans and their goods to be of the pre-pottery stage. And he laid sole claim to the find. At that moment a seed of resentment was planted. Daniels let her family know that as Flora's helper, she had actually discovered the well-preserved female mummy.[39] Probably to their relief, she never expressed any desire to possess this dried creature.

Together Flora and Daniels worked feverishly for several days to clear the contents from the crevice. They found it necessary to cover their noses with towel masks because the dust stirred up was noxious and foul smelling. From time to time Flora stopped long enough to make a few cursory notes about the nature of the deposit and its arti-facts. In his haste some lesser objects were overlooked or thrown aside in the spoil dirt. Daniels carefully gathered up hundreds of loose beads and put them in one of the baskets. Transporting the arti-cles required many arduous trips up and down the tiresome slope. As the pair thrashed through the snagging vegetation, some ties and wrappings on the bodies were torn free and lost. A later search for them proved fruitless.

Back at the Flora house, Daniels used a vacuum upholstery brush to clean bits of hide, the cradleboard, baskets, and beads. Flora spruced up the mummies and used sandpaper to remove a crusted substance from a sandstone pipe.[40] They then alerted three known authorities on regional prehistory of their spectacular find. Harold Gladwin and Paul Martin did not respond, but Earl Morris came posthaste.

As he scanned Flora's letter describing the material recovered from the Falls Creek rock shelter, Morris must have winced at the lack of common sense displayed in handling the prized female mummy. The letter read,

> I am still a little "shaky" with excitement from a recent find, as yet to be fully excavated. It is a dry crevice north of Durango, left by our pre-pottery B.M. II. 18 of the 19 burials had hair on the head. One adult is so marvelously preserved that you may doubt my description. Skin almost completely intact. Full head of hair, eyebrows, eyelashes, finger and toe nails, body hair, etc. In attempting to give her a much needed bath with gardenhose and scrub-brush, I was surprised to find the skin soften, could move the lips and tongue, adjust features, open the eyes and see the pupil of the eye on intact eyeballs.[41]

Later this mummy was judged to have been about twenty-two years old at time of death from an undetermined cause.

Thus far in Flora's archaeological experience, skeletons, even skulls, were abstract objects, sanitized and dehumanized. But the mummies were powerfully human, with distinct identities. He could select no ordinary names for these extraordinary individuals. Esther, the exceptionally well preserved young woman, was named after a cartoon character Flora had seen a year earlier in the *Denver Post*.[42] Perhaps it was prophetic that this figure was depicted as a Neanderthal maiden riding on a stone slab harnessed to a dinosaur. The youth was christened Jasper by Daniels. The old crone was Grandma Niska, Oniska being an Ohio Indian name recalled from Flora's boyhood. The bejeweled child became Tannis. Despite these personalizations, however, Flora suffered no qualms about disturbing their eternal peace: grave robbing was an age-old and widespread practice.

Appalled at the shower bath that could have led to rapid decay of the desiccated bodies but intrigued by the tantalizing finds described, Morris stopped in Durango en route to Boulder from the huge Awatovi excavations in Arizona. He found the Flora house under quarantine because a child had scarlet fever. There followed what would have been a comedic scene were it not so highly charged for all parties: separatèd by a window, one by one the two men and Daniels examined some three dozen artifacts and several grotesquely dried humans that Flora's wife held up for inspection. To each other they commented, yes, the stone necklace was superb; no, the baskets were not as elaborately decorated as others known. At that moment, the amateurs and the professional were on common ground: they all wanted to know more.

Morris recognized the specimens at Flora's house as being of the Basketmaker II culture. He had worked with similar materials in Canyon del Muerto in Arizona and Moqui Canyon in Utah, but he had never suspected these Basketmakers were in the Animas district, the lower section of which had been his boyhood home. The first Basketmaker finds had been made in Grand Gulch, Utah, in the 1880s and 1890s by men from Durango and the tiny ranching community of Mancos, who doubtless would have been just as amazed as Morris to know of their presence on Falls Creek.

Always stimulated by the prospect of new discoveries, Morris plotted a future course of action. In another time and place, red warning flags might have been raised over the impropriety of a prominent scientist's becoming involved with the grubbing of a known pothunter. But not in the northern Southwest before World War II. In fact, much of the regional archaeology could not have been accomplished without the information and hard work provided by interested, untrained laymen. And if anyone understood the compulsion to search for artifacts, it was Morris. He had been at it since he was a youngster. To him, there was no ethical conflict between a professional and personal approach. He justified the latter as a means of preventing antiquities from falling into less appreciative hands.[43]

So, on this occasion Morris decided that once he verified the authenticity of the collection and reassured himself of its cultural affiliation, he would secure the necessary excavation permits through the Carnegie Institution in Washington, D.C., the influential body for whom he worked under A. V. Kidder. Because Flora and Daniels asked him to appraise the collection, it never occurred to him that they might have their own plans for further excavation. His permit request would include a ten-mile tract radiating in all directions from Durango. If the Basketmaker II people had been in one nearby locality, he reasoned, they must have been in others. Hopefully, there would be additional caves with deposits of fragile specimens. Morris would hire his new ally, Flora, to scout out the territory for other indications of possible Basketmaker II presence. The permit request would be addressed to both the Departments of Agriculture and the Interior, under whose custody much of southwestern Colorado was administered. Nowadays such a sweeping permit would not be forthcoming, but at the time, it was not seen as overly ambitious.

Several weeks later, the scarlet fever quarantine having been lifted, Morris returned to Durango to examine the specimens more closely. Pleased with the results, Morris found Flora eager to continue tracking down evidence of what he was now calling "the cave men." There was, however, a hitch. Flora confessed that the collection of human remains and artifacts had been illegally exhumed on Forest Service lands. Although he claimed to have believed the shelter to be on private land, he had failed to check. In addition, three years earlier he had dug in the adjacent alcove without determining land ownership. As it turned out, both shelters were within the San Juan–Rio Grande National Forest, and without a permit to excavate, Flora and Daniels were liable to felony prosecution under the Antiquities Act of 1906.[44]

This put Morris in a difficult situation. Because the specimens were both unique and, in some respects, of high quality, he wanted to incorporate them into his own anticipated research. Still, he had a feeling that Flora, who assumed proprietorship, might capriciously sell them at the first opportunity. What should he do? He could notify Jesse Nusbaum, regional archaeologist for the Department of the

Interior and superintendent of Mesa Verde National Park, that the specimens were secured illegally from federal holdings. A friend of Nusbaum's for a quarter century, Morris knew, however, that his colleague would like nothing better than to arrest a recognized pothunter and confiscate his extraordinary haul amid considerable fanfare. Morris quickly ruled out telling Nusbaum because he did not want to betray Flora's trust. As he said to Kidder, chairman of the Division of Historical Research at the Carnegie Institution of Washington, he could not blame Flora for his actions because, without constraint, the NYA boys were ripping open valley sites.[45]

Other problems included the fact that federal proceedings might implicate Gladwin, for whom Flora dug illicitly in the South Shelter. In addition, Flora had mailed charcoal and wood fragments from the burial crevice to Haury.[46] Morris's particular quandary was that he could not buy the collection outright for the Carnegie Institution because that would put the organization in a position of seeming to sanction illegal excavation. At the same time, he did not want to lose control over what he considered an assortment of special archaeological significance.

Undoubtedly recognizing Morris's quandary, Flora had his own agenda. He wanted to cash in on what he believed was a bonanza. In October, after Morris had declared his intention of taking up the study of the Durango Basketmakers, Flora informed him that he considered the Falls Creek assortment to be worth $2,000 on the commercial market, a hefty sum in 1937. He hinted that he might, however reluctantly, part with it. A few months later he followed up, writing to Morris that "I have been forced by financial difficulties to place the material I have 'in hock.' Only definite action within a short time will save the material from going 'via the underground railroad' to doctors and private museums."[47]

Morris believed Flora was bluffing. It was highly unlikely anyone would accept the collection as collateral on a loan, especially if the circumstances of its recovery were known. Still, he was fearful of having it slip beyond his grasp. Having already determined that the University of Colorado Museum (his sponsor since college days) had no money for further acquisitions, he obtained Kidder's permission to arrange a transaction for the Carnegie Institution.

The following February, Morris went to Durango to present Flora with a Carnegie check for $300. The receipt was worded to imply that the money was for rights to study the specimens for an eighteen-month period, but both men tacitly understood it was a sale and that Flora relinquished all further claim to the items. Or so Morris thought. He would come to rue the words "to study." He removed the articles to his home in Boulder and several months later paid Flora an additional $200. The arrangement was a devious way to obtain the specimens while at the same time protecting Flora. The artifacts would be included with others gathered in the course of authorized work, and there would be no mention of exactly how they were found. Nusbaum was informed of the transfer and agreed to it. One interpretation is that Flora broke the law, but Morris, Kidder, and Nusbaum, three of the most respected archaeologists of the day, only bent it.

In return for her help in clearing the burial crevice and restringing some of the beads scattered throughout the fill, Flora gave Daniels one of the repaired necklaces.[48] It comprised 238 beads of black lignite and pink and cream hornstone with a pair of bone pendants attached at the lower end of the loop (Fig. 1.4). Perhaps originally it had been worn by Esther. Morris saw the necklace but did not request that it be included with the objects he purchased on behalf of the Carnegie Institution.[49] He probably assumed that when he prepared a report on the planned excavations, he would be permitted to examine it more closely and that eventually it would be placed in whatever institution was selected as the final depository for all the recovered artifacts.

Fig. 1.4. Restrung Basketmaker necklace of black lignite and pink and cream horn-stone beads (these were originally strung on a cord of human hair), with a pair of bone pendants at the strand ends. *Courtesy Center of Southwest Studies, Fort Lewis College, Durango, Colorado.*

Falls Creek Rock Shelters Excavated

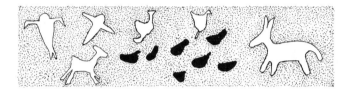

In July 1938 Morris arrived in Durango ready to take on the local Basketmakers. He was accompanied by Robert Burgh, a young draftsman with whom he had become acquainted during 1934 stabilization work at Mesa Verde. Because Flora had been unable to locate any more alcoves or other promising sites of the pre-pottery period, Morris decided to launch his campaign at the Falls Creek shelters.

Upon visiting the overhangs for the first time, Morris was unimpressed (Fig. 1.5). In his journal (now in the University of Colorado Museum archives) he noted on July 7, "They are by no means alluring to one who has worked in real cave country, yet since they offer the only prospect of dry B.M. II material that Flora has been able to find in weeks of scouting, they must be worked to the limit." As he poked around the enormous sharp-edged blocks that obstructed much of the North Shelter floor space, he thought he detected evidence of artificial terracing, as if to create level living areas. If this was so, there might be traces of habitations and other domestic patterns that heretofore had not been identified in Basketmaker II sites. He was unaware of Flora's discoveries made two or three years earlier. The weathered tops of vertical slabs probably lining storage cists were visible, as were a few corncobs.

Fig. 1.5. Opening to North Shelter, Falls Creek Valley. *Courtesy San Juan–Rio Grande National Forest.*

Arrangements were made to use a three-room shack on a ranch at the base of the cliff as a bunkhouse. The following week was devoted to hauling off piles of junk that had accumulated around the premises, digging a privy, improving the trail to the sites, killing off a resident rattlesnake colony, and assembling field equipment. After years of enduring the isolation and hardships of work in the hinterlands, Morris found the proximity of Durango's supply sources most welcome.

Flora was included in the work crew in return for having alerted Morris to this potentially important research opportunity. Not only was he more conversant with local antiquities than anyone else, but his demonstrated dendrochronological skills would be useful. As Morris wrote Douglass, the developer of this dating technique, "This chap, Flora, although uneducated, is somewhat of a genius and an indefatigable worker. He hovers over tree rings as a gambler would over his cards and, I gather, has done some pretty creditable dating."[50] This was Flora's first daily field association with an accredited archaeologist, and he passed the test. Later Morris was to write, "Flora is one of the most intelligent observers and best archaeological excavators I have ever come across."[51] It was high praise from a master, who nevertheless must have gaped at Flora's unconventional tool of choice—a sharpened hunting knife.

Oley Owens and Oscar Tatman, two farmers from Aztec who had dug for Morris on each of his Southwestern projects since 1916, also came to camp. To Morris, they were like silent partners who between them probably had learned more about successful field methods than most contemporary professionals. All their skills were called into play in the difficult task at hand.

The remainder of the crew comprised Paul Franke, son of the chief ranger naturalist at Mesa Verde National Park; Frank Lee, member of the Durango archaeological society and NYA supervisor who later attained a degree in anthropology from the University of Colorado; and H. E. Gardner, a local man in need of a job. None then had any formal training or experience in this kind of work, but as shovel hands, they were not expected to do more than follow orders.

Work began at the North Shelter, where the steeply slanted floor was a jumble of weighty stone slabs and piles of smaller rock that had scaled from the ceiling after the site had been vacated (Fig. 1.6). The large blocks could not be blasted out for fear of loosening tons of fissured rock and obliterating any archaeological materials beneath or around them. Danger to the crew was another consideration. Only by hours of brute labor with sledges was the zone cleared. Two NYA helpers dug three lateral trenches leading away from the excavated area next to the cliff face, manned wheelbarrows to cart off the overburden, and dumped it down the talus slope. The dust raised was almost intolerable. Tatman, veteran of many cave digs, suffered so severely that he had to avoid the area until this initial work was done. Daniels was on site nearly every day making drawings of the pictographs (Fig. 1.7).

Once the preliminary clearing was accomplished, the workers outlined four distinct man-made terraces leading downslope from

Fig. 1.6. North Shelter in 1938 prior to excavation, showing narrowness of possible living area and extensive drift of rocks and earth since abandonment. Flora stands at right center. *Courtesy University of Colorado Museum, Boulder, Colorado.*

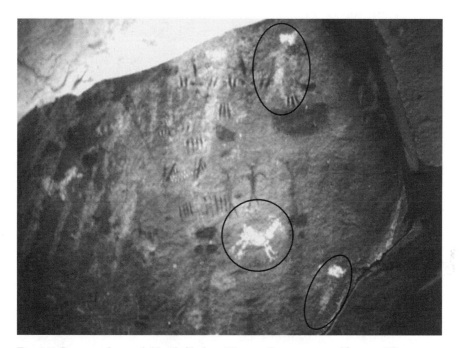

Fig. 1.7. Pictograph panel, North Shelter. Human figures, *top and bottom right,* are tur-
quoise with white headdresses. Central quadruped is white. Remainder of elements
are dark red. *Courtesy San Juan–Rio Grande National Forest.*

north to south that were held secure by rough rocks scraped aside
when they had been leveled. Excavations commenced on the upper-
most of these smoothed areas because visible slabs partially outlining
a cist had been discovered. All terraces had experienced prolonged
periods of moisture, the result of centuries of summer clouds boiling
up over the mountains and dropping their wind-swept loads. Substantial dampness had rotted all delicate objects, and Morris lost
hope of recovering further perishable artifacts. Inevitably this
enhanced the value of the Flora collection.

　　Although the yield of perishables was disappointing, two-and-a-
half months of tedious, painstaking brushing and troweling through
up to nine feet of darkened, human-related deposits revealed partial
outlines of what appeared to be use-hardened house floors, numerous
storage cists of several styles dug below or placed on floors (Fig. 1.8),

Fig.1.8. A number of living surfaces and cists on North Shelter Terrace II after excavation. Construction here dates to the A.D. 200s. *Courtesy University of Colorado
Museum, Boulder, Colorado.*

floor pits that were interpreted as places where hot rocks might have
been stacked, implements of various materials, portions of dried animal and vegetal foodstuffs, bits of human bones and strands of cordage thrown out of the burial crevice during Flora's agitated pot-
hunting, and graves lacking pottery offerings.[52] In all likelihood,
Flora's earlier trenches cut into and mixed cultural deposits in the
South Shelter, but the same kinds of occupational evidence were
present in both alcoves (Fig 1.9).

The Falls Creek shelters were not simply cemeteries or granaries, as so many of the Utah and Arizona Basketmaker caves then
seemed to be. They were where people long ago had eaten, worked,
slept, and died. Many of the human remains had turned to soft brown
mold. Only half of the twenty-four skeletons found outside the burial
crevice were in good enough condition to save. The bones of eleven
infants and one child were almost disintegrated. The fragile remains

Fig. 1.9. Flora surveying the excavated portion of the South Shelter in 1938. Hardened floors and storage pits are exposed. *Courtesy University of Colorado Museum, Boulder, Colorado.*

of this age group survived more readily inside the dry crevice. There, six of the nineteen burials were children.

Preparing a photographic record of the work was the sort of challenge Morris enjoyed. Without standing walls of prominent structural features in the sites, he decided to point his camera downward toward the cleared areas from some height. Fortunately, there was a pine tree in a suitable position near the front of the northern alcove. Standing with one foot on a slat he had nailed to the tree and the other braced against the shoulder of an NYA youth, Morris was able to balance the cumbersome ten-year-old American Museum of Natural History box camera and its black cloth long enough to hold his breath and take a series of exposures. Thick oak brush afforded a comparable platform at the South Shelter.[53]

At the end of the summer, Morris was satisfied that his future analyses would add a new dimension to the understanding of daily life at what he considered the opening stages of the Basketmaker-Pueblo continuum. Because his earlier work with the Basketmaker culture in Canyon de Chelly was inconclusive due to aboriginal disturbance of cultural deposits, he was especially pleased with his conclusion that use of these Durango shelters had been almost entirely restricted to the Basketmaker II horizon. There had been some later, rather minor Basketmaker III use, but its study was postponed.

Furthermore, Morris and Burgh had a larger sample of stone and bone tools than had been recovered in any previous Basketmaker work. They were unhappy, however, that they were not better able to define a specific house type. Whatever form of construction might have been raised above the floor level remained the kind of nagging mystery that keeps archaeologists awake at night. Morris wrote that he and his associate spent frustrating hours hopelessly trying to interpret every rat hole, root cast, or surface irregularity as a depression for wall or roof supports but in the end realized that they would have to look elsewhere for an answer to this question.[54]

The fill dirt within the shelters was peppered with many chunks of charcoal and a lesser number of wood pieces that Flora carefully gathered but, as examination years later would show, did not consistently document.[55] He was given time to attempt their dating. Some results were checked by Haury during a visit to the excavations. When fieldwork concluded, Morris instructed Flora to divide the wood samples into even lots to be forwarded for final dating to Gila Pueblo and to the Laboratory of Tree-Ring Research. Flora's personal appeal to Douglass for help in dating some two thousand specimens went unanswered.[56]

At the very time that the Carnegie work was in progress, Gladwin, the iconoclastic upstart, was attacking what he called the Douglass school of tree-ring dating.[57] A serious rift between the two men developed when Gladwin became very vocal in his objection to the Douglass methods of correlating measurements of ring widths and their use in cultural interpretations. More and more, Gladwin's personal attention was given to new photographic devices, new instrumentation, and what proved to be more abrasive methods of preparing wood surfaces. Flora's expertise was behind the development of a continuous microphotographic system for tree-ring dating that used a ten-power scope as a lens and sixteen-millimeter film synchronized to move ten times the speed of the moving stage. This process facilitated viewing by enlarging the tree-ring one hundred times. However, Gladwin's dating results often differed markedly from those derived by conventional methods.

For twenty years Morris supplied Douglass with archaeological wood from sites of all cultural stages and was among the first true believers in the dating results, but he was sufficiently flexible to consider conflicting readings of the Falls Creek materials. He was firmly convinced that the set of dates obtained from either Gladwin or Douglass would be among the earliest yet detected and possibly would reach into the pre-Christian era. If so, it would be a first.

Word was out that Morris had another interesting dig going, so during the summer of 1938 a stream of colleagues came to observe. Some drove up from Chaco Canyon following the annual meeting of regional scholars that after World War II would become known as the Pecos Conference. Among them were Winifred and Paul Reiter, Stuart Northrop, and W. W. "Nibs" Hill, of the University of New Mexico; Nan Cook, a regional ethnographer; Anna Shepard, ceramic specialist; Emil Haury; and Charles Amsden, curator at the Southwest Museum in Los Angeles. Morris carefully included Flora and Daniels in discussions with these visitors and in so doing helped salve the hurt left from Paul Martin's blunt refusal to examine skulls they considered unusual. Outwardly at least, they were accepted for what they were—enthusiastic students of their regional past.

If Flora was irked that Morris was being praised for demonstrating that some Basketmakers did indeed live in houses and that these particular individuals may have been biologically distinctive, he did not reveal it in a 1939 revision to his earlier paper on local prehistory. He did, however, indirectly stake his own claims. He wrote, "It was indeed an inspiration to have many tentative details verified by the Carnegie crew including Basket Maker II floors, seemingly a different physical type than the recognized Basket Maker people, the 'basin' metate, chipped projectiles and blades, time of occupation, duration of occupation, etc."[58]

During the next winter the notable mummy Esther, who like other showbiz stars went by a single name, hit the road. Morris dispatched her to Washington for an annual Carnegie Institution meeting. The *Durango News* reported that in the exhibition hall, with two dozen booths featuring various Carnegie projects worldwide, Esther stole the show.[59] The article credited Flora (not Daniels) with Esther's discovery, but Morris was the obvious beneficiary of her fame. He proudly stood beside her for a picture that appeared in *Science News Letter* (Fig. 1.10).[60]

While in the East, Esther's body was X-rayed to try to ascertain the reason for her early demise. Nusbaum, the Mesa Verde superintendent, also wanted to know if, before burial, her mouth had been filled with kernels of corn or colored stones. Quantities of these objects frequently were found scattered near Basketmaker human remains. The X-ray results were negative.

At the time Esther was making headlines back East, Flora submitted a long article to the *Durango News* outlining the Falls Creek work of the previous summer and the analyses of various classes of material that were to be undertaken.[61] In the same issue of the newspaper, Flora relayed a request from Carnegie archaeologist Kidder for skulls removed from sites within a ten-mile radius of Durango to be sent to Harvard University, through Flora, for comparative studies. Behind this request can be sensed the great extent of uncontrolled digging taking place. This was confirmed when Flora shipped at least fifty-eight skulls contributed by local collectors, apparently without any sort of documentation, to the Peabody Museum, where physical anthropologist George Woodbury was to study them. What followed was another of the muddled affairs that came to characterize so much of the pursuit of Durango antiquity.

After two years, when it became obvious that Woodbury was not going to follow through on his proposed study, several Harvard graduate students made a cursory examination of the skulls before returning them to Durango. No formal report was written. The present whereabouts of any of the specimens are unknown.

It is most unfortunate that the actions of amateurs and professionals alike short-circuited an opportunity that has not come again

Fig. 1.10. Earl H. Morris stands by a 1938 Carnegie Institution of Washington exhibit of some of his findings in the Four Corners area. Deleted from this photo, the mummy Esther, adorned with a lengthy olivella-shell necklace wrapped many times around her neck, was displayed in a glass case to Morris's left. I have chosen not to include her picture out of respect for Native American wishes. *Lister Collection.*

for serious comparative physical analyses of what likely were two different populations occupying the same territory at different times. In the beginning stages of the explorations of regional prehistory, basic questions concerning possible successive human migrations into the area by diverse groups might have been answered. Not the least benefit might have been to rein in Flora's wild imagination, which for years to come would muddy interpretive waters.

After a limited exhibition at the University of Colorado Museum in Boulder, Esther next traveled to Mesa Verde National Park. A glass box was prepared so that museum visitors could view her wizened charms from all sides. Writing in the *Toledo Blade* of June 29, 1939, Ernie Pyle, soon to gain fame as a war correspondent, said he was in park naturalist Don Watson's office when she arrived in a wooden crate labeled THIS SIDE UP. When they opened the container, Watson was repulsed. Esther was just plain ugly because of prunelike shrinkage that had reduced her weight to a mere sixteen pounds and contorted her features over the centuries. By many standards, she never had been a beauty in life; in death she had become a curiosity. Regardless, the display was installed. The thousands of visitors who walked through the museum stared at Esther, called her by name, and bought postcards featuring her facial grimace and bony torso. Navajo workers at the park complained of dizzy spells whenever they passed near her case. She was at best famous, at worst, a sideshow.

In June 1939 Morris brought some items from the Carnegie holdings to the Durango Public Library, where Daniels's Indian Room was expanding through contributions from many of the nearby collectors. Among them were digging sticks used by the ancient peoples in their farming activities, part of a cache of twenty-seven such objects that Temple Cornelius, a sheepherder turned pothunter, had retrieved from a cave in Pump Canyon south of Durango.[62] Cornelius also loaned some yucca fiber sandals from an amazing hoard of 175 examples of such footgear that he found in another cave on Mesa Mountain. Flora contributed assorted pottery from several dozen sites he had opened.[63] Included in the Carnegie contribution were the Falls Creek mummy Jasper in his burial hide, two baskets, a cradleboard, and two necklaces once belonging to

Tannis. Morris did not know that at both Mesa Verde and Durango, the labels next to the exhibited mummies listed him as their discoverer. Those credits, one provided by Flora's comrade-in-arms Daniels, inflicted a wound to Flora's ego that festered and never healed.

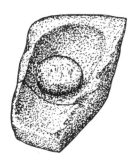

Explorations in Falls Creek Flats

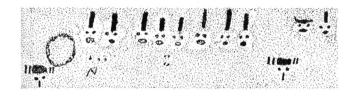

In his revised paper on Durango prehistory, Flora stated that he knew of at least forty Basketmaker II floors in the Animas district.[64] Either he withheld that information from Morris, or the sites were deemed unsuitable for study. Back in the field in 1939, Morris and Burgh instead turned to six of the twenty sites partly trenched earlier by Flora and to some extent by his NYA helpers (Figs. 1.11-1.14). They each consisted of one or several associated living rooms dug down into the ground and thus were true pithouses. Several surface chambers made of materials that later decayed were located on rises above the floor of a small opening at the northern end of Falls Creek Valley. From the pithouses in particular, excavators hoped to obtain information about possible construction methods for the structures indicated the season before in the rock shelters.

In this, Morris and Burgh were disappointed once again because settlement pattern and style of domicile differed significantly from what had been exposed the previous summer. The pithouses were comparable to others Morris had dug in the La Plata district; that is, there was evidence on the earthen floors for a system of four or six vertical posts that supported slanted pole-and-mud walls, perhaps covered with tules, and either a cribbed or flat roof. Lateral ventilation shafts and central pits where open fires obviously had been kindled were typical (Figs. 1.15-1.17). Surface rooms were contiguous

Fig. 1.11. NYA crew members clearing overburden from Basketmaker III site Ign 7:36 in Falls Creek Flats, 1939. A pithouse and seven contiguous surface rooms were uncovered. *Courtesy Charles Brockway, Helen Sloan Daniels Collection.*

rectangular units of poles and mud arranged in an arc at one side of the pithouses. Only foundations remained. Morris regarded them as storage facilities.

From the architecture and the presence of the same sort of gray or black-on-gray pottery with which Flora's excursion into regional archaeology had begun, Morris judged all the sites in Falls Creek Flats to be Basketmaker III, postdating the deposits in the rock shelters (Fig. 1.18). Dendrochronologist Douglass, who spent a week at the excavations poring over tree-ring charts, dated their construction to the mid-700s, a time regional archaeologists would now consider the early Pueblo I period.[65] Flora was convinced that he read dates some 350 years earlier. This was an error that Douglass attributed to Flora's having overlooked some microscopic rings and being content with a near rather than precise reading. Part of the problem may have been the difficulties encountered in trying to date rings in scopulorum juniper, a kind of conifer commonly used in construction.

Fig. 1.12. Flora cleans a small piece of pottery near the encircling banquette and ventilator opening at site Ign 7:36, Falls Creek Flats, 1939. *Courtesy Charles Brockway, Helen Sloan Daniels Collection.*

Regardless, on this first encounter with the father of dendrochronology, Flora felt no need to correct his own findings. He was becoming ever more intent on satisfying his notion that the natives of the Animas district were older than others were willing to admit.

If Flora's dates for the pithouses were correct, it would have made the Basketmaker II and Basketmaker III occupations contemporaneous, with pottery producers and those lacking this technology living side by side. This was a situation totally at odds with the sequential Pecos Classification by which Anasazi archaeologists arranged their data. Morris forthrightly rejected Flora's dates and accepted those of Douglass and Gladwin.[66] Whether he acknowledged it or not, Flora was overruled.

For the first time the work of the 1939 season defined in professional terms the dominant period of prehistoric occupation of the upper Animas region. Even so, Morris was disheartened. He was so intent on solving the Basketmaker II architectural riddle that the

Fig. 1.13. Flora photographing at site Ign 7:30. Note the dense growth covering the Falls Creek Flats Basketmaker III sites. *Courtesy Charles Brockway, Helen Sloan Daniels Collection.*

familiar later material was of no special interest at the time. When the 1939 season ended, he put the bulk of his new excavation data aside, publishing only very brief papers in 1949 and 1952, hoping for better luck next time. He died before completing his work.

One clue to Morris's discontent with the results of the 1939 program is revealed in a shipment of fourteen specimens of skeletal material he made to the Peabody Museum at Harvard. Remains recovered in six other burials were too fragmentary or decomposed to save. Morris carelessly wrapped the bones in newspapers and scribbled field specimen numbers on the outside of the bundles without putting any identification on the bones themselves. At the Peabody Museum a laboratory assistant assigned the unpacking task not unexpectedly threw the wrappings away without noticing the numbering. It seemed the comedy of errors in Durango archaeology would never end. Morris must have been chagrined when Donald Scott, director of the museum, chided him, "You know what you or I

Fig. 1.14. Site Ign 7:31, located on a ridge between the Falls Creek and Animas Valleys, was cleared by NYA crews prior to excavation by the Carnegie team. A pithouse and five surface rooms were surrounded by a circle of cobblestones. *Courtesy Charles Brockway, Helen Sloan Daniels Collection.*

would say of anyone who was digging and committed a comparable sin of omission."[67]

Working diligently from a separately submitted list, the Peabody Museum staff made a match with nine of the remains. Only five were in good enough condition for study. All were male skulls exhibiting no deformation. Once again, no report was written, and another opportunity to contribute knowledge about the Old Ones of Durango was lost.

A happier result of the 1939 digs was that the amateurs' cooperative efforts were scientifically fruitful. After Daniels had traveled throughout the Southwest in the late 1930s to learn how archaeological records were kept, she saw to it that the NYA digs were described in detailed handwritten notes and drawings housed at the Durango Public Library. Her efforts to conform to professional standards were exemplary. Among the sketches were some of the objects from the North Shelter burial crevice.

Fig. 1.15. Pithouse at site Ign 7:23, Falls Creek Flats. Morris, using a bulky ten-year-old camera, was perched high in a tree when he took this photograph. Note the extensive amount of wood (dated to the A.D. 700s) that had collapsed onto the ban-quette from the upper walls. *Courtesy Charles Brockway, Helen Sloan Daniels Collection.*

Fig. 1.16. Cleared surface room of site Ign 7:30, Falls Creek Flats, showing slab-based construction. *Courtesy Charles Brockway, Helen Sloan Daniels Collection.*

Fig. 1.17. Morris clings precariously to a treetop to take photographs of a pithouse far below at site Ign 7:30. *Courtesy Charles Brockway, Helen Sloan Daniels Collection.*

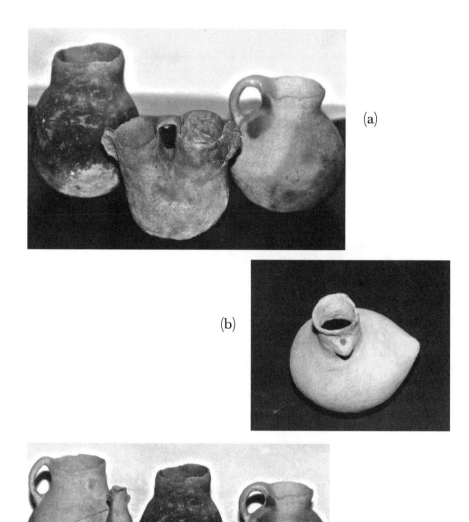

Figs. 1.18a-c. Assorted Basketmaker III earthenwares from the Helen Sloan Daniels collection obtained in the Durango area through NYA excavations during the late 1930s. *Courtesy Center of Southwest Studies, Fort Lewis College, Durango, Colorado.*

Following the 1939 excavation season, Flora spent four months at Gladwin's tree-ring workshop in Santa Barbara, California. During that time his technical sensibilities were offended by a process then being practiced by Gladwin and his associates of sandblasting sample surfaces. Other tree-ring specialists likewise were critical of this method, but perhaps tart-tongued Flora spoke out. At any rate, Gladwin abruptly severed his ties to Flora, as he said, amid a shower of sparks.[68] Two opinionated men could not compromise. Flora stated his version of events as follows: "In 1939 a deal was apparently made in which all Durango tree-ring data (including Zeke) was to go to that camp [Gladwin's]. I was only a pawn but was able to withdraw and thus upset plans."[69] In actuality, he was fired.

Back in Durango, Flora continued to build a collection of wood samples from sites all around the northern Southwest to supplement his hoarded specimens from the Falls Creek work. Acquaintances supplied fragments they gleaned on outings, and others Flora searched out himself. He spent long evenings hunched over his scopes and plots and carried on a voluminous correspondence about his findings. Slowly the rigidness of opinion that was to characterize his future began to emerge.

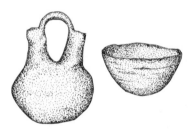

Talus Village

In the spring of 1940 Flora suggested to Morris that a possible Basketmaker II site on the west side of the upper Animas Valley might warrant study. Five years earlier he had uncovered a hardened living surface there.[70] The site was on a steep hillside near Trimble Springs on the ranch of Kenneth Logan, an archaeological society member who also had shoveled into the zone and encountered some skulls and bits of stone tools. The scree-covered slope appeared to have been leveled in one area in a fashion similar to the terraces in the Falls Creek alcoves. One unalerted to the faint traces of human modification of the surface would have walked over the spot without a second glance. However, Flora's cut revealed human-deposited debris to a depth of about three feet. Ceramics were absent. Still seeking a prototype for the local Basketmaker II residential architecture, Morris and Burgh decided to set up camp. They named the site Talus Village.

A new crew member that season was James Allen "Al" Lancaster. He deserves special mention not because of particular involvement with the Durango Basketmaker story but because his long career in Southwestern archaeology exemplifies a phenomenon no longer possible in a discipline that now demands an advanced degree for the lowliest field task. Like Flora, Lancaster came into research on regional prehistory via the Great Depression. He was untrained but smart and needed an income. In the late 1920s, unable to provide for his young family on a bean farm in southwestern Colorado, he took a job on a digging crew assembled by Paul Martin.

On behalf of Chicago's Field Museum of Natural History, Martin proposed to excavate a series of sites in the western Montezuma Valley. Included in his plans was Lowry Ruin, a large masonry houseblock situated on a homestead adjoining that of Lancaster's in-laws. Like most others living in that part of the state, Al and his family occasionally roamed the region's many ruins and had a lively curiosity about farmers of an earlier time who faced survival in an often inhospitable land. But unlike Flora, Lancaster never was a pothunter.[71]

Given the opportunity under Martin's guidance, Lancaster soon demonstrated a talent for the practical skills of a competent field technician. He was promoted to Martin's dig boss for several seasons, then worked for J. O. Brew on Harvard excavations in southern Utah. In 1934, he formed part of a National Park Service stabilization crew directed by Earl Morris that repaired Cliff Palace at Mesa Verde. It was the beginning of a long friendship between the two men.

After the 1940 stint with Morris at the Basketmaker II Talus Village, Lancaster continued perfecting his excavation and stabilization techniques. He worked on a number of projects, including one with Haury at an important Hohokam settlement in southern Arizona, but his principal activities over the next thirty years were with National Park Service excavators and Navajo stabilizers at Mesa Verde. Again, unlike Flora, he left the bold cultural reconstructions to the academics but did contribute to a number of published reports. He was highly respected for the role he played and as a consequence received several honors. When he died in 1992 at the age of ninety-eight, bean farmers, archaeologists, and Navajo masons sat side by side at his memorial service, each feeling that Al Lancaster had been a meaningful part of their working lives.

Excavation at Talus Village was exhausting because of the slanting gradient of the terrain and the difficulty of detecting occupational zones buried by centuries of loaded runoff and sloughed soil (Fig. 1.19). As trenches ate into sections of the incline, slight changes in

Fig. 1.19. Initial clearing of the Basketmaker II hillside site known as Talus Village (Ing 7:101), 1940. *Courtesy University of Colorado Museum, Boulder, Colorado.*

soil color or compactness were the only clues to the presence of many saucer-shaped earthen floors of one-room structures. They were stacked up against the hillside on two terraces held in place by a rock border, and they often cut through each other as successive building episodes took place (Fig. 1.20). A bewildering maze of different kinds of cists, warming pits, and holes for unknown purposes pockmarked the floors (Fig. 1.21). Some held the bony mortal remains of former residents, few with grave offerings. Diggers were rewarded with many stone and bone tools, but objects made of fibers had rotted. Pottery was not present.

In general, the excavations were a revisit to the rock shelters, with the same range of material goods and little doubt that they were contemporaneous. They confirmed that some of the early Basketmakers lived under cover on hogbacks and hillsides. Exactly what kind of shelters they erected remained a troubling question until just a week before the work was scheduled to end.[72]

Fig. 1.20. Tiers of partially cleared earthen floors stacked against a slope at Talus Village. When a structure was no longer usable, it was dismantled to make room for a later structure built above it. This occupation dates to approximately A.D. 200 to A.D. 350. *Courtesy University of Colorado Museum, Boulder, Colorado.*

With Morris on his knees beside him, Burgh traced the imprint of short footing logs laid horizontally around the outer ring of a floor and in one section found several pieces of wall logs still in place. The men decided that above the floor a house shell was composed of horizontal logs, with quantities of mud mortar to hold and chink them into a flattened or truncated dome roof. This created an architectural feature rather like a hard orange cut in half and placed upon a saucer. No vertical posts within the circumference of the room were necessary to sustain this sort of construction. Morris was amazed that he had not suspected such a logical solution to a building problem, especially in a forested environment. After all, the mountains were dotted with nineteenth-century log cabins laid up in the same way. Maybe the prehistoric homes were circular rather than rectangular because short logs were more easily handled without metal axes and winches. Or perhaps there was some underriding convention that dictated a

Fig. 1.21. A confusing mass of storage cists crowded successive house floors at Talus Village. *Courtesy University of Colorado Museum, Boulder, Colorado.*

home should be round. Regardless, the abundance of charcoal surely was due to extensive use of timber in building.

Morris ended his Durango research on this successful note but was personally distressed. In addition to the serious illness of his wife, Ann, he had trouble coping with Flora's growing contentiousness. At the time, Morris did not realize that Flora was afflicted with a strong sense of territoriality and resented Morris and Burgh's intrusion onto his turf. It was he, after all, who had first discovered the Basketmaker II floors for which Morris and Burgh were being congratulated. Flora further longed for public acclaim for his Falls Creek burial discoveries and what he saw as his pre-eminence among local antiquarians.[73] At the same time, Flora was insecure about his lack of formal schooling in the science. He did not have Gladwin's *savoir vivre.*

There was another side to camp disharmony that summer due in part to a current scientific fallacy that was taken to extremes by Flora, who possessed only a smattering of knowledge about human evolution but nevertheless held a set of inflexible opinions. Because of him, an argument revolved around the physical characteristics of the recovered human remains. Up until the late 1930s, regional prehistorians were of the opinion that the Basketmakers and the later Pueblos were two distinct physical strains, the Basketmakers possessing long, or dolichocephalic, skulls and the Pueblos having rounder, or brachycephalic, skulls. Morris, who had handled hundreds of such remains from both Basketmaker and Pueblo contexts, thought the Falls Creek Basketmakers were biologically distinctive. His reaction as expressed to Kidder was, "The skulls impressed me particularly; the majority are very small, very broad, with extremely low foreheads. This bunch might represent a family of cretins or the like, but if they are typical of the contemporary population, the latter would appear to have been a different strain of Basket Maker than we have known heretofore."[74] He echoed Flora's viewpoint, and without realizing it, his off-the-cuff remarks probably fueled his helper's fantasies.

As he worked with the materials, Morris modified his assessment somewhat. He described the Falls Creek Basketmaker II people as being short in stature and having low-vaulted mesocephalic skills with prominent brow ridges. He did not think they were handsome in appearance, and he still felt they represented a different Basketmaker migration into this part of the northern Southwest than that which had taken place elsewhere. He did not consider them to be anything other than Basketmakers.

By the time the 1954 Morris and Burgh report was written, physical anthropologists were in agreement that Basketmakers and Pueblos were one basic breeding population, which they termed the Southwest Plateau stock.[75] Differences in shape of skulls were due to use by the Pueblos of a hard cradleboard that deformed the soft bones of infants (Fig. 1.22). Most often in the San Juan region the flattening was lambdoid, or applied to the upper occiput at a fifty-to-sixty-degree angle.[76] Flora rejected the deformation idea as "silly."

The scientists described the Southwest Plateau physical category with enough latitude to allow for regionalizations, and the Durango people were apparently seen as one variant of a widespread type of

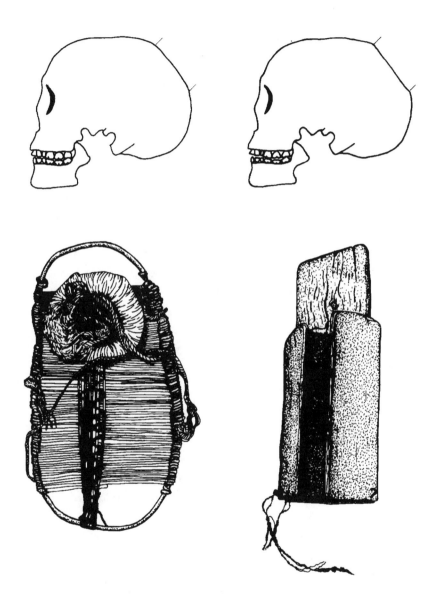

Fig. 1.22. The typical flexible cradleboard used by Basketmakers, *bottom left,* caused no deformation of the infant's skull, *top left.* The hard cradleboard, *bottom right,* preferred by later Pueblos tended to cause a permanent flattening of the infant's skull, *top right.*

early Native American.[77] In addition to having heavy facial features, at first they were thought to have walked with bent knees because of the tilt of the joint surfaces of their shin bones. Later these unusual surfaces were recognized as facets resulting from the habit of squatting flat-footed. Otherwise, they were generic Basketmakers.

Flora converted "Durango Man," as he now called the local Basketmakers, into a Neanderthal, one of a number of Old World fossils preceding modern humans. Most scientists believe *Homo sapiens neanderthalensis* was widespread in Europe and the Middle East anywhere from 150,000 to 35,000 years ago, or roughly the Middle Pleistocene period. Neanderthals disappeared in Europe about the time modern *Homo sapiens sapiens* appeared there. Flora termed his Basketmaker representative a mutant who was half ape and half human. He said Durango Man lived at high altitudes along the Animas in order to track and kill bison grazing in the valleys below. Flora ignored the charred remains of domesticated corn and the stone implements used to process it, thus glossing over the probability that these people were part-time farmers rather than full-time hunters.

As Daniels's 1937 letter to the Field Museum of Natural History concerning skull differences noted, Flora had posited a Neanderthal connection from his first finds of Basketmaker II skulls. However, this radical idea seems to have solidified in his mind during the spring of 1940. From that time on, he was a man possessed and turned a deaf ear to all contrary evidence. Brew, the Harvard archaeologist who specialized in Southwestern prehistory, wrote him, "I would not be a friend to you if I did not point out that the pictures of skulls which you sent me do *not* show the characteristics of Neanderthal Man."[78]

Flora did not budge then or ever from his set-in-concrete notion. Never mind that European scholars said the Neanderthal branch of the human family tree died out thousands of years before the New World was peopled. Never mind that no Neanderthals had been discovered in north China or Outer Mongolia, generally regarded as the points of origin for hunters migrating across the Bering Strait. Never mind that no heavy stone implements of the Mousterian cultural period—diagnostics for Neanderthal presence elsewhere—were found locally. Never mind that no bison bones turned up in the Animas Valley excavations.

The specter of Gladwin looms large in this rigid attitude of Flora's. The two men certainly had discussed the apparent uniqueness of the Durango Basketmaker II. For Gladwin, these people were products of a crossbreeding between Australoid and Negroid strains of humans from what he proposed were the first two New World migrations, which ended some thirteen thousand years ago.[79] Several physical anthropologists of the day speculated upon this same theme. Flora, however, stood alone. The basic difference in the approach of these two men to their quasi-heretical ideas was that Gladwin viewed his as an enjoyable game of eternal chess. For Flora, there was no levity.

Flora's warped perspective was recorded many times, thanks to an ignorant or disinterested press who might have been better served by consulting recognized authorities before publication. One Flora account, written in the voice of the mummy Esther, reads,

> Although I was X-rayed from head to toe, you need only to see my photo to realize that I was very primitive. Just look at my jaw and my bull-like neck. I really have no forehead as the top of my head starts just above the ears, my brain box is back of my ears instead of above them as yours is. This accounts for the heavy neck, thrust forward. Yes, we had the unbalanced head of the animal kingdom and our heads bobbed up and down as we shuffled through the game trails in a crouching, stiff-legged walk. My ancestors were probably the first group of people to cross from Asia, by way of the Bering Strait.[80]

When Morris tried to point out some of the gross errors in this interpretation, Flora became argumentative and attributed the rejection of his theory to academic jealousy. The battle was joined. "A ranking amateur is one so successful he is discriminated against by the profession," he wrote. And, "The first reaction of organized archaeologists to any discovery made by an amateur is adverse and belittling."[81]

Flora was entitled to his own fanciful ideas, but when he presented them in print as established fact, Morris felt his own credibility and that of his institution were assaulted. It was then that he realized the pitfalls of working with someone lacking scientific caution. At summer's end in 1940 the two men parted on unfriendly terms. Morris removed Flora from the Carnegie payroll and requested return of all the Falls Creek tree-ring specimens.[82] Flora only partially complied. He never supplied a report on the tree-ring studies he presumably undertook. Furthermore, unknown to his superior, throughout the Carnegie project Flora had stockpiled a large sample of charcoal specimens for himself. He was guilty of stealing artifacts that could be expected to yield significant data.

Flora's brief but tumultuous paid career in Durango prehistory terminated at the end of the 1940 field season. He had provided some valuable assistance to Gladwin and Morris, the two most prominent researchers into the area's past. On his own he also did untold damage. Although he sometimes wrote of the amateur's threat to full scientific recovery, he himself lacked any apparent feeling of guilt. Inexplicably, he must have felt he was above reproach. At times he boasted that in a seven-year period he opened from five hundred to one thousand graves and collected from twelve hundred to two thousand pottery vessels and other artifacts within ten miles of Durango. Even if these figures were overblown, much of prehistorical value doubtless was lost. Few of his finds were documented with the kind of precise detail required for accurate cultural reconstruction, and except for the pottery collection sold to Gila Pueblo and a limited number of items excavated for that foundation, it is not known where most retrieved specimens now reside. The category of material that Flora did save—and that would bring him some deserved thanks—was a large assortment of tree-ring samples that would substantiate the early nature of the occupation of the high north country.

The loss of professional connections inflicted a blow to Flora's self-esteem that he compensated for by writing a series of newspaper articles designed to cement his reputation as the town's resident archaeologist. Increasingly, it became a darkening story line pitting the astute, maligned amateur against the baffled, unscrupulous scientist. To him,

Ph.D. translated as "piled higher and deeper."[83] Again, there was Gladwin's shadow. In some of that individual's writings he imagined a cartoonish character of an inept professorial type named Dr. Phuddy (Phuderick) Duddy.[84] In so doing, he displayed a disdain for academicians that fueled Flora's discontent. Trouble lay ahead.

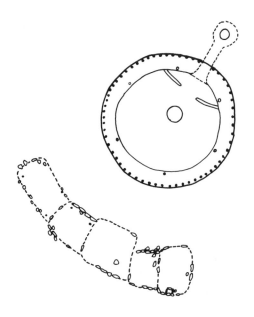

Clouded Postscript

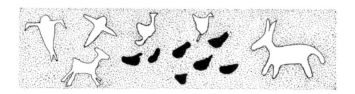

Meanwhile, Daniels, who had been under Flora's influence from the beginning of their association, likewise had her own misgivings about the way archaeological studies were going. First, she resented seeing the specimens excavated in the Durango area by the Carnegie project being taken away. Moreover, because the Animas district was her prehistoric universe, Daniels expressed concern that those who brought it to scientific attention were not getting the help or commendation they deserved. This concern reflected the need for cooperation between nonprofessionals and paid researchers if both were to share in an increasingly technical endeavor. She commented, "We have spotted sites that Mr. Morris has never taken the time to see. He says that he already has so much started that he may never finish that he declines to take on any more. This area was developed to the extent of finding the divergence of types which he merely adopted in part, so we still must keep punching it out for ourselves."[85]

To do just that, Daniels and Flora undertook a series of columns—some of which were reprinted in the *Durango News* and *Durango Herald Democrat*—that they later collected under the title *Sherds and Points*. These articles treated a range of topics concerning the aboriginal past of the Animas district. When the reporting was straightforward, it served a worthwhile purpose, promptly presenting useful information to a wider audience. The articles' value was reduced by the authors' sometimes narrative approach, presumably to make the subject matter more palatable to the general public. It was another Gladwin tactic, but in his case, the treatment was generally humorous.

Regrettably, the series became a forum for Flora's mounting strident antagonism toward the archaeological establishment. For him, this meant Gladwin, Nusbaum, and Morris. Without naming them specifically, he constantly accused them of "self-aggrandizement," doubtless seeing in others his own faults. He angrily claimed that a form letter was being circulated nationwide warning professionals against having any dealings with three Durango amateurs, assuming he was one of them. This intemperance merely served to increase the polarization between involved factions. Unintentionally, Flora also revealed his lack of scientific grounding when he stated he wanted to avoid "one man's report made uninteresting by bibliographies, French measurements, and questioned tradition," translation: no references, no metric system, no open-mindedness.[86]

Prepared under the auspices of the San Juan Archaeological Society, *Sherds and Points* was mimeographed and sent to several dozen specialists in the field as a demonstration of the amateurs' good intentions, as well as to air their grievances. Complimentary replies came in from Carl Guthe, University of Michigan; J. O. Brew, Harvard University; Charles Amsden, Southwest Museum; Leonard Leh, University of Colorado; and Emil Haury, University of Arizona.[87] These men wisely hoped to encourage responsible reporting by their avocational colleagues. However, E. B. Renaud, University of Denver, wrote Flora and Daniels a thinly veiled criticism of Morris and his pot-hunting reputation. In Renaud's view, there could not be two standards of conduct toward protecting the integrity of aboriginal materials. Douglas Byers, editor of *American Antiquity,* and C. T. Hurst, editor of *Southwestern Lore,* invited a follow-up article by Flora or Daniels on the difficulties to be overcome between the two camps. Such a response was not forthcoming.

Renaud's opinion revealed a basic stumbling block to harmony between the two opposing groups engaged in regional prehistoric inquiries: the dearth of general public education about how to approach—and guard—the nation's heritage. The prevailing attitudes hardened into a confrontation between those who wanted to excavate using their own methods (in particular, those with ruins on their property) and those who saw such activity as destructive to finite ground truth. Until the amateurs were willing to learn and the professionals to instruct, each respecting the other's point of view, there could be no resolution. As Douglas Byers noted in a guest column in *Sherds and Points,* "The failure to know more about archaeology is the amateur's handicap. Why? Because the professional hasn't taken the opportunity to help and educate the amateur by telling him what the problems are."[88]

Lack of communication between amateurs and professionals was illustrated by the proposal before the Durango Library board to expand the Indian Room into a permanent museum. Morris was never fully informed of these plans. Undoubtedly, had he known, he would have arranged to have an adequate representative collection sent there. As it was, the entire Carnegie artifact assortment, with the exception of the materials from the North Shelter burial crevice, was donated to the University of Colorado Museum in Boulder, four hundred miles away on the Front Range of the Rockies. Though deflated and feeling cheated of artifacts from the Carnegie collection, the locals were partly to blame for the dilemma that Flora quaintly described as a "freeze-out."[89] During the subsequent war years, collectors withdrew their loaned specimens from the Indian Room, the archaeological society stopped meeting, and plans for a museum were tabled.

After the Carnegie work in the Animas district was stopped, a cave originally excavated by Nusbaum near Kanab, Utah, yielded the earliest date yet determined for a Colorado Plateau site—A.D. 217. Douglass, who announced the dating, stated that the figure was arrived at through comparison with a beam from Talus Village (Ign 7:101). Flora, in what was becoming his typical disregard for the facts, sent the obliging *Durango News* a note that the very oldest date so far determined for the Southwest came from humble Basketmaker huts on the outskirts of town. Douglass and Morris fumed, to no avail.[90] As it turned out, the Kanab date was later shown to be erroneous and the

Falls Creek shelters did indeed yield the earliest tree-ring dates. Flora was vindicated.

Now and then a touch of humor poked through the cloud of Flora hostility. In *Sherds and Points* he created an author he called Sherd Temper, who wrote amusingly about Bee-em (Basketmaker), Peewon (Pueblo I), and Peetooi (Pueblo II).[91] Once more, Flora was emulating Gladwin. Later he had a business card prepared that listed his professions as he perceived them: dendrochronologist, archaeologist, and horologist, in that order. Tongue-in-cheek, he noted his hobbies as grave robber, game exterminator, and mummy excavator; his specialties as making A-bombs, counterfeiting, and dermograting; and his outstanding failures as movie actor, writer, and laborer. Poking fun at himself in this way underscored the poignancy of his unmitigated anger at the world.

During 1941 and 1942, Morris's hopes of settling down to an analysis of the Durango Basketmaker II sites dwindled. He was burdened with a backlog of unfinished work; the outbreak of World War II, which took away his laboratory assistants; a delay in obtaining critical tree-ring dates because Douglass was engaged in war-related work; and his wife's terminal illness. The boxes of specimens sat unopened in his workroom.

As 1943 dawned, a bombshell arrived from Flora, demanding return of the burial crevice collection. He claimed it had been "rented" to Morris for a study period of eighteen months, and that deadline had long expired.[92] Morris was stunned at this new twist on their old agreement and felt justified in refusing. Flora subsequently dashed off a series of hateful letters to Kidder and his higher-ups at Carnegie and to Haury, accusing Morris not only of stealing Flora's artifacts but giving them as souvenirs to his friends.[93]

Another letter from Flora to Morris told of a new find. "Recently a cave was reported to me on the Pine River Drainage. Investigation proved it to be contemporaneous with the Falls Creek Caves. An outstanding feature was an unburied house nearly intact to the eaves."[94] If this were bait to get his former sponsor back into the field, Morris did not take it. However, he did notify Nusbaum. Nusbaum, wanting to avoid another Falls Creek fiasco, asked an avocational archaeologist in Bayfield, Colorado, to inquire whether such a site had indeed been discovered.[95] Surely every casual digger would be alerted. No one had news of any such site. Nor has one been verified in the more than fifty years since. Nonetheless, Flora wrote Douglass that he removed thirty beams from the mysterious structure.[96]

Meanwhile, Flora's epistolary barrage against his perceived archaeological enemies continued until it was obvious there was no recourse but for Morris to ask the government to confiscate the burial crevice goods. Morris wrote the National Forest and National Park Service authorities in the Durango district to explain the circumstances surrounding the plunder.[97] He suggested that the human remains at the Peabody Museum of Harvard University be allowed to stay there for study. Unknown to Flora, most had been cleaned of skin tissue and hair to permit key observations. Flora was also unaware that Tannis, the Bead Girl, had been disposed of years earlier after her remains grew odorous pink mold, the result of her sojourn beneath a leak in Morris's roof. Morris proposed that the thirty-seven other objects removed from the Falls Creek burial crevice be permanently deposited in the Mesa Verde museum, the closest suitable facility to the find area.

Pleading his cause, Flora protested to anyone who would listen that even had he sought an excavation permit, Nusbaum would have denied him because Nusbaum favored only those who provided kickbacks to the Mesa Verde museum. Flora must have known, however, that Nusbaum had no authority to grant excavation permits on Forest Service lands, and the charge made against him was patently false.

On September 10, 1945, J. B. Huston, acting secretary of agriculture, signed the confiscation orders eight years after the illegal act occurred.[98] Prosecution was forestalled because the government lawyer in charge felt the statute of limitations had expired. Flora attempted damage control by putting a new spin on the recent events. Determined to have the last word, he mailed a statement to the *Durango Herald Democrat* that was picked up by the *Denver Post* stating that "Flora, deciding that 'Esther" and a companion mummy, 'Jasper," had overspent their stay in Carnegie Institution took steps to have them placed permanently in the Mesa Verde park museum."[99]

He had come to believe they were six thousand years old, the most important finds ever made on this continent, and he was seeing that they were protected.

If Flora's alleged adversaries thought that was the end of the Esther affair, they were soon disappointed. Exactly a month after the confiscation, a three-column article appeared in the *Durango News* that rocked them. It repeated Flora's outlandish Neanderthal drivel and in unmistakable terms accused Morris of conspiracy and the Mesa Verde staff of arranging a deal. The piece, obviously written by Flora himself, said in part:

> The anthropologist that studies the skulls bemoans the fact that an outsider, an amateur, has definitely proven what they could only guess at before. There was a primitive type of man that did not walk quite erect slouching through the hills of North America a long time before and up until the time of Christ. But then the thought occurs to him that no one will believe the amateur if the scientist does not back him up with a report. If he stalls long enough, now that he knows the clues he might be able to find his own and get the credit.[100]

Nusbaum exploded. He was a large imposing figure, with a booming voice and quick temper. He could easily intimidate. He stormed into the office of the owner of the paper, Judge John B. O'Rourke of the Sixth District Court, demanding an apology for the article that he felt vilified Morris, the Carnegie Institution, and Mesa Verde National Park. He protested the reams of archaeological misinformation that the account irresponsibly gave readers. Judge O'Rourke lamely responded that he regretted the article, but he had not been in town when it appeared. He remembered Morris as a 1908 classmate at the University of Colorado and, to make amends, invited him to write a response to be published in the paper in the near future.

The Carnegie executive officer, Walter Gilbert, asked Morris not to answer in the belief that silence would be the best weapon against Flora's egotism. Morris grumbled but bit his tongue. Nusbaum, nevertheless, threatened a government libel suit against the paper and, on behalf of science, asked a number of fellow archaeologists to write the paper to complain about printing such far-fetched fantasy.

While all parties were still smarting over the newspaper-article upset, another shocker came to light. The authorities learned that three of the Falls Creek specimens loaned to the Durango Public Library for its exhibit—a cradleboard and two necklaces—had disappeared and consequently could not be turned over to the Mesa Verde museum. Nusbaum threatened another lawsuit. As secretary of the library board, beleaguered Judge O'Rourke convened an emergency joint meeting of the board and Mesa Verde administrators that erupted into a firestorm.

Many raw nerves were exposed. Some citizens harbored a deep resentment against Morris and Burgh in particular and federal agencies in general because of a perceived lack of concern for local interests. For their part, the government officials thought the local amateurs had brazenly flouted the law.

Daniels took the lead. She asserted that Flora was an employee of the NYA (actually he was an unpaid volunteer) when the Falls Creek incident occurred and that she and Flora, through the NYA and after the fact, had asked for an excavation permit in 1937. She wanted a trench dug at the base of the pictograph panel to prevent further vandalization. She was unaware that such disturbance surely would have negatively impacted the archaeological evidence. Fortunately, her application had somehow been tabled. Meanwhile, Morris, with the backing of his influential institution, acquired the coveted permit and usurped their territory.

Dumbfounded at her assertions, Nusbaum explained that nonprofessionals were not qualified for a permit under the terms of the Uniform Rules and Regulations of the Antiquities Act. Furthermore, even if Flora had been an NYA associate when he unearthed the specimens, he could not rightfully have claimed their ownership. Nor, of course, could the NYA, without an excavation permit. If Daniels participated in removal of the antiquities from the site, she, too, was guilty of violating federal law.

Daniels, who was responsible for the artifacts at the library, then explained that in 1939 she allowed Flora to remove the now disappeared Falls Creek objects for the benefit of a photographer who proposed to write and illustrate an article for *Life* magazine.[101] Pumped up by the prospect of national coverage, Flora accommodated this request without any authorization from Morris. It was Morris, of course, who supposedly controlled the specimens and was director of the legitimate excavations. The photographer and Flora first carried the objects–two baskets, two necklaces, a cradleboard, and the mummy Jasper–to Flora's home, where some pictures were taken of the amateur diligently at work in his shop. The two men then took the mummy and other specimens up the hillside to the North Shelter for some on-site shots. Jasper, minus his buckskin burial wrapping, and the two baskets were returned to the library. The cradleboard and the two necklaces were not. Each of the necklaces was twenty feet in length, one composed of olivella shells, the other of tiny juniper berries. They had been shown off with Esther at the well-publicized Carnegie exhibit the previous winter. Daniels offered no explanation for not requesting the missing items' return. Her smoldering indignation at what she regarded as outside interference was obvious.

It was a morass of cross-purposes. Forest Service personnel had thoughtlessly ignored a legitimate inquiry by a citizen. An overzealous digger and a well-intentioned accomplice had failed to understand the threat their probings posed to a prehistoric record. A scientist did not immediately inspect the site from which the invaluable items were taken or advise the discoverers against any further disturbance. All were responsible for the current situation.

Charges and countercharges notwithstanding, all present at the meeting were convinced that Flora had walked off with the beads and cradleboard, but no one wanted to confront him. Perhaps Daniels was reluctant to do so because of her opposition to what she saw as a high-handed government takeover. Further, she and Flora were no longer on speaking terms. In view of Flora's inescapable irrationality, the National Park Service men did not want to confront him either, fearful that if he had not done so already, he would sell or destroy the items out of spite.

After learning that *Life* magazine had rejected the photographer's article, Nusbaum contacted Eric Douglas, curator of Indian art at the Denver Art Museum, asking him to track down the Denver-based photographer in hopes that the negatives or prints could be located to identify the missing items. Curiously, none of the objects had been documented before being installed at the library. The inquiry yielded nothing. Watson, the Mesa Verde park naturalist, then took on the unpleasant task of meeting Flora face-to-face. After enduring a six-hour harangue, Watson knew only that Flora claimed he could not remember whether or not all the specimens had been returned to the library. If they were not there, he had no idea where they were. A picture taken in August 1942 of Flora, Jasper, and the cradleboard showed otherwise. Nevertheless, the government officials decided to wait for further developments.

One day in 1962 Arthur Thomas, then the Mesa Verde superintendent, looked up from his desk to see Flora standing before him. Twenty years after he had taken two Basketmaker necklaces of shell and seeds from the Durango Public Library display and then steadfastly lied about it, Flora did an about-face. He "donated" them to the Mesa Verde museum, where a small label, unread by most viewers, acknowledged his generosity. The following year in a similar gesture, Flora at last parted with the cradleboard. It must have been a wrenching experience for him. Subsequently, he provided descriptions and photographs of other specimens, including two pieces of hide cut from Jasper's missing burial robe.

During the uproar over the Flora matter, neither Morris nor Daniels mentioned the Falls Creek stone necklace still in her possession. Morris's silence probably can be attributed to respect for her help during the excavations and her prominent role in the community. He assumed that someday she would reunite the necklace with the rest of the Falls Creek collection in the Mesa Verde museum and that the transfer would be handled discreetly. Daniels, however, had no such intentions.

Only through small-town gossip did news of the existence of the necklace finally reach the Mesa Verde staff. Again, it was Watson's thankless job to try to retrieve what legally was government property.[102] Daniels admitted to having the object but vowed that she would not relinquish it to Mesa Verde. Without success Lewis R. Rist, forest supervisor, formally requested its return.[103] Government officials opted to let the matter rest. There already had been too much controversy over these artifacts. In July 1948 the burial crevice case was officially closed.

Twenty years later, Daniels at last relented and gave the strand of Basketmaker beads to the Center of Southwest Studies at Fort Lewis College.[104] There it rests securely in a safe, essentially as unknown as it was for the preceding two thousand years.

The publicized confiscation proceedings and Flora's loud and frequent protestations of mistreatment did little to quell the animosity he had stirred up among local amateurs toward academia nor did it put a damper on the collecting fever still raging in some breasts. These feelings were fanned to fever pitch by the *Durango News,* which in 1950 thoughtlessly printed an article about condescending professional attitudes and the intrinsic right to pot-hunt.[105] Flora's influence is obvious in the following statement: "Basin amateurs have consistently found prehistoric artifacts in the past few decades, while their learned brethren smugly tell them the find doesn't amount to much. Yet they study the stuff after it's found and even appropriate it from the amateurs." The author, Harley Ashbaugh, Jr., went so far as to suggest five subdivisions in town where the digging might be profitable and further commented, "If anyone gets the idea he'd like to go hunting for artifacts, there are plenty of yet unexplored caves in the area." Meanwhile, other news releases reported archaeological finds made within the city, giving specific locations and number and kinds of artifacts.[106]

Although Morris earlier had produced two very brief articles about the Durango Basketmakers, it was not until 1954 that he and Burgh finally published their monograph on the local ancients.[107] Descriptions of artifacts and execution of maps were Burgh's responsibility; Morris wrote the interpretive sections. Their combined efforts yielded an outstanding study that decades later remains a primary resource. Included was an appendix by Helen Sloan Daniels on the pictographs that initiated the whole troubling affair. If the paintings correspond to the site's occupation, they are the oldest tree-ring-dated examples of rock art in the Southwest.

In preparing their monograph, Burgh and Morris were unable to study Daniels's Basketmaker necklace and were therefore forced to refer to it only obliquely. In the 1940s Daniels wrote a description of the necklace for the Durango Public Library Museum Project notes that was more formally published in 1976.[108] Nor was Morris able to reexamine the cradleboard and two necklaces that had vanished from the library display. In discussing the cradleboard, he had to rely on a photograph and a description by Daniels that appeared in the library NYA notes. The seed and shell necklaces were only mentioned in Flora's included notes on the burial crevice finds. In the monograph's preface, Morris tactfully acknowledged the contributions of Daniels and Flora. Even so, after years of verbal abuse, he could not resist a final rebuttal: "His [Flora's] facile interpretations to the findings provided unceasing stimulus. So often were they at variance with our own that the effort to weight the facts against the theories evolved by his agile thinking kept us constantly alert, and, we believe, on the right track."[109] Reading between the lines clearly shows the yawning abyss between this professional and this amateur. Not surprisingly, Flora deplored the lack of a special section in the report on Esther and the failure to include photographs of Jasper or Grandma Niska. According to Flora, Morris was "blackmailed" by Gladwin and Nusbaum not to tell the true story of the Neanderthals.

At the end of World War II, Flora returned to Durango from a brief job as a welder at the Los Alamos Scientific Laboratories in New Mexico to open Zeke's Watch and Western Jewelry Shop. After ten years, he sold the business and retired due to poor health. A trail of writings and actions suggests one problem was a worsening dementia.

Among a dozen manuscripts Flora wrote after retirement on a variety of topics in physical science were two dealing with archaeology. One discussed long-distance trade in aboriginal America. The other was the story of the Neanderthal Grandma Niska of Falls Creek. Flora's overwrought imagination had her dying of childbirth far from home. In his fantasy, her body lay out in the mountains over the winter and was finally brought back to the rock shelter in four pieces that were deposited in the burial crevice. The articles were returned by a New York literary agent with the comment that slipping "facts" into a manuscript was bad enough, but that they could easily be caught by readers and proven incorrect was worse. Never one to doubt himself—even in the face of well-informed opinion—Flora again prevailed upon the obliging local newspaper to run the Grandma Niska fairy tale as if it were fact.

Expectedly, Flora continued to hike the hills looking for the Old Ones. The zest and zeal of earlier days had dissipated, but he did claim to have located some forty to sixty Basketmaker II open sites (Fig. 1.23). Years earlier he had written to Douglass, "I believe I informed you that we at Durango have learned to locate hillside Basketmaker II sites where they were not even supposed to exist. For nearly a year, a few of us have been following the floors far enough to prove the culture—obtain a sample beam or two—and cover the whole site back."[110] This was the kind of exploration in which Flora had always reveled.

In 1966 Flora contacted my husband, Robert H. Lister, who had set up the Mesa Verde Research Center, to suggest that excavation of some five Basketmaker II sites north of Durango might be fruitful. Hoping to secure some wood samples to pin down more precisely the time of Basketmaker II presence in the upper Animas Valley, a party of University of Colorado students led by William Biggs was sent to investigate. In addition to Flora, William L. Morris, a local man whose father had worked for Earl Morris at the Falls Creek rock shelters and Talus Village, joined the group. Their site identification proved to be correct. One partial earthen floor and several cists comparable to those at Talus Village were outlined (Figs. 1.24a-1.24c).[111] One unusual feature was parts of three stacks of horizontal logs spaced about the floor perimeter and held in place by mud. The excavators interpreted them as possible pilasters to support a cribbed roof. Flora later claimed that fifty other floors at the site were overlooked. Few artifacts and no remains of foodstuffs were recovered. A tree-ring sample from the dwelling yielded important terminal phase dates in the late A.D. 300s. The student report was never completed.

The following summer, the university students, accompanied by archaeologist Jack Smith, examined a series of other places that Flora

Fig. 1.23. One of a number of possible Basketmaker II sites discovered by Flora, site Ign 7:103 is probably located in the vicinity of Talus Village (Flora's map is illegible). The vertical slabs likely define a living area. *Lister Collection.*

thought represented Basketmaker II habitations. He said these pre-dated the Basketmaker III "submerged tipis," as he now described pithouses. Excavations encountered no evidence of living surfaces or artifacts. Flora blamed the lack of positive results on academic ineptitude, not his own misinterpretation. The project was aborted. This was the last time a professional party tried to conduct fieldwork with Durango amateurs.

In fairness to Flora, it should be noted that surface indications of Basketmaker II remains in the open in this region are extremely subtle. The floors of dwellings were shallow and often filled to the surface with burned debris, leaving little or no sign of architectural features. In his obsessive drive to demonstrate an early cultural horizon, Flora may have seen things that were not there, or he may have been more perceptive than others in reading the ground. Because he left no legible maps giving precise locations of his suspected sites, the truth likely will never be known.

(a)

Figs. 1.24a-c. These three photographs were taken at Basketmaker II site Ign 12:46, located on a hillside east of Falls Creek Valley. Fig. 1.24a shows the site in 1966, before excavation; Fig. 1.24b shows a crew member clearing a floor and remains of a roof beam; Fig. 1.24c shows grinding stones and a partial floor surface after excavation. *Courtesy Mesa Verde Research Center, Mesa Verde National Park.*

(b)

In the 1960s, Robert and I published a book about our friend, Earl Morris, in which the Falls Creek project was discussed.[112] Flora immediately wrote the American Civil Liberties Union asking for help in bringing charges of slander against us. In the same letter he also expressed a desire to collect royalties from the postcards on sale at Mesa Verde bearing the likeness of Esther. Because he was the person who found her, Flora said Esther was his "moral and legal property"; no one had sought his permission to use her picture in this commercial way.[113] Feigning shock, he seemed to have forgotten that

(c)

shortly after he found her, he was more than willing to sell Esther for a price. Because both accusations were without merit, no action was taken by the ACLU or any other group.

Flora's flagging spirits were temporarily revived in 1967. During an extensive reappraisal of tree-ring materials gathered from all sectors of the prehistoric Southwest, William Robinson and Bryant Bannister, staff members of the Laboratory of Tree-Ring Research, called upon him, seeking specimens accumulated primarily during his digs thirty years earlier. Flora claimed some two thousand such pieces of charcoal and wood, including more than fifty (concealed from Morris) from the fill at the Falls Creek shelters and the burial crevice. Earlier in 1949 he had told Edmund Schulman, also of the tree-ring laboratory, that he retained one thousand dating plots.[114] What the men from the tree-ring laboratory learned was that in preparation for his move to New Mexico during World War II, Flora had packed small samples in egg cartons and larger pieces in apple boxes and stored them in an outbuilding on his Durango property. There they remained, untouched for a quarter century, while mice and black widow spiders made their homes among them, and dust, extreme temperature changes, dampness, and sheer neglect took their toll. The men were told to take whatever might be useful.[115]

The renewed interest in his wood samples must have pleased Flora. For many years he dutifully sent specimens and plots of readings to the Laboratory of Tree-Ring Research and to Gila Pueblo and asked for help in verifying his dating efforts. Understandably, he was angry that rarely did he receive any response. Only Douglass escaped his castigations. Nevertheless, in private, Douglass often judged Flora's work to be flawed, but failed to guide this eager dendrochronological convert toward more critical analysis.[116] It was another example of lost opportunity to bridge the academic gaps between amateur and professional.

Eventually the analyses of these pieces from Flora's supply were undertaken in Tucson by Jeffrey S. Dean. He acknowledged the discipline's debt to Flora for having saved what others of his time probably would have discarded as trash.[117] Judging from the mass of household receipts, cancelled checks, medical bills, correspondence, and rejected manuscripts found at his home after his death, Flora's specimens, once precious but by the 1960s virtually meaningless to him, might have survived simply because of their owner's apparent inability to throw things away.

The Durango tree-ring restudy was not without its problems, many of them due to Flora's poor record keeping and the loss through the years of identifying documentation. The difficulties were compounded when the collections were divided and duplicate or differing numbers were assigned to the same sites and specimens. The Gila Pueblo collection suffered physical damage, further confusion of labels, and torn bags that allowed mixture of samples as these fragile objects were shipped from place to place. During the war years, when the Gladwins moved back to California, the Gila Pueblo materials accompanied them. Ten years later, after Gila Pueblo disbanded, the specimens were given to California Institute of Technology in Pasadena. From there, they were later passed on to the tree-ring laboratory in Tucson to be housed with Douglass's collections from some of the same sites. What should never have happened to sensitive time markers did, but, by great good luck and assiduous work by Dean, these bits of old house timbers and hearth sweepings yielded the earliest set of tree-ring dates for the Southwest.

On the one hand, the report containing this exciting information must have been extremely gratifying to Flora. On the other, he surely was crestfallen because he remained certain that the mummies from Falls Creek were at least a thousand years older than the wood indicated.[118] Disappointed that the readable tree-ring record could not confirm this idea, he sought the aid of E. B. Sayles, University of Arizona, to get funding for carbon 14 dating of some juniper beads, shells, and fragments of hides he still had that came from the Falls Creek burial crevice.[119] One buckskin may have been the burial shroud removed from Jasper. Although it is uncertain whether any action was taken, Flora did keep abreast of technical advances in matters of site dating.

Meanwhile, Homer Root, whose relic collecting had inspired Flora three decades earlier, retired from the ministry in the 1950s to open a small shop on the outskirts of Durango that sold mineral specimens and objects made of gnarled wood. Undoubtedly, he continued digging through the years, but news of any such activities was drowned in the flood of Flora publicity. Whether he ever attempted to acquire acceptable field techniques or concerned himself with baffling questions of prehistoric cultural dynamics is unknown. Nevertheless, his local reputation as a person interested in the Indian past led to a part-time curatorial job at Fort Lewis College.

He must have taken pleasure in being among growing collections of artifacts donated by various individuals, which to him represented archaeology. On campus he made posters about the ancient peoples to be sent to local schools and meetings. When a text was required, he merely repeated Flora's ideas. As an outlet for his considerable artistic talents, he created mosaic displays by permanently gluing small artifacts to stiff backing materials. With a citizenry that half believed in tall tales of Durango Man, who would object to trailing floral sprays composed of twelve-hundred-year-old arrowheads, chips of colored stones, and bone awls? One is tempted to say that this could have happened only in Durango, where even at that late date, amateurism in the science still seemed a virtue.

It was no surprise, therefore, that in 1965 the college administration approved Root's plan for an archaeological field school in Ridges Basin, where a number of known ruins on private lands might provide specimens for the school museum. Students would experience the excitement of exploration and digging, and no federal excavation permit would be required. An added plus, the area's proximity to campus would eliminate the need for a field camp.

The inspiration for Root's program may have come from the University of Colorado field school that had recently renewed operations at Mesa Verde National Park after a nine-year hiatus. The main difference in the programs, of course, was in the background of the personnel. Root was an avid pothunter with no experience in fullfledged excavation, publication, or teaching. The staff at the University of Colorado school comprised highly trained professionals with many years in the field and classroom who had extensive technical bibliographies to their credit.

During four seasons (1965 through 1967, and again in 1969), Root and Fort Lewis College students dug in five pit structures, at least thirty-one surface rooms, and many trash middens from which forty-three burials were removed. Probably because Root expected the pithouses to be oval or circular in outline, he followed a novel plan of laying out a pie-shaped grid, which was excavated a slice at a time.[120] Recording of measurements, structural features, and artifacts was inconsistent and incomplete, as was the photographic record. Even the location of sites was so imprecise that some cannot now be identified. Specimens of least interest to Root, such as potsherds or the stone scraps left from the manufacture of projectile points, were not retained or tabulated, but Root did maintain a hand-lettered ledger account of other objects, accompanied by elaborate polychromatic drawings of some of them. He never produced a report on the work or undertook any interpretation other than classifying the sites as late Basketmaker III. From a professional standpoint, the program was little better than looting, although it did give the students some exercise and blisters and the museum some artifacts. When excavations ceased, little knowledge had been gained, and pieces of an archaeological record had been forever destroyed.

The profession at large must bear some responsibility for this assault on prehistory. Had protests been lodged with the college authorities, the resulting damage might have been prevented. Here was yet another instance of the lack of communication between amateur and professional that had plagued Durango archaeology from its inception.

As a result of Root's tenure, Fort Lewis College added anthropology to the curriculum and hired a professor with a new advanced degree in the subject, John C. Ives. In addition to teaching undergraduate courses, in 1967 and 1968 Ives directed excavations in Ridges Basin that complemented Root's program. In the early 1970s, after Root's departure, Ives supervised a student survey and excavation of two sites on Blue Mesa, where much of Root's and Flora's pothunting had been conducted. Ultimately, Ives left the faculty without publishing the results of his work.

The 1970s saw the climactic disintegration of Flora's mental health. Few individuals with whom he had any archaeological dealings escaped blunt accusations of falsifying records, stealing artifacts, wrongfully claiming finds that had been Flora's, or being downright ignorant for discounting the cultural theories Flora wholeheartedly believed in. It was during this time that he was handed another cause.

After protests by the American Indian Movement about disrespect for the Indian dead, Esther was placed in storage at Mesa Verde. It was a move long overdue. Flora, however, soon lodged a complaint with the park superintendent and the National Park Service regional director, decrying her removal.[121] According to Flora, when the public discovered that Esther had been discovered by Flora near Durango—not, as the museum label erroneously read, at Mesa

Verde–the park staff responded by hiding Esther away. "His" mummy was stuffed into a box in a garage, head down, face pressed in, and she was rotting and being eaten by insects. He did not divulge the source of this information, but he demanded that Esther be put back on display. If that were not possible, he would loan the park a life-size poster to exhibit. The Park Service's response was that, first, Esther was the government's property, and it was under no obligation to exhibit her then or into perpetuity. Second, she was being cared for properly and was available to qualified researchers only.

Continuing his diatribe, Flora complained that the dioramas in the Mesa Verde museum, admired by public and professional visitors alike since the WPA days of the 1930s, gave a false impression of the prehistory of the region. As Flora saw it, the preparators had known the truth but were fearful of telling it because they would have lost their jobs. The real story was as only Flora recognized it: the Basketmakers were Neanderthals. He mailed copies of this tirade to forty individuals around the Southwest.

In a last-ditch effort to get Esther reinstated as the principal attraction of the Mesa Verde museum, Flora hired the Durango law firm of Kirschenmann, King, Dawes, and Ker to take legal action, charging some nebulous federal offense. Esther was only at the museum because of Flora, and if she were not displayed, he would be forgotten. Once the lawyers winnowed chaff from grain, the case was dropped.

And then there was "Rent-a-Mummy," the unresolved dispute harking back to the February 1938 agreement between Morris and Flora on the Falls Creek finds. Flora calculated that Morris had had possession of Esther for a total of 497 days between February 8, 1938, and June 20, 1939, for a sum of $500. That amounted to a "rental" charge of $1 per day (the remainder of the burial crevice specimens apparently were free of charge). From June 20, 1939, until September 10, 1945, the date of formal confiscation by the government, Esther was a guest of Mesa Verde National Park. Therefore, Flora maintained, the government owed him quite a hefty sum in rental fees, for which he presented a bill.

The discredited billing was followed by a Durango radio interview in which the hyperbolic Flora expounded on his shopworn theme: the Basketmaker II were Neanderthal without doubt.[122] There was nothing new here. This time, however, Flora cited Carleton S. Coon, eminent physical anthropologist, as agreeing. What Coon actually wrote Flora was that some Neanderthal blood may have flowed in the veins of the first Native Americans, but there was absolutely no proof.[123]

Still, Flora persevered. Not only the recognized Basketmaker II but also the Basketmaker III, who lived on until well after A.D. 700, were Neanderthal.[124] This line of reasoning was because his confused mind then had them all with undeformed typical Basketmaker skulls. However, when they met up with the Pueblos, the skull shape changed because, as he explained, "the low, far-back brain-cavity of the Neanderthal was being pushed up and foreward [*sic*] to fill in the sloping forehead and thus make Basketmakers and Pueblos look more like each other for marriage."[125] Sadly, continued Flora, when the two peoples mated, their offspring were sterile–the mules of the human chain. Because they could not reproduce, the races died off. That explained why the Colorado Plateau was vacant after A.D. 1300.

Here ended Flora's science fiction.

The era of turbulence in the Durango archaeological community, academic and amateur, came to a close in the 1970s. Root died in 1977. Coincidentally, the two people who began the Falls Creek caper forty years earlier passed on in 1979. Helen Sloan Daniels died quietly in her sleep. At age seventy-seven, terminally ill and confined to a wheelchair, bitter, and unrepentant, Zeke Flora put a gun to his head and pulled the trigger.[126]

As the old guard faded into memory, the dawn of ecological archaeology in the Durango sector brought with it loftier goals than mere collection of artifacts, goals to be accomplished with a host of up-to-the-minute field and analysis techniques. Thus far, more recent archaeological activity, centered south and southeast of Durango, has brought regional prehistory into sharper focus. This mounting new information underpins the reinterpretation of ancient life on the upper Animas to follow.

Notes

1. Daniels, 1940A.
2. Smith, 1986, 67-70.
3. *Great Southwest* (newspaper), April 18, 1893.
4. Atkins, 1993, Appendix H, 295-296; Daniels, 1976, 9; Smith, 1981, 4.
5. Phillips, 1993, 104.
6. Lister and Lister, 1990, 68.
7. Lister and Lister, 1990; Smith, 1981.
8. Kidder and Guernsey, 1919; Lister and Lister, 1968 (1993), 57-64; Morris, 1939, 19.
9. Flora, 1940B.
10. Daniels, 1940B.
11. Daniels, 1936-1940, intro., and 1976, 9-15.
12. Cassells, 1983, 226-227.
13. Flora letter to Jeffrey S. Dean, September 25, 1974, Archives, Laboratory of Tree-Ring Research, University of Arizona.
14. Lister and Lister, 1968 (1993).
15. Lister and Lister, 1987 (1996), 1990.
16. Flora, 1941.
17. Haury, 1988.
18. Morris letter to Harold S. Gladwin, September 6, 1934, Archives, University of Colorado Museum; Archives, Arizona State Museum.
19. Morris letter to Harold S. Gladwin, September 6, 1934, Archives, University of Colorado Museum.
20. Dean, 1975.
21. Flora, 1940B; Gladwin, 1957, 53.
22. Gladwin traded some of the pottery to the Field Museum in Chicago, the National Museum in Copenhagen, the Southwest Museum in Los Angeles, and the museums at the University of Arizona and the University of New Mexico. The remainder of the collection is now at the Arizona State Museum, Tucson. Files there list specimens GP346-361 and GP4982-5013 as having been purchased from Flora in 1935.
23. Flora, 1940D; Gladwin, 1957, 55-57.
24. Flora, 1940E.

25. Douglass letter to Emil Haury, December 3, 1935, and Haury letter to A. E. Douglass, December 1, 1935, Archives, Laboratory of Tree-Ring Research, University of Arizona. A photograph of the wood section with the date A.D. 649, signed by Haury, hung in the Indian Room of the Durango Public Library.

26. Haury and Flora, 1937, 7-8.

27. Daniels, 1936-1940; *Durango News,* July 28, 1939.

28. Hooton, 1947, x.

29. Haury, 1988, 24; Vivian, 1990, 396-397.

30. Daniels, 1940B.

31. Duke and Matlock, 1983, 25.

32. Martin letter to H. S. Daniels, March 25, 1937, Archives, Center of Southwest Studies, Fort Lewis College.

33. Susan Davies, pers. comm.

34. Flora letter to A. E. Douglass, November 18, 1935, Archives, Laboratory of Tree-Ring Research, University of Arizona.

35. Daniels, 1936-1940.

36. Daniels, 1976. Part 1 of a 1936 Durango Public Library Museum Project index of artifacts dug without permit from the South Shelter and donated by Flora included corncobs, other plant remains, manos, and an infant cradleboard.

37. Daniels, 1976, 8.

38. Morris and Burgh, 1954, 40.

39. Susan Davies, pers. comm.

40. Morris letter to Don Watson, January 18, 1947, Archives, University of Colorado Museum.

41. Flora letter to Earl Morris, September 7, 1937, Archives, University of Colorado Museum.

42. Flora, 1940E.

43. Lister and Lister, 1978, 17.

44. 34 Stat., 225 16 USC432.

45. Morris letter to A. V. Kidder, November 23, 1937, Archives, University of Colorado Museum.

46. Flora letter to Emil Haury, December 2, 1937, Center of Southwest Studies, Fort Lewis College.

47. Flora letter to Earl Morris, October 28, 1937, Archives, University of Colorado Museum.

48. Daniels, 1976, 28-29.

49. Morris letter to I. F. Flora, May 2, 1938, Archives, University of Colorado Museum.

50. Morris letter to A. E. Douglass, August 7, 1938, Archives, University of Colorado Museum.

51. Morris letter to J. B. O'Rourke, November 6, 1945, Archives, University of Colorado Museum.

52. Morris and Burgh, 1954; Morris letter to R. E. Clark, July 9, 1945, Archives, University of Colorado Museum.

53. Daniels, 1976, 34.

54. Morris and Burgh, 1954, 50.

55. Dean, 1975, 2.

56. Flora letter to A. E. Douglass, October 10, 1938, Archives, Laboratory of Tree-Ring Research, University of Arizona.

57. Haury, 1988; Vivian, 1990, 397.

58. Flora, 1939.

59. *Durango News,* January 13 and February 3, 1939.

60. *Science News Letter,* December 24, 1938.

61. *Durango News,* January 13, 1939.

62. *Durango Herald Democrat,* April 30, 1939.

63. According to Flora's numbering system, these were Ign 12:10, Ign 12:23, Ign 12:26, Ign 12:27, Ign 16:51, Ign 17:10, Ign 17:18, Ign 17:23, Ign 17:31, Ign 17:45, Ign 17:51, and Ign 17A:2. Ign 12 was the area of Durango; Ign 16 was south of town and west of the Animas River; Ign 17 was south of town and east of the Animas River. Durango Public Library Museum Project, vol. 3, 1938.

64. Flora, 1938-1939.

65. Douglass letter to Earl Morris, August 20, 1941, Archives, University of Colorado Museum; Flora letter to A. E. Douglass, July 25, 1941, Archives, Laboratory of Tree-Ring Research, University of Arizona.

66. Morris letter to A. E. Douglass, April 16, 1940, Archives, University of Colorado Museum.

67. Scott letter to Earl H. Morris, November 13, 1939, Archives, University of Colorado Museum.

68. Gladwin letter to Deric O'Bryan, March 5, 1940, Archives, Arizona State Museum; Gladwin letter to Jesse Nusbaum, December 4, 1945, Archives, Mesa Verde National Park.

69. Flora letter to A. E. Douglass, June 20, 1941, Archives, Laboratory of Tree-Ring Research, University of Arizona.

70. Flora letter to Edmund Schulman, April 7, 1953, Archives, Laboratory of Tree-Ring Research, University of Arizona.

71. Adams, J. L., 1994, 71-72; Cassells, 1983, 234-235.

72. Morris and Burgh, 1954, 8-26.

73. Flora letter to Earl Morris, January 3, 1943, Archives, University of Colorado Museum; Flora letter to Jesse Nusbaum, September 29, 1944, Archives, Center of Southwest Studies, Fort Lewis College.

74. Morris letter to A. V. Kidder, November 4, 1937, Archives, University of Colorado Museum.

75. Seltzer, 1944.

76. Reed, 1949, 106-119.

77. Snow and Sanders, 1954, 89-92.

78. Brew letter to I. F. Flora, n.d., 1967, Archives, Center of Southwest Studies, Fort Lewis College.

79. Gladwin, 1947, 108-112.

80. *Durango News,* October 3, 1947.

81. Flora, l940A.

82. Morris letter to Jesse Nusbaum, October 8, 1944; Morris letter to Edmund Schulman, February 14, 1948; and Morris letter to Edmund Schulman, March 25, 1949, Archives, University of Colorado Museum.

83. *Durango News,* March 10, 1941.

84. Gladwin, 1947, 20-21.

85. Daniels letter to C. T. Hurst, April 2, 1941, Archives, Center of Southwest Studies, Fort Lewis College.

86. Flora, 1940C.

87. Daniels, 1940A.

88. Byers, 1941.

89. Flora, 1940D.

90. Douglass letter to Jesse Nusbaum, September 27, 1941, Archives, Laboratory of Tree-Ring Research, University of Arizona.

91. Flora, 1941.

92. Flora letter to Earl Morris, January 12, 1943, Archives, University of Colorado Museum.

93. Flora letter to Jesse Nusbaum, September 29, 1944, Archives, Mesa Verde National Park; Flora letter to Emil Haury, September 24, 1944, Archives, Center of Southwest Studies, Fort Lewis College.

94. Flora letter to Earl Morris, February 19, 1943, Archives, University of Colorado Museum.

95. Nusbaum letter to Frank Morse, February 19, 1943, Archives, Mesa Verde National Park.

96. Flora letter to A. E. Douglass, January 1, 1942, Archives, Center of Southwest Studies, Fort Lewis College.

97. Morris letter to San Juan National Forest, January 13, 1945, Archives, San Juan National Forest. Personnel included were regional forester John W. Spencer, acting regional forester R. E. Clark, forest supervisor Lewis R. Rist, acting regional attorney Walter J. Ise, and acting director of the National Park Service Hillory A. Tolson.

98. Declaration of Ownership and Designation of Depositories for Certain Objects of Antiquity, October 1, 1945, Archives, San Juan National Forest.

99. *Durango Herald Democrat,* October 1, 1945.

100. *Durango News,* October 12, 1945.

101. Daniels, 1976, 21.

102. Watson letter to Lewis R. Rist, February 2, 1947, Archives, San Juan National Forest.

103. Rist letter to H. S. Daniels, February 13, 1947, Archives, San Juan National Forest.

104. Daniels, 1976, 28-29.

105. *Durango News,* September 6, 1950.

106. Duke and Matlock, 1983, 28-29.

107. Morris, 1949, 1952; Morris and Burgh, 1954.

108. Daniels, 1936-1940, 12-13, and 1976, 28-29.

109. Morris and Burgh, 1954, iii.

110. Flora letter to A. E. Douglass, August 24, 1941, Archives, Laboratory of Tree-Ring Research, University of Arizona.

111. Biggs, 1966.

112. Lister and Lister, 1968 (1993), 160-168.

113. Flora letter to American Civil Liberties Union, December 7, 1968, Archives, Center of Southwest Studies, Fort Lewis College.

114. Flora letter to Edmund Schulman, May 27, 1949, Archives, Laboratory of Tree-Ring Research, University of Arizona.

115. Dean, 1975, 5.

116. Douglass letter to Earl Morris, August 20, 1941, Archives, University of Colorado Museum; Douglass letter to Jesse Nusbaum, September 27, 1941, Archives, Laboratory of Tree-Ring Research, University of Arizona.

117. Dean, 1975, 7.

118. *Durango News,* July 13, 1949; Flora letter to Edmund Schulman, April 7, 1953, Archives, Laboratory of Tree-Ring Research, University of Arizona.

119. Flora letter to E. B. Sayles, January 22, 1959, Archives, Center of Southwest Studies, Fort Lewis College.

120. Duke, 1985, 24-138.

121. Flora letter to John Cook, November, n.d., 1976, Archives, Mesa Verde National Park.

122. KDGO, *Senior Saturday,* December 1, 1976.

123. Coon letter to I. F. Flora, December 14, 1967, Archives, Center of Southwest Studies, Fort Lewis College.

124. Flora letter to Ian Thompson, June 2, 1974, pers. prop.

125. Flora letter to Barry Fell, June 15-October 16, 1977, Archives, Center of Southwest Studies, Fort Lewis College.

126. *Durango Herald,* March 25, 1979.

PART II
The Ancients of the Upper Animas District

Their Mountain Fastness

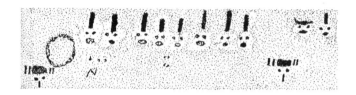

In Pleistocene times on four occasions, sheets of glacial ice stubbornly crept southward from the Rocky Mountain continental spine to reshape the Southwestern world that Esther and her kind would later know. Two pre-existing troughs in their paths were chiseled broader and deeper, their escarpments sheared more vertically, exposing millions of years of complex geological deposition, faulting, and uplift. The floor of the primary valley, the Animas, was gouged at an elevation of sixty-five hundred feet. To the west, separated by a resistant ridge, the lesser Falls Creek Valley, also known as Hidden Valley, was cut at an elevation approximately six hundred feet higher than the Animas.

The Animas Valley cut through terrain riven by deep clefts and pierced by rugged peaks, opening out toward the south. The glaciers that carved this and surrounding valleys eventually fanned out and spent themselves in terminal moraines. Deep alluvium accumulated behind these barriers. Following the slow retreat of the ice in the early Holocene period, the sparkling waters of icy springs, cascades, and snowmelt coursed downward through the valley toward the San Juan drainage working their way westward along the break between the northern mountain and southern, high desert provinces. The upper Animas area formed a transitional zone between the two.

Falls Creek Valley, running north-south for only a few miles, remained a world unto itself. It is walled on the east by several high, rocky fins rising into Animas City Mountain at the south. The western boundary is an abrupt cliff whose most prominent feature is the thick, white Dolores Formation, a composite of sandstone, shale, and conglomerate that dips sharply southward. A number of jagged recesses have weathered out of bottom layers of that formation, two of which are fairly large. Now known as the North and South Shelters, they face generally southeast.

The yawning mouth of the southernmost alcove is visible from the valley floor seven hundred feet below because, during storms, a gushing volume of water has cut a channel down and away from the recess. The opening, 180 feet long, is 33 to 46 feet high and 84 feet deep and now is thickly drifted with hillocks of thin tabular spalls broken from the rear alcove walls and ceiling. Much more floor space may have been available for human use in the past.

The overhang a bit higher and several hundred feet to the north is nearly obscured by vegetation. The pine that Earl Morris climbed to take pictures still towers at mid-section. This relatively low, narrow recess, no more than 33 feet deep, runs upward from south to north for approximately 228 feet at a steep angle. The shelter roof has a maximum height of only thirty feet.

Morris described both rock shelters as misshapen and threatening, certainly a far cry from the grand vaulted amphitheaters of the western sectors of the Colorado Plateau that could have housed the U.S. Capitol. From the less impressive Falls Creek shelters, scree pours down and levels out in cramped bottomlands now cut by a sluggish intermittent watercourse that in aboriginal times may have been boggy marshes.

Over time the sculptured landforms rising in tiers from the valley floors to high mountaintops became rich with a plant diversity that probably is not much different today. However, paleoenvironmental studies are needed to confirm this. Ridge faces and crests now are stabilized by thick mantles of conifers such as fir, pine, and spruce at the higher elevations and pinyon and juniper lower down. Above are dense pockets of white-barked aspens standing ramrod straight. Thick scrub oak, serviceberry, and Oregon grape crowd into rocky drifts spilling downslope. Swordlike yucca and gray-green sage carpet the terraces. In summer, meadows flutter with billowing lettuce-green grasses and clumps of variegated wildflowers surrounded by thickets of reeds, chokecherries, cottonwoods, alders, and willows.

Moisture allowing this abundant flora to flourish comes from winter snows and summer rains that average eighteen to twenty inches annually. Precipitation varies both in amount and seasonal occurrence, leading ecologists to conclude that alternating warm/dry and cold/wet conditions have prevailed cyclically. Here can be found ponds that were once meanders and marshes that are remnants of extensive wetlands of the past. Seeps ooze at bedding planes, and here and there a waterfall gushes over an escarpment.

Even with modern encroachment, the lush domain is the natural habitat of a wide variety of fauna. The mammal population ranges from large animals such as deer, elk, mountain lions, bears, and coyotes to smaller creatures like porcupines, beavers, rabbits, squirrels, and chipmunks. Trout swim beneath cold waters, while ducks and geese, pausing on their long migrations, float on the surface. On lower slopes rattlesnakes slither among the rocks. The same variety of animal life likely has been present for a very long time.

Their Way of Life
As Seen by Morris and Burgh

    Against this paradisiacal natural backdrop, Earl Morris and Robert Burgh prepared a coldly factual report on what they considered a Basketmaker II horizon. Their work served as the springboard for later, more humanized cultural reconstructions that would nevertheless remain incomplete. Because the North Shelter cache of perishables was limited in quantity and variety and no comparable artifacts ever have been recovered in the district, information about any potential textiles or basketry containers–for which these people were named–is lacking. More important, because their spoken tongue is unknown and they had no written language, the taboos, stories, songs, ceremonies, social interconnections, and tribal wisdom that bind a people together remain unknown.

    The people who once occupied the two openings in the western cliff of Falls Creek Valley and the hillside near Trimble Springs to which Zeke Flora led the Carnegie diggers were of primary interest. To learn how they compared with their known contemporaries, Morris dispatched those human remains that could be salvaged to Harvard experts in physical anthropology. Included were the skeletons or skulls of five infants, five adolescents, and five adults, as well as a miscellaneous assortment of stray bones, all removed from the North

Shelter burial crevice. Ten of these specimens were partially desiccated, and three others retained small bits of skin tissue. The mummies known as Esther and Jasper and that of an infant wrapped in a hide bundle were kept in Colorado and later were deposited at Mesa Verde National Park. From the legitimate excavations at the North Shelter, Morris was able to reclaim skeletons or skulls of six adults, two adolescents, and three children. Two adult skeletons were removed from the South Shelter, but one was too fragmentary to be studied. Ten more adult specimens and the broken skull of one child were submitted from Talus Village.

When the fieldwork was being carried out, regional scholars still believed that the Basketmakers and later Pueblos were of different racial stock. Morris suspected at least a three-way split, because to him the upper Animas district Basketmakers appeared to be distinct from those of the Four Corners. The absence of the dominant dolichocephaly, or long-headedness, that characterized the classic Basketmakers troubled him.[1]

By the time Morris published his site report in 1954, he had, at least in part, been answered. Through a study of Basketmakers and Pueblos from a wide area of the northern Southwest, a researcher, Carl C. Seltzer, had shown that the two peoples were directly linked genetically to each other, to the fundamental breeding populations that came into the New World out of northeast Asia, and to some modern Native Americans in the Southwest.[2] No Neanderthals were among them. The parameters of the Southwest Plateau grouping to which they were assigned were flexible enough to allow some variability. Seltzer found fault with field archaeologists for loose terminology regarding human remains because this lax terminology led to the erroneous claims of racial distinctions. In fact, the Basketmakers were not as dolichocephalic nor the Pueblos as brachycephalic as claimed.[3]

The physical anthropologists studying the few sufficiently intact remains of Falls Creek Basketmakers characterized them as short. The females, whose height was less than five feet, were significantly smaller than the males. The tibia bones of both sexes bore facets formed by flat-footed crouching with buttocks on heels, which caused a slouched posture. The skulls were described as "interesting," but otherwise were not unusual. They were undeformed, comparatively small, and not strikingly long-headed. Foreheads were low, faces were short, brow ridges were prominent, and features were rugged. Analyses of jaw formation did not indicate, as Flora believed, that these Basketmakers relied primarily on meat in their diet. To the scientists, the prognathism, or projection of jaws beyond the upper face, was average. Study of the mummies yielded common characteristics of straight, coarse black hair and dark skin.[4] On the basis of the bare skulls, Morris privately thought the people almost simian in appearance. A less-than-erect carriage would have strengthened that impression. (Modern students now think this slouched posture was misinterpreted in earlier studies.)[5] Still, Morris chose to let the appendix to his report on the human remains stand without adding his personal opinion.[6]

The physical studies confirmed that life was not easy for these people. Adult teeth were abraded by stone grit loosened in grinding foodstuffs. Abscesses were common. Arthritis, spina bifida abnormalities, and healed scalp wounds were detected. There was possible evidence of syphilis. Lack of sanitary facilities, exposure, proximity to accumulated household refuse, and rodent and insect infestation were conditions that shortened lives. Although starvation was not a problem, malnutrition was.

In the late 1930s, forerunners to the Basketmaker II had not been defined, but Morris and his colleagues believed them to be small bands roaming the Colorado Plateau, living off whatever nature provided, always following a common pattern for survival. This, then, was the hypothesized Basketmaker I phase of the Pecos Classification, a phase of undetermined duration and characteristics. Morris thus assumed that the beings who first came to Falls Creek Valley and vicinity followed a basic hunting-and-gathering subsistence strategy supplemented by a limited corn agriculture that had already been identified among Four Corners Basketmakers. His excavations in the upper Animas district proved him correct.

Had coprolite, stable carbon isotopic data on bone, or pollen analyses been archaeological practices at the time, more would be known of the role of native plants in the diets of those early Basket-makers. The imbalance of data favoring the dominance of corn over nondomesticates may be due in part to the methodology then current or to the greater potential for preservation of cobs as opposed to edible seeds. One small bit of fecal matter contained seeds of sunflower and skunk brush. Other than a few vetch seeds, the only reported undigested wild plant food from the Carnegie digs was a bag of tiny amaranth seeds in a leather pouch found in the North Shelter burial crevice.[7] Surely acorns, pinyon nuts, juniper berries, prickly pear cactus, saltbush, lamb's-quarter, chokecherries, and other edibles that must have been abundant along the slopes and bottomlands were consumed as ground flour or potherbs or were eaten raw.

One indirect clue to the importance of such foods was a number of grinding implements. Roundish basins worked into boulders of various sizes held small objects that were pulverized by a shaped, hand-held cobble. Similar artifacts later were found to be common milling tools among the area's early foragers.

Unlike some groups in less blessed regions, the local Basketmakers did not go without meat. The importance of game hunting was demonstrated by the more than two hundred chipped stone projectile points recovered. Although they varied in size, shape, and material, Morris and Burgh believed they were all used on darts propelled by wooden atlatls, or throwers, of which they found four fragments. The successful use of these weapons accounts for the abundance of deer bones—and the tools created from them—in the domestic refuse. Deer would have been easy prey even with the use of awkward atlatls because these animals habitually stand motionless for long periods of time. Other fauna doubtless hunted by similar means were bighorn sheep and black bear, probably more skittish and difficult to bring down. Smaller animals represented in the bone waste include marten, marmot, beaver, porcupine, and rabbit. Reed snares with a running noose (one such specimen was recovered), woven nets, and wooden clubs likely were used in their capture.

The foodstuff of greatest cultural significance among early Durango area settlers is maize, *Zea mays,* or corn. Because corn—an annual plant—requires tending in order to flourish, its presence implies a pivotal redirection from a lifestyle based on hunting and gathering to one incorporating agriculture. Regional archaeologists agree that horticulture–however cursory–diffused northward from Mexico during the dimly illuminated pre-Christian era. The exact date of this critical watershed and the composition of plant types involved had not been determined when the Durango Basketmakers came under scientific scrutiny, but in the greater Southwest, it was generally believed to have been at least four thousand years ago.

The large sample of maize stalks, cobs, tassels, shanks, and kernels retrieved during the Carnegie work proves that the upper Animas district Basketmakers were at least part-time farmers and that corn was becoming a primary food staple. Examples of reclaimed corn were charred, uncharred, and mouse-eaten but nevertheless informative to ethnobotanists from the University of Michigan who undertook their analysis.[8] Most corn samples came from scattered refuse and therefore could not be correlated with specific features or dated wood, but they confirm a dedication to an annual cycle of planting, tending, harvesting, and consuming.

The most striking aspect of the Durango maize collection is the heterogeneity of corn hybrids.[9] Prior to this work at the Falls Creek rock shelters, researchers thought Basketmaker corn was primarily of one type, with other hybrids being introduced later by Pueblo farmers. But here four distinct strains were present, with the Hohokam/Basketmaker Complex predominating. Other types identified were Eastern Complex, Tropical Flint Complex, and Mexican Complex. The Hohokam/Basketmaker Complex is described as having cigar-shaped, medium-sized cobs and unindented flour- or flint-type kernels; presumably, it had adapted to the relatively high elevation. Later studies show wide variation in corn types to be typical of much of the northern periphery of the Anasazi realm and suggest these new farmers were influenced from a number of directions. The relationship of ancient corn types to each other and to modern Pueblo strains needs further analysis.

A second domesticated plant known to the upper Animas Valley settlers was squash. Although ethnobotanists believed the local squashes were different from other Basketmaker examples, they could not determine their species because the few rinds and seeds recovered were so poorly preserved. These squashes were probably *Cucurbita pepo,* common elsewhere in the Southwest.

Garden plots of corn and squash may have been planted on south-facing slopes rather than valley floors, due to the slower spring-time warming and marshy ground encountered at those lower elevations. If so, dry farming dependent upon rich soil deposits and early-season subsurface moisture, runoff, and summer rainfall was the prevailing practice, as it would be throughout the Basketmaker residency. On these uplands, corn could generally survive without supplemental irrigation or intensive maintenance. Certain wild plants, such as lamb's-quarter and amaranth, were probably allowed to colonize gardens.

Even under optimal conditions, the region was a marginal agricultural zone. Native plants had long before adapted to the environment, but newly cultivated ones had not. Long-term climatic records for the district show that the necessary number of frost-free days for corn to mature (115 to 120) often is not reached. In the past, as today, sowing two weeks early or harvesting two weeks late could prove disastrous. Add unpredictable rainfall to the unpredictable frosts, and the staying power of the Basketmaker II for several centuries becomes all the more remarkable. The underlying uncertainty of crop returns emphasizes a probable continued reliance upon plant foraging to supply a high percentage of foodstuffs.

Some of the corn and squash harvest, of course, was earmarked for the following year's planting. Looking toward the future and selecting the largest, fullest kernels and seeds was inherent in successful farming and improvement of the stock, but it also represented a steadfast faith in spring's rebirth and reinforced the Basketmakers' probable animistic beliefs. Although Morris and Burgh did not note it in their upper Animas district explorations, storage facilities likely preceded human habitation at the shelters.

Harvesting techniques—whether for native or domesticated plants—are difficult to document archaeologically. Preparation methods for turning these harvested plants into edible food, on the other hand, are revealed by much of the usual artifact inventory. Among the typical artifacts were stone grinding slabs, or metates, with a central rectangular trough suitably sized for a hand-held, shaped stone, or mano, to be pushed back and forth. The end next to a kneeling grinder was left open to allow the finished product to be brushed into a basket or other container. Metates of this sort are ubiquitous among native Southwestern farmers of corn and securely place the upper Animas district Basketmakers in that grouping.

In the absence of earthenware receptacles, another important adjunct to the Basketmaker II food preparation process was basketry. This was a craft with a known venerable ancestry, a craft that remains essential in the lives of some modern Native Americans. In other localities, Morris had discovered clay liners for basket panniers. These were meant to keep seeds from becoming embedded in the coils when they were roasted. No such liners were encountered in the Falls Creek deposits, either because they had crumbled or dissolved or because they were never used. However, large dumps of baseball-size, fire-reddened rocks suggest that these rocks—and possibly hot coals—were used for boiling or parching food in what must have been basketry containers. Diggers recovered some shallow, open tray- and bowl-shaped baskets that could have been used for these purposes. Other baskets may have been carried on the back, held secure by a forehead tumpline, the interiors of their large, tapered forms sealed with pitch in order to hold water.

Another clue to the extensive manufacture of baskets was several bundles of prepared splints and 387 awls made from animal-bone splinters. Such awls, commonly used to push peeled and softened willow splints into place, were polished to a satiny surface finish through frequent use.

Morris and Burgh were especially interested in the few surviving Falls Creek basket specimens because of their concurrent work on a definitive monograph dealing with the prehistoric Pueblo basketmaking craft as a whole. Of the six coiled baskets in the collection Flora took from the North Shelter burial crevice, Morris wrote Kidder, "The basketry runs true in shape, but is unlike anything I have come across in that the foundation consists of a single flattened rod padded above and enclosed in a bundle. There are no decorative patterns."[10]

Subsequently, Morris and Burgh described these specimens and a number of fragments as being close-coiled, with half- or one-rod-and-bundle stacked foundations sewed with both interlocked and uninterlocked stitching. They identified the weaving technique that used half-rod and one-rod foundations with that of Fremont (and Great Basin) peoples living to the northwest in Colorado and Utah rather than with the workmanship of traditional Basketmakers of the southwestern Colorado Plateau in northeast Arizona and southeast Utah.[11] The lack of decoration made the Falls Creek baskets drab in comparison.

From this skimpy evidence, the archaeologists tried to reconstruct mealtime in Falls Creek Valley. Bones tossed aside in drifts of refuse were too splintered and fragmentary to retain butchering marks. It is presumed that cooks skewered chunks of venison on sharp sticks and held them over hearth flames. Others cracked boiled or raw bones for marrow or oil and opened skulls for brains. Small skinned animal carcasses probably were broiled whole over hot coals. When the feasting was over, toolmakers, jewelers, blanket weavers, and hide tanners selected unconsumed raw materials for their crafts. Some skins and bones were stockpiled; others were discarded.

When fresh vegetables were in season, corn, perhaps still in husks, was roasted over embers or put into preheated pits. Elsewhere, cobs skewered onto short sticks indicate spit cooking. These were the original roasting ears and must have been an anticipated treat. That fresh corn was eaten is proven by cobs showing that soft kernels had been removed.

Most corn was dried, sometimes left on cobs after curing in the autumn sun but more often shelled to conserve space in the storage cists. It was prepared by the women in various ways. Coarsely ground, it was mealy and, with the addition of water and perhaps some native amaranth seeds, suitable for a flavored mush cooked by dropping hot rocks into water-tight baskets. Finer grinds produced a flour that when combined with animal fat, ash, and water could be shaped into cakes or thin sheets for baking on hot, flat rocks. Succotash could be made by boiling whole kernels together with wild vetch beans, some remnants of which were taken from the South Shelter deposits.

Cucurbits added the essential amino acid tryptophan to the diet. These gourds were convenient because they could be eaten raw, or dried and stored for later use. Because they needed no containers, squashes or pumpkins probably often were roasted whole over coals. Some of the seeds were parched in basketry trays. The dried gourd shells made containers for many uses.

Once Morris and Burgh at least partially understood how the Falls Creek Basketmakers subsisted, they turned their attention to shelter, hoping to establish the earliest Basketmaker house type yet known. Morris immediately assumed that the necessary building materials were plentiful. Timber of all sizes and kinds must have been in virtually inexhaustible supply, and mud was readily available. Writers of archaeological reports almost universally overlook mud as a critical resource. However, soft, wet, clinging mud was what held together the timbers and later the cobblestones and sandstone blocks of masonry construction. The dirt needed to make mud is everywhere on the Colorado Plateau, but the water often is lacking or very limited. Not so in the upper Animas district, where from weeping banks and soggy bogs beside perennial waterfalls, gloriously sticky mud came ready to use. When one source was exhausted, there were always others. In addition to its practicality in terms of available raw materials, these early builders may have viewed mud-and-timber construction as a symbolic tie to the earth below them—source of the mud—and the sky above, into which the timber beams once soared.

Because the floor of the north alcove sloped steeply, the Falls Creek Basketmakers needed to create level spaces on which to build their domiciles. This was no easy task for people without metal tools or mechanical devices. Ponderous slabs of rock must have been pried aside using poles and human muscle. It was then a matter of loosening hard, compacted soil with pointed sticks, scraping the ground with faceted stones, and carrying off earth with baskets. Finally, each prepared spot, wide enough for only one or two dwellings, had to be banked with stones to prevent slumping.

Inasmuch as two seasons of arduous effort by the Carnegie crew produced only partial earthen floors, much of the proposed reconstruction was educated conjecture. The rock shelter residents, like most early builders, were found to favor round dwellings. The oval-to-circular house floors, thinly coated with mud plaster, were scooped slightly below surface level, with perimeters of footing logs placed on the surrounding ground. Contrary to frequently restated descriptions, the houses were surface, not pit, structures. Bedrock or heavy stony soils precluded deep excavations. What remained of the floors of these habitations indicated rooms that at best estimate ranged from eight to twenty-five feet across.

Why the Falls Creek Basketmakers did not utilize the abundant supply of thin sandstone slabs present in the South Shelter to lay up walls is puzzling. For unknown reasons, they preferred to laboriously hack logs, limbs, and wooden slabs and stack them up using mud cement to create single-unit structures that may or may not have been sufficiently high for an adult to stand erect inside. The free-standing walls may or may not have sloped inward into a cribbed, domed roof closure. In some dwellings, the cliff face formed the back wall. There may or may not have been an opening in the roof. If central heating was provided by hot rocks in a sandy floor basin, as Morris and Burgh suggested, no hole would have been needed to vent smoke, but the desire for light and fresh air might have made one essential.

Because the relevant portions of floors had crumbled away, the excavators could not be certain that the houses were entered through a floor-level crawl hole that could be closed by a stone slab or piece of hide. One researcher suggests the missing floor portions may have included actual antechambers through which entry was gained.[12] Flora had, in fact, noted such a vestibule in his first encounter with a Basketmaker II structure, but because he never published results of his diggings, this information was not available to others.[13]

The adoption of architecture–at this site or elsewhere–was a major advancement entailing consequential changes in lifestyle; however, there was a substantial drawback to the design of the Falls Creek dwellings. With a single aperture, the rooms must have been cavelike–dark and stuffy. Although assorted implements were recovered on intact floors, and grinding stones were secured on top of interior clay pedestals, it is probable that most daytime activities took place outside.

Even in winter, open-air work might have been possible. Sparkling skies are cloudless approximately three-fourths of the time due to the elevation and atmospheric clarity of the upper Animas district. Snow could have been brushed aside, crude windbreaks of branches thrown up, and roaring fires set with the twirling of a wooden drill (one such specimen was recovered in the trash) to keep scantily clad flint knappers, basket weavers, and meal grinders warm while they worked. Their babies, cuddled in swaddling bands of rabbit fur, probably watched from the cradleboards propped against rocks. Admittedly, few exterior fire beds for heating or cooking were recorded by excavators, but there is little doubt that they once existed. How could rocks for parching, boiling, or warmth have been prepared? With no interior fires for light, and winter darkness typically enveloping mountain valleys at an early hour, one can envision the Falls Creek settlers wrapped in hides or yucca fiber blankets softened with strips of rabbit fur, stretched out on twined tule mats spread over their unyielding dirt floors, feet extending toward the hot rocks piled in the room's center, probably thinking longingly of spring.

Aside from providing snug quarters for sleeping or escaping severe weather, the habitations were veritable warehouses. Inside each was from one to a half dozen or more storage cists. They were dug beneath the floor, built on its surface, or sometimes both. Subterranean cists often had ring collars of adobe at floor level. Others had domes made of stacked thick coils of clay in a process not unlike that later used to build earthenware vessels. Some cists were lined with sandstone slabs; some were not. Some were small; some were large. There was a clear emphasis in these dwellings on interior storage, even though aboveground facilities severely reduced already limited floor space. Forestalling freezing or raiding of precious foods may have motivated this practice. Additional cists were crammed between the habitations. The most important inference to be drawn from the abundance of cists is that these people had both the need and opportunity to hoard large quantities of edibles. The excavators estimated that one cist could have held as much as forty-five bushels of shelled corn kernels.

The siting of open-air Talus Village on terraces laboriously cut into a steep incline paralleled a practice observed in the rock shelters. As rebuilding took place, successive platforms were stacked atop each other, eating into the cliff. The rise of land at what probably was the rear of the houses was a shield from wind and cold. That downslope drainage was a problem is confirmed by the presence of rows of rock next to the slope to divert runoff.

The study of Talus Village helped prove that when there were no natural features to provide protection from the elements, the local Basketmakers did erect permanent habitations in the open in the same style as in the alcoves. Flora's estimation of their number may have been too high, but certainly more houses existed than were found at this locale.

Superposition of floors and the limited space on the leveled building spots at all three examined sites makes it obvious, in conjunction with tree-ring dating, that there was a successive rather than simultaneous occupation there. The excavators reported a total of forty-eight floors cleared, often two or three deep, with seven stacked up in one portion of Talus Village.[14] Flora thought the pancaked floors more correctly would be numbered at thirteen to twenty-three.[15] There probably were no more than a dozen dwellings in use at the three locations at any one time: four at the North Shelter, two at the South Shelter, and six at Talus Village.[16] Each was large enough only for a nuclear family of four or five. Unless future work proves otherwise, the Basketmaker II population in the upper Animas district never was very large. In all likelihood, the settlers built on the slopes rather the valley floor because, as Morris and Burgh suggest, the heights are actually warmer in winter than the lowlands, where cold air settles.

A mystery regarding the known Basketmaker II houses in this region is why they all appear to have burned. The true pithouses that followed suffered a similar fate, but in their case, the conflagrations could logically be attributed to open fires that were fanned by drafts of air from ventilator shafts and ignited walls and ceilings of exposed dry timber, brush, and shredded juniper bark. Experiments and archaeological evidence, however, do not bear out the accidental house fire theory.

One explanation for the Basketmaker II fires may be that if the dwellings were not well maintained, they quickly fell into disrepair. Snowmelt or pelting August thunderstorms would have dissolved copious mud chinking and whatever exterior mud coating might have been applied, allowing wall and roof to collapse. When later reoccupation was desired, it would have been easier to salvage usable materials, burn the rest, scrape the debris over the front edge of the terrace, and start afresh. Archaeology seems to confirm this sequence of events, although the question remains as to whether the fires were intentional or accidental.[17] Both types of fires may have occurred.

It is noteworthy that the last of the superimposed houses–as well as those representing only a single occupation–also burned. This suggests that there may have been a deep-seated philosophical rationale for destroying one's home upon abandonment that mandated returning the site to its natural state. If this were so, it did not extend to the removal of trash. Warfare also might have been responsible for the burning of some structures.

In enumerating basic human needs, there is the matter of clothing. Although Morris often remarked that come rain or shine the Basketmakers dressed in their own weatherbeaten skins, this was not entirely true. Some of the bodies recovered by Flora still wore bits of loincloths or aprons. The loincloths were belts woven from yucca fibers or human hair. From these belts hung long fringes of fiber cords or cedar bark that were passed between the wearer's legs and caught in back by the belt. According to Helen Daniels, the mummy Jasper wore a kind of leather jerkin across his upper body.[18] Flora simply notes a wrapping of hide.[19] Tatters of fiber sandals and one of leather tumbled out of the debris. A throw of hide or fiber must have comforted nude shoulders in cold weather.

An unusual item of winter wear was twilled sandals made of bulrushes that grew in marshes below the rock shelters. Because of the sandals' width, it is suspected that a lining of loose shredded bark was worn between sandal and foot. The tule fibers surely were not sufficiently durable to have been practical for traversing rocky terrain but may have served well over soft snow.

Even with such no-nonsense wardrobes, these Indians were not above human vanity. There is no evidence of body tattooing or painting, but they did have an unabashed fondness for jewelry. Hundreds of beads from necklaces, pendants, or bracelets sprinkled the deposits. The effort, skill, and patience needed to gather colored rocks, bone, berries, and tiny shells from far-off waters and then shape, polish, drill, and string them on cords painstakingly woven of vegetable fibers or human hair stretches the imagination. Two necklace chains of black lignite and pink-to-red hornstone, each made up of hundreds of beads, are more than two feet in length. Morris called them the finest Basketmaker ornaments found to that time.[20] The strands of beads created from juniper berries or olivella shells were some twenty feet long and obviously were looped many times around the wearer's neck. One choker was composed of a short leather neck cord to which was attached a black lignite pendant encrusted across the top with five small shells.

Another important consideration in understanding Basketmaker life was the hardware they devised to carry out necessary tasks. The Carnegie excavators were fortunate: the upper Animas district sites they opened produced the largest, most varied display of such goods known to that time. Common implements were nothing more than roughly shaped or faceted all-purpose, cobble tools for felling trees, smoothing ground, shaping stone slabs, and cracking large animal bones. None were hafted. Other stones were ground down to work hides, plaster floors, weight atlatls to increase their leverage, or serve other unknown purposes. Knives, drills, scrapers, and gravers were skillfully chipped from quartzite, obsidian, agatized wood, or hornstone. With the exception of obsidian, most of these resources were available in the vicinity.

As for other resources, the yucca plant native to North America was invaluable to these settlers. Its fruit provided nourishment and its root made soap, but, most important, its stout leaf fibers formed the binder twine, the string, the warp and weft that held most of the portable and wearable goods together. Residue from the dry burial crevice contained examples of its usefulness; others are known from contemporary sites elsewhere. These uses included cordage, belts, bands, nets, tumplines, and blanket foundations that were insulated with rabbit fur and occasional bird feathers. Some of the cordage employed an S twist rather than the Z twist used by the Western Basketmakers (the letters indicate the direction in which the fiber twists were pulled).

The excavations yielded what appear to have been implements indispensable for separating longitudinal fibers from the flesh of yucca leaves, a process called decortication. These were 119 shaped deer ribs and scapulae that became serrated along their working edges as they repeatedly scraped down a leaf surface. Several identical notched ribs have been reported from local Basketmaker II sites, but they are uncommon elsewhere.[21]

Two twined yucca fiber bags and fragments of several others with encircling bands of red, black, and tan are identical to known examples from Basketmaker debris in southeast Utah and northeast Arizona. They seem out of place with the other Falls Creek textile specimens, but that may be because the full range of local textile production is unknown. Conversely, they may represent trade items.

Among bone artifacts, gaming pieces loom large. Those who denounce present gambling casinos on Indian lands as demoralizing influences upon innocent Native American communities should know that two thousand years ago, upper Animas district Basketmakers squatted around their piles of heated stones and passed long winter days or nights throwing dice. As Morris and Burgh state, "Sporting blood was strong in the veins of the Durango people."[22] It is hard to believe that competitive games did not entail betting and even harder to imagine that gambling was gender specific.

Common to those of most Basketmaker and Fremont groups, the upper Animas gaming pieces were small, thin plates of mammal bone that were cut into circular, rectangular, or lenticular shapes and scored on one or both surfaces by various linear patterns. The forms and markings surely had numerical or other significance. The chips may have been made in sets, such as the thirteen pieces found together in a Talus Village burial. The rules of the game are unknown, but the pieces clearly demonstrate that there was more to Basketmaker life than hardship and wondering where the next meal was coming from.

It was no surprise that earthenwares were not recovered in the principal zones excavated at either the rock shelters or Talus Village, because their absence is one of the distinguishing features by which the Pecos Classification identified Basketmaker II. However, the local residents may have known of pottery in use elsewhere. Certainly from their own constructions, they were aware of the plasticity and cohesiveness of moist mud and of its hardness when burned. Occasionally, they fashioned small unfired clay figurines; the partial remains of one were found during the Carnegie digs.

It may be that the absence of pottery was at least partly a matter of choice, not ignorance of technique. If the Animas district Basketmaker II were semisedentary, pots would have been too cumbersome and fragile to move around on lengthy collecting excursions. Furthermore, the mountain climate dictated that pottery making be a summer activity (which would have conflicted with gathering time) so as to avoid the freezing of wet clay and permit sufficient drying time to avoid explosions when baked.

Because these prehistoric tribes had no written language, attempts to understand their ideology are perplexing and unverifiable. Still, to gain some insight into Basketmaker beliefs, researchers turned to two types of evidence found in the rock shelters: burial customs and pictographs.

The manner of disposal of the dead reflects both a culture's practicalities and philosophy. The bodies that were laid to rest in the debris of the North Shelter burial crevice were flexed and trussed to save space in the cramped area between rock slabs. Others were flexed and placed in unused cists or in the spills of earth, rock, and cinders pushed between dwelling platforms or over the edges of the building terraces. There were no multiple burials such as among Western Basketmakers. Burial sites in loose debris were selected because digging graves into packed, rock-laden earth with nothing but a stout, pointed stick would have been gut-wrenching at best and impossible if the ground were frozen. In addition, there may have been an impulse to keep loved ones nearby rather than leaving them in more distant surroundings. Such localized burials might also have been one way of establishing family or kin-group ownership of a particular territory.

Bodies of the dead were oriented so that heads generally did not point south. Among present-day Pueblo Indians the cardinal directions have symbolic meanings. It would be surprising if that were not so from the earliest times. The researchers did not know whether disturbances of some graves, including disarticulation of skeletons, might have caused anguish. Obviously, some intrusion of graves was done by the Basketmakers themselves, not to remove goods left with the dead but to put later deceased to rest. Further, if comparisons with present Pueblo attitudes are acceptable, the corporeal entity was regarded only as a vessel for the spirit.[23] At death the flesh and bones lost their purpose, freeing the spirit to merge with the wind, the clouds, and the breath of life that enveloped the natural world.

Graves found in the open no longer contained many offerings because damp conditions over time had rotted the burial goods–and frequently the bones themselves. However, most of the bodies placed in the relatively dry crevice in the North Shelter were covered with hides, bark, or robes of fur and fiber and were accompanied by bags, baskets, jewelry, and other articles, some of which represented considerable sacrifice. None were in large twined bags, as was typical of Western Basketmaker burials. Also notably absent was the pottery that would characterize virtually all later prehistoric Pueblo graves and attract greedy modern collectors. Respect for the dead, and the concept of an afterlife are inherent in these Basketmaker practices.

The pictographs that first brought attention to the Falls Creek Valley shelters are another avenue into the Basketmaker mentality. It is easy for modern observers to imbue the surviving rock art with false mysticism, but by the same token, it clearly was not mere doodling on inviting expanses of blank rock. Simply reaching the heights at which some of the paintings were executed required serious motivation, not to mention derring-do.

Although the pictographs in question repeat some themes, such as flute players, birds, and spirals, common to a generalized Basketmaker background, taken as a whole they are unlike most examples on the Colorado Plateau.[24] The well-known San Juan Anthropomorphic Style, with its large representations of handprints, atlatls and darts, square-shouldered humans with headdresses and other costuming, or human scalps is absent. Nor are the drawings reminiscent of late Fremont rock art. The human and quadruped animal forms do bear some semblance to petroglyphs at the Alva Site at the northwest end of the Uncompahgre Plateau. That alcove site was undated but aceramic.[25]

The Falls Creek Valley panels and another one recently found in the upper Animas district are characterized by the very small scale of the elements (nothing exceeding approximately eight inches in height) and the crudeness of their execution. Using a palette of white, red, black, green, and yellow mineral pigments against the reddish or tan native stone, the artists created some concentric nested circles, a few wiggles, and figures that can be identified only as human or animal.

One reaction to the lack of definition and detail is that these folks were bunglers with the brush. This interpretation is fortified by the fact that none of the recovered artifacts indicate much concern with graphic expression. On the other hand, perhaps these paintings were intended only as simple sketches of a vision or prayer. They may have been a dreamscape. Many of the figures do appear hallucinatory, making one wonder what was smoked in the several tubular stone pipes recovered from the deposits. The frequent bird figures may have been inspired by observation of the seasonal movements of these creatures along the Animas flyway.

In contrast to the amorphous depictions are some fifty nearly identical abstractions interpreted as masks. Lined up horizontally and painted in red, each consists of eyes, nose, and usually a swipe of color that may have represented a cap or feather; sometimes the masks are emphasized by pairs of bordering vertical parallel lines. Their arrangement in rows suggests ceremonial dancers. Or perhaps they were ancestor or clan records. It is our loss that the meanings, perhaps not just to non-Indians but to Native Americans as well, have vanished in the mists of time.

Not surprisingly, because there is no proven way to date rock art, current specialists disagree about the age of these pictographs. They may be Basketmaker II representations. Sally Cole sees an earlier heritage in some of the painted abstractions and in incised or impressed imagery of plants, parallel wavy lines, and paw prints on at least one aboveground clay cist dome.[26] Maybe in the case of the cist, the designs represented a supplication for bountiful harvests to stock the larder. Or maybe they were the result of the temptation to playfully manipulate soft clay.

Polly Schaafsma and Jane Young think the masks are a product of later Basketmaker III painters.[27] Unquestionably, they show more careful drafting skills than the other elements, but whether that in itself indicates less antiquity is debatable.

By the time the Morris and Burgh report on the Durango Basketmaker II was published, tree rings had established a time span for the North Shelter of A.D. 46 to A.D. 260.[28] One date of A.D. 198 was read for the South Shelter. Talus Village dated circa A.D. 175 to A.D. 324. Morris thought the North Shelter was where the district's occupation likely began. Over the years, he expressed the belief that because the rock shelters were the most primitive sites he had explored in his long career, tree rings would surely push the Anasazi timetable back into the pre-Christian Era.[29] They did, but Morris never had the satisfaction of knowing how much. In any case, by the mid to late fourth century A.D., the inhabitants had vanished from the humble houses in the upper Animas district that Morris and Burgh explored.

Archaeological endings like this are thought-provoking and sobering, often because emptied ruined dwellings suggest failure. The dwellings are mysterious because the underlying reasons for their abandonment are not always apparent. For Morris, such was not the case with these sites because he believed that somewhere in the vicinity, the Falls Creek Basketmaker II slowly evolved into the Falls Creek Basketmaker III. He was wrong.

Their Reconsidered Place in the Scheme of Things

After four decades, the work of Morris and Burgh remains a classic in its field. Notwithstanding, those same four decades have seen the number of people engaged in ancestral Pueblo research swell to hundreds working on many levels, with a consequent proliferation of data and ideas. It is therefore timely to re-evaluate—and amplify for the interested public—a record that has become increasingly complex. Such a review reveals how much has been learned about the early peoples and how important further research is to a more complete understanding.

By the late 1930s when the Durango fieldwork was underway, regional scholars recognized two prehistoric sedentary entities in the Southwest: one was the Colorado Plateau Anasazi, on whom research had begun fifty years earlier, and the second was an adaptation, known as the Hohokam, to the low Arizona deserts along the Salt and Gila River drainages that Gila Pueblo staff members vigorously studied during the 1930s. A proposed third component to the prehistoric collage, this one situated in the mountain and basin country separating New Mexico and Arizona and called the Mogollon, was being hotly debated.

The dozen or so years that elapsed between excavations and publication of the Falls Creek rock shelters and Talus Village, distressing to Morris and feeding Flora's gristmill of bitterness, allowed a conceptual fruition in the discipline that could be plumbed in the effort to appreciate past cultural processes. The validity of the Mogollon had been accepted, albeit begrudgingly in some quarters. Morris hastened to compare his Basketmaker materials with those of Mogollon groups once living several hundred miles due south and found numerous resemblances in architecture and portable goods. He concluded, "The identities and similarities are too many to preclude the possibilities that both were developed from a single more ancient and more simple culture."[30] He called for a study of what was then known as Early Man.

Although not yet definitively articulated, what Morris thought of as the Early Man period is now conceived as two successive cultural expressions that in past millennia appeared throughout the Southwest. The first is generally referred to as Paleo-Indian because it exemplified a lifeway characteristic of Paleolithic hunters of the Old World but present among the first human inhabitants of the New World. The second, more recent expression is generally called Archaic.

Paleo-Indians appear to have had little impact on the region that Morris was most concerned with, because glaciation of the San Juan Mountains continued at least intermittently until approximately nine thousand years ago. By that time most of the Pleistocene megafauna upon which the Paleo-Indians preyed had vanished. Still, in warm periods when ice flows blocking corridors into the mountains melted, some relict populations of *Bison antiquus* and similar large animals may have grazed the uplands. This could account for a few large, lanceolate, well-made stone spear points recovered in widely dispersed localities. None has been found associated with the bones of extinct or modern types of fauna. However suggestive, random surface finds of human artifacts such as these must necessarily be treated with caution because they could have been recovered and then dropped by later peoples.

Paleo-Indian stone points reported from the general Animas district number only a handful. Several came from the Ridges Basin, a depressed plateau rising just southwest of the regional commercial center of Durango.[31] Another partial point was recently picked up in the flats below the alcoves on the west side of Falls Creek Valley. It was identified as a Plainview point, which at its type location on the Texas prairie could be considered approximately nine thousand years old.[32] Although Zeke Flora claimed he recovered similar heavily patinated artifacts underneath some unidentified trash, it is not likely they pertained to that refuse, except as objects found elsewhere and recycled by later atlatl-wielding Indians. Four or five other large spear points have been reported as lying on the surface of the backcountry toward the headwaters of the San Juan River, one on a mountainside at an elevation of more than ten thousand feet.[33] Based on this paucity of evidence, scientists concede that there were some Paleo-Indians wandering along the upper Animas and the mountain ramparts beyond, but their presence was at best ephemeral. On the basis of typology of the points, they assign these big-game hunters to the Llano, Folsom, and Plano complexes, as defined in other sectors, none with any connection to Morris's immediate project.

As the large game animals became scarce, the Holocene climate grew warmer and drier. Populations increased, and a somewhat variant lifestyle was adopted. Nomadic bands evolved basic technologies that enabled them to survive on whatever modern species of animal and plant life they encountered. This ageless subsistence pattern kept Archaic groups mobile as they followed the rhythms of seasons in order to fully exploit the spectrum of edibles. They likely stayed in lower elevations than those who stalked the big game. Their use territory was more restricted. It is possible that they even may have manipulated the biotic landscape, perhaps through fire, in order to enhance their chances of survival.[34] The archaeological record does not indicate specific divisions of labor, but analogy with modern peoples in the same regions and on the same cultural plateau suggests that the men were the primary hunters—at least of large animals—and the women and youngsters were more frequently the plant gleaners and preparers of food.

Among the first concrete examples of this hypothesized Southwestern Archaic developmental stage to be investigated was the Cochise Culture, so named by the Gila Pueblo researchers. It was localized in bleak basins of southeastern Arizona. Of the three successive periods the archaeologists outlined there (the earliest possibly dating back seven thousand years), it was the final San Pedro phase that caught Morris's attention. Here was a potential source from which the Durango people, as well as the early Mogollon who occupied the area between them and the Cochise domain, might have evolved. In a summary of San Pedro characteristics, he noted "a gathering-hunting economy; a profusion of ground and chipped stone artifacts; a crude house type, with a fire area and undercut storage pit; but *no pottery*."[35] Moreover, the time frames of the San Pedro and Durango developments generally meshed: 1500 B.C. to 200 B.C. This posited relationship of San Pedro Cochise to upper Animas groups through a Mogollon intermediary was a bold interpretation by a cautious man, necessitating a grand five-hundred-mile migratory sweep over time from the playas carpeted with greasewood and creosote bush edging down to the north Mexican sierra, up through the more elevated headwaters of the Gila River, to a refuge at the stony foothills of the Rockies.

Another possible point of origin for the Durango people was only 150 miles away in western Colorado. In the 1930s and 1940s, a clique of tyro enthusiasts explored the rugged canyons and tablelands south of Grand Junction, Colorado, in search of Indian relics. They concentrated primarily on the blocky landform of the Uncompahgre Plateau, which runs diagonally from northwest to southeast, pointing toward the lower end of the San Juan Mountains. At the base of its escarpment are many shallow alcoves where the collectors observed campsites littered with ash and charcoal; milling stones; bits of flaked stone implements, including large corner-notched projectile points; shreds of rough cordage; and a few slab-lined cists. They found no burials with pottery such as lured their Durango counterparts.

Information about the finds was relayed to several regional scientists. The person most interested, Clarence T. Hurst, also had no formal archaeological training but was a professor of zoology at Western State College in Gunnison, Colorado. Hurst became so caught up in the excitement of testing a number of Uncompahgre sites that he led efforts to organize a statewide archaeological society with chapters in areas where the examination of prehistory had become popular. The local Durango archaeological society joined this larger organization. Hurst also oversaw the society's small quarterly journal, *Southwestern Lore,* and for several decades used it as an outlet for modest reports on his own work.[36] The writing was chatty and often lacked sufficient detail to be of much use to the professional archaeological community, but it did not stray into Flora-like fantasies.

Undoubtedly, Morris was aware of this archaeological activity taking place virtually next door to his own, but he apparently did not consider it relevant to Falls Creek prehistory. He likely viewed it as the work of amateurs among the remains of a hunting-gathering society having no great antiquity. This may have been an unfortunate blind spot. Instead, he looked far to the south, where the Gila Pueblo archaeological staff had high professional credibility.

Looking southward for Indian origins was a long-standing, deep-rooted trend in Southwestern archaeology. The first U.S. encounters with San Juan Basin ruins in the mid-nineteenth century mistakenly attributed them to the Toltecs or Aztecs of Mexico. A little later, the fundamental technologies of agriculture and pottery making—as well as many lesser aspects of material culture—usually were described as diffusing northward from higher Mexican cultures. The idea that the Anasazi evolved out of a hunting-gathering society located off the Colorado Plateau to the south was therefore a reasonable extension of this rationale. The semiarid land of western Colorado north of the Dolores River was generally discounted as having much impact on cultural developments farther south.

Even with the touted critical importance of the hunting-gathering stage in the formulation of the prehistoric Pueblo cultural statement, specialists were slow to take serious field or conceptual interest in this elusive horizon. One reason is that it takes a truly dedicated researcher to become excited over the artifactual findings of most open sites of this period when there are potentially more exotic things waiting to be discovered. Furthermore, the wellsprings of financial support typically expect more bang (that is, tangible goods) for their bucks. In Southwestern archaeology it always has been much harder to sell postulations than pots.

In addition, technical methods to date the findings more precisely were either nonexistent or inaccurate until the post-World War II introduction of radiocarbon dating. Though not yet perfected, the technique had the tremendous advantage of being applicable to periods before the use of wood construction, thus allowing the time-scale to be pushed back much further than was permitted by tree-ring dating. At last some temporal specificity for the earliest stages of native cultures was promised.

As inquiries heated up, scientists saw that over perhaps as many as five millennia before the Christian era, Archaic groups filled in previously little-used areas of the West, from the Canadian border into Mexico. Some of them slowly rooted themselves physically and spiritually in the often unforgiving land that since the 1800s has been known as the Colorado Plateau. Work in the early 1950s by Marie Wormington, Denver Museum of Natural History, and Robert Lister, University of Colorado, demonstrated that one of the areas over which they ranged was the Uncompahgre Plateau.[37] The results of their research came too late to be useful for Morris. What they found was a culture geologically dated within the first millennium B.C., living in cliffside alcoves. No formal shelters were present, but open hearths and slab-lined cists for storage of plant foods were observed. Basin metates, one-hand manos, a notable mix of stone dart and arrow points, one-rod-and-bundle basketry, and rabbit fur robes constituted the artifact inventory.

Elsewhere in the northern Southwest, what appear to have been some formalized human burials, clay and twig figurines, and huge panels of iconographic art on rocky cliff faces mirrored mystical religious consciousness. It was obvious that Archaic culture was not rudimentary. A major project directed by Jesse Jennings, University of Utah, in caves scattered about that state's vast, desolate interior basin, reinforced this conclusion by producing a wealth of perishables to complement the repertory of less fragile goods being taken from contemporary open sites.[38]

Together, the artifacts from both open-air and protected occupations confirmed the degree to which the minds and hands of the simple wanderers made the available natural resources work for them.

Although technical sophistication varied among Archaic bands, some of them were seen to have turned bone, antler, shell, stone, wood, fibers, hides, fur, and unfired clay into clothing, jewelry, tools, gaming pieces, icons, weapons, pigments, basketry, pipes, fire drills, and other everyday paraphernalia. These cultural artifacts represent a stunning display of intelligence and tactile abilities.

It was not until thirty years after the publication of the Morris and Burgh report that scientific attention turned to the hunting-gathering stage of development in the Durango region. In the 1980s, government-mandated surveys of cultural resources likely to be impacted by economic development led researchers, working under business contracts, to look for evidence of Archaic penetration of the highlands skirting the upper Animas district. Two such development projects were a possible diversionary enterprise on the Animas River that would impound water in Ridges Basin, and the removal of hazardous waste from a smelter dump to Bodo Canyon, both localities just a few miles south of Durango.

In these regions surveyors noted more than four dozen large and small campsites that they attributed to Archaic bands roaming these areas, once or repeatedly over many years, on their seasonal collecting and hunting cycles.[39] All that remained to mark their passage were surface scatters of debris left from the creation and use of stone spear points and knives, complete or partial large corner-notched points, a few worn stones needed for milling seeds and nuts, and occasional reddened rocks cracked from old cooking fires. If habitations of any kind had been in use, they were not recognized. Nor was evidence of corn noted. On the other hand, no excavations of these sites were undertaken, probably because the exuberance of Archaic culture seen in more protected spots was absent.

Precise dates are unknown for the first Archaic-stage cultures of the northern Colorado Plateau.[40] These cultures may have been in place by the third or second millennia before Christ. One scenario has them arising from the dreary, windswept arroyo country to the southeast, where archaeologist Cynthia Irwin-Williams identified five diagnostic stages of an Archaic background she termed the Oshara Tradition. This would put the Archaic source geographically closer than the arid basin-and-range province further south. This idea has yet to be proved.

More likely, the hunter-gatherers of the general Animas area may have been part of a wide but thin distribution of early nomads spreading from the grayed, castellated panorama of eastern Utah and west-central Colorado. They may have been attracted by improved environmental conditions in the evergreen uplands that allowed richer harvests of herbaceous seeds and crops of nuts. Or conversely, it may have been a warm/dry period in the lowlands that was behind the territorial shift.

If, over the centuries, Archaic groups were in the highlands just ten miles to the south, they surely were also in the Falls Creek and upper Animas Valleys. One hundred years of modern farming activities have no doubt eradicated many unobtrusive surface indications of that prehistory, but nevertheless, Forest Service personnel making surveys of the Falls Creek Archaeological Area have come across discarded lithic materials strewn over bottomlands and upper reaches of Falls Creek Valley that they believe to be Archaic.[41]

One suspects that in spring as the sun warmed the earth, foragers drifted into the heights to gather tender buds of new plant life, and hunters stalked animals drawn to water holes. Like their descendants, these people doubtless felt a oneness with the land and drew inner strength from the majestic mountains, forbidding yet protective as well. They lingered as seeds, tubers, berries, and grasses matured in the low-lying areas and then, as fall approached, moved up the slopes to harvest pinyon nuts and acorns. With the drop in temperatures, they may have sought refuge on high ledges and hilltops, away from the cold settling in hollows in shadow by mid-afternoon. Others may have retreated back down the valley corridors toward the relative warmth of the San Juan River depression. These are speculations to be substantiated by future research.

One of the warm/dry cycles typical of the lowlands of the northern Southwest is thought to have occurred during the fourth or third century B.C.[42] It may have prompted peoples already having adopted limited corn agriculture to migrate toward the uplands. The darkened mouths of the Falls Creek rock shelters invited some of them to stay.

The first to seek a suitable camp at the North Shelter found in the lowest part of the opening a narrow, level floor of compacted sand that over the ages had been washed down grain by grain from the escarpment above. Another comparable natural platform slightly farther up the cave floor was separated from the lower platform by a steep irregular slope. It was these two level areas, nestling against the cliff, protected by the overhang, that people chose to occupy.

If any sort of dwellings were erected on these two terraces, they were destroyed by later construction. A number of shallow slab-lined cists sunk next to the cliff face or in the incline between the two terraces may have been their work. Other cists are suspected to have been covered with heavy rockfall after the shelter was no longer used. R. G. Matson categorically states that storage cists were associated with this first occupation and dates them to just before A.D. 50, but neither Morris and Burgh nor Jeffrey Dean specifically confirm this.[43] At the lower level, in front of the massive sandstone wall forming the rear of the cave, is a closetlike space created by parallel vertical slabs broken from the matrix and fortuitously topped by a horizontal rock that formed a roof. Into this spot, daily refuse drifted, gradually creating a soft cushion for the dead. Flora referred to it as the burial crevice.

The only remaining clues to the first living zones of the North Shelter were pockets of soil stained by waste and lumps of charcoal lying beneath or beside four later overriding house floors plastered down by liquid mud. The charred wood from the debris yielded a series of informative tree-ring dates. Six dates from the upper level (Morris and Burgh's Terrace III) and fourteen dates from the lower level (Morris and Burgh's Terrace IV) may have resulted from the presence of humans three centuries before Christ. However, in most instances, outer growth rings of the samples may be missing, throwing off the accuracy of dating. Further, there is always the possibility that long-dead wood was gathered from the hillsides to be used as fuel or for construction and that the ring dates therefore do not pinpoint actual occupation. Dean, the dendrochronologist responsible for determining these dates, considers them indicative of a pre-Christian-era occupation.[44] Six other samples date to the early first century A.D.

In the same time frame, one wood specimen from the burial crevice dates to 291 B.C. (the outer rings are missing) and another to 81 B.C., probably close to the actual cutting date. Thirty-one pieces of charcoal from the South Shelter predate the Christian era and were collected either during Flora's work for Gladwin or during the later Carnegie Institution excavations. Unfortunately, they are without provenience. At present, these pre-Christian-era charcoal samples from the Falls Creek shelters have yielded the oldest tree-ring dates (none of which represent cutting dates) in the Southwest.

Corroborative evidence that humans occupied the locale this early on comes from corn recovered from trash brushed into the burial crevice. Three samples of corn kernels gathered by the Carnegie crew as it cleaned up after Flora's rummaging recently were radiocarbon accelerator dated to 181 B.C., 368 B.C., and 377 B.C.[45] Other corn scattered in the fill of both overhangs might be even older. These dates make clear that some people in the vicinity were at least attempting to grow corn at a period earlier than previously known for this part of the Southwest, and they were doing so at high altitude in a marginal climate.

The basic corn type was described as Hohokam/Basketmaker Complex influenced by the Mexican Complex, but the lot as a whole is notable for heterogeneity that now is believed typical of many early northern peripheral sites.[46] Because it was studied as a unit, without any differentiation between early or late deposits, any morphological changes in the plant during what is now seen as more than half a millennium of cultivation were not detected. Because of decay, only a negligible amount of charred corn was recovered at Talus Village. None was reclaimed nearby in the two open sites at Tamarron and Ign 12:46 that were excavated later.

The corn was planted either on the south-facing slopes below the shelters (elevation, more than seven thousand feet) or in the nearby Animas Valley (elevation, sixty-five hundred feet). Dependent on spring subsoil moisture and summer precipitation, this corn was meant to supplement the stores of collected native foods, not replace them. Unfortunately, the excavation report does not reveal whether refuse taken from cists not associated with dwellings included parts of corn plants. That information might confirm that the cists were created for corn storage by the alcove's first residents. Nevertheless, until such time as analyses of stable carbon isotopes in human bone from the Durango area can be made, there is little reason to think that the appearance of corn meant total sedentism or substantial reliance upon that foodstuff.[47] The shelters probably were seasonal base camps to which the bands returned sporadically. As elsewhere, these peoples had a taste for montane rock shelters along a stream drainage, to which they returned from time to time.[48]

The introduction of corn agriculture in the Anasazi domain now is generally believed to have taken place between the first and second millennia B.C., primarily to the south and west of the upper Animas area.[49] The Falls Creek corn, although not of that antiquity, is the oldest so far identified in the immediate vicinity. Notwithstanding, its age and the fact that it was probably raised at an elevation of seven thousand feet or more is not unique for western Colorado. It is matched in both respects by corn from Cottonwood Cave on the Uncompahgre Plateau, an area that in the Christian era became part of the traditional territory of the Fremont rather than Anasazi peoples. A sample recovered in 1947 by Hurst now yields a date of 270 B.C.[50] Doubtless, similar results from other western Colorado sites will be forthcoming, as they have been from south and central Utah.[51] It is noteworthy that much of the early corn has come from relatively high elevations where the advantage of extra moisture was balanced against shorter growing seasons. Cottonwood Cave itself is at an elevation of seven thousand feet.

The age of the corn, the large number of comparable tree-ring dates, and goods recovered from the general deposition within the Falls Creek alcoves (including one-hand manos, basin metates, half-rod- or one-rod-and-bundle basketry, twilled tule fiber sandals, and large corner-notched projectile points that some archaeologists classify as Elko and others as San Pedro) all suggest an early use of the two rock shelters that was not defined by Morris and Burgh, possibly by people from a Great Basin Archaic tradition.[52] The tree-ring sequence for the Durango sites that Morris and Burgh knew when their fieldwork ended began at A.D. 46, a bark date from two chunks of charcoal from ponderosa pine logs that had been discarded in refuse.[53]

A personal bias entered the picture when Morris discounted two tree-ring dates of 98 B.C. and 107 B.C. determined by Gladwin from charcoal found below Floor 8 on the lowest terrace of the North Shelter. Although he recognized this as the place of earliest occupation, Morris wrote Schulman at the Laboratory of Tree-Ring Research, "Of course the dates that Gladwin gives are way off the beam."[54] Instead, he ultimately accepted the Schulman date of 59 B.C. as representing the start of the chronology.

Some scholars now would call the first occupation of the Falls Creek rock shelters Late Archaic, with some corn farming. They perhaps would consider it allied to the En Medio phase of the Oshara Tradition in central New Mexico, the Los Pinos phase of the upper San Juan slope as proposed by R. Gwinn Vivian,[55] or perhaps an extension of the Uncompahgre Complex of central Colorado.[56] Mark Stiger, Western State College, confirms contemporaneity and basic similarity between Formative Period materials Hurst recovered fifty years ago at Tabeguache Cave on the Uncompahgre Plateau with those of the first occupation of the Falls Creek rock shelters.[57]

Others following the Pecos Classification prefer to use the inception of horticulture as the beginning of the Basketmaker sequence. This now would push the Basketmaker II back in time from A.D. 1 and divide the resulting long chronology into Early and Late.[58] In this interpretation, the first Falls Creek occupation would be considered Early Basketmaker II. However, the lines of demarcation between the two broad horizons of Archaic and Basketmaker, at best merely artificial taxonomy to bring order to a plethora of data, have become even more blurred with continuing research because architecture, subsistence measures, settlement patterns, and range of artifacts can no longer be considered certifiable distinguishing features.

In the case of the Falls Creek rock shelters, using modern methods to test an undisturbed deposit (if such still exists) would help clarify some of the present confusion and hopefully shed light on the important social and economic questions of culture continuity, adaptive strategies, and adoption of maize agriculture. Such a study might reinforce the growing feeling among many students that Basket-maker II was essentially an elaboration of the Archaic base and that Basketmaker III represented the real beginnings of the ancestral Pueblo continuum. William Lipe, specialist in Basketmaker research on Cedar Mesa in southeastern Utah, sees Basketmaker II as transitional, with the Late Basketmaker II (post-A.D. 1) as having a greater commitment to agriculture.[59]

Flora would have taken great satisfaction in some recognition of a formative stage underlying that of the local Basketmakers. In 1953, a year before the site report appeared, he wrote Schulman, "As you undoubtedly know, I never could concede the culture here at Durango starting at the time of Christ. One carbon 14 dating I have received was 1400 B.C. The B.M. II culture we are primarilly [*sic*] dealing with goes back through two distinct phases of cultural levels prior to the obvious and excavated top floors of the caves and Ign 7:101 [Talus Village]. There is, in addition, a parallel culture that seems to predate by far the known B.M. II."[60]

Once again, Flora may have been expressing his obsession with what he believed to be the great age of local antiquities. Or, as another aspect of the Durango conflict between amateurs and professionals, he may have been privy to items withheld from the hated "doctors." Sad to say, these materials remain unknown. Nor is it known what artifact in his possession was radiocarbon dated.

If the gap of nearly a century from A.D. 50 to A.D. 150 is not simply a happenstance of tree-ring sampling, the rock shelters appear to have been vacated during this period.[61] This information was not available to Morris. If the dwellings were indeed abandoned, this would more or less correspond to archaeologist Michael Berry's belief in a regionwide hiatus between the late first century B.C. (the end of his proposed Early Basketmaker II period) and A.D. 200 (the beginning of his proposed Late Basketmaker II period).[62] The usual reasons for such a withdrawal are depletion of readily obtainable resources and/or a climatic change.

When people returned to the Falls Creek rock shelters, they came in greater numbers and with the knowledge of simple architecture. Whether that skill was acquired elsewhere or developed on the spot either in Late Archaic or Basketmaker II times has not been determined. The continuity from the earlier occupations is likewise uncertain, but it was this second occupation that Morris considered a variant of Basketmaker II. To convince his colleagues that his assessment was sound, he scoured the extant literature to produce a comparative list of the worn and discarded precipitates of life, which showed a slightly more than 70 percent correlation between the Animas artifacts and what were considered the classic remains of the western Colorado Plateau, particularly those associated with the Kayenta Branch of the Anasazi.[63] Such comparative trait lists were standard techniques for demonstrating likenesses or dissimilarities. The obvious utilization of the Animas sites for domestic purposes and those of Grand Gulch in southeastern Utah and March Pass in northeastern Arizona for what was then believed to be storage and burial accounted for some distinctions.

According to Dean's 1975 reappraisal of the tree-ring chronology, domestic construction in both of the Durango shelters began in the late second century A.D. and continued periodically for the ensuing century and a half.[64] This activity took place as much as five hundred to six hundred years after human beings first made their way up the cliff to the alcoves and corresponds to a period of major drought farther south that once more may have driven tribes back to the high country.[65] At the North Shelter, floors were smoothed down on the two lower levels used by the original residents, and two additional platforms were flattened upslope to the north. The higher level, the most difficult to access, was not built on until late in the third century.[66]

In summary, based upon the data available to him, Morris considered the Falls Creek rock shelters to have been continuously used by the Basketmaker II for approximately the first two centuries of the Christian era. Three centuries later, a Basketmaker III family lived at the front of the South Shelter but did little more than wander through the North Shelter. One interpretation would substantially modify his reconstruction, positing two episodes of occupation separated by a century of abandonment. The first period substantially spanned 450 to 500 years before the time of Christ, when a group of people made use of the alcoves. It is not known that they erected habitations, but they probably did build cists for storing corn and nondomesticated plant foods. Most regional archaeologists would classify this culture as Early Basketmaker II. Thus far, this represents the only known incidence of this horizon in the Durango vicinity. The second occupation, lasting from the A.D. 200s into the A.D. 300s, featured culturally related groups who lived in small habitations, engaged in corn agriculture, but probably continued to undertake seasonal foraging. They were members of the Late Basketmaker II category.

Unless future work produces earlier tree-ring or radiocarbon dates, it appears that in the third and fourth centuries A.D., groups sharing the same cultural orientation as that uncovered in the rock shelters also built houses in the open on the ledges and hillsides of the upper Animas district. Had there been suitable alcoves present, other than the North and South Shelters, they might have preferred to live in them. Thus, just as in the Kayenta and other areas, use of rock shelters preceded these open habitations by centuries.[67] If Flora's assessment was correct, as many as sixty houses in the upper Animas served the population there. Talus Village may have been a rarity among open sites in having several units in use simultaneously. The other sites noted by Flora seem to have been single, isolated structures.

If the number and variety of storage cists is indicative, the second wave of colonists was firmly committed to corn agriculture. They were clearly full-fledged Basketmakers. However, even with architecture and this incipient farming, there likely was a fluid seasonal occupation such as would characterize a transitional stage between a hunting-gathering subsistence economy partially buttressed by planting of cultigens (Late Archaic-Early Basketmaker) and full-scale farming (Pueblo). The rich biomass of the environment may have delayed acceptance of the residential "tethering" necessitated by tending gardens. Or the unpredictable climate may have forestalled heavy dependence upon farming. In either case, the individual house units were frequently rebuilt, as though they might have collapsed while standing empty for a time. Moreover, even though some pockets of refuse were nine feet deep, the general volume of cave waste seems small for so prolonged a period of use.

In addition, there is the choice of localities in which to live. These Basketmakers had an obvious preference for ridge crests, upper slopes, and benches, many of which were difficult to reach at elevations of seven thousand to eight thousand feet and were well removed from arable land. This has been confirmed by two professional excavations done after the Carnegie work. One took place on a rock-strewn hillside to the east of the shelters and was carried out by University of Colorado students, who uncovered a house floor and several cists (Ign 12:46).[68] A single habitation with four subfloor cists and heating basin (5LP326) was found by a state highway contract crew on a high bench at more than seventy-seven hundred feet elevation near Tamarron in the north end of the Animas Valley.[69] Flora's photographs and scanty notes on local explorations, and Forest Service reconnaissance of the Falls Creek Archaeological Area show a similar settlement pattern. In no instance was there appreciable aggregation into clusters of domiciles or evidence of any particular permanency, even though there was repeated usage of the same locations.

The shelters may have been built at high elevations to escape the chill of the valleys, as Morris and Burgh suggest, or they might have been used only in winter, when neither foraging nor farming were practical. They might have been places where special activities, such as the making of stone or bone tools or the weaving of baskets and textiles, were conducted.[70] Realistically, at least eight months out of twelve were not productive for the Basketmaker II people in terms of harvesting plant foods. The number of storage chambers at some sites may indicate the amount of food necessary to get the hunkered-down people through very long, frigid winters and chilly springs. Successful planting of new crops could not take place until after the last frost, which often came in late May or early June. Many foodstuffs other than corn or squash likely were stashed in these containers. From the considerable number of basin metates and one-hand manos recovered, one can infer that wild foods in some quantity continued to be processed with these traditional gatherer implements.

One interpretation of the settlement pattern is that either autonomous family units or small lineage groupings lived together during plant-dormant seasons in the upper Animas localities least subject to harsh weather extremes. When the snows melted and temperatures rose, all able-bodied members of the group worked lower garden plots, where it was anticipated that subsurface moisture, summer rains, or stream overflows would hasten germination and promote plant growth. These activities would have come too early in the season to have interfered with foraging. Subsequently, the old, sickly, or very young may have been left behind in temporary adjacent field houses, of which currently observed lithic scatters in the Falls Creek Archaeological Area might be remnants, to monitor fields, pull unwanted weeds, and keep rodents and deer from eating green sprouts.

Prior to harvest, the more vigorous then may have undertaken a prolonged hunting and collecting round in lower elevations to replenish depleted stocks of plants and seeds. After corn harvest, the collectors may have moved to higher ground to reap pinyon nuts and juniper berries. This interpretation sees the early Durango Basketmakers as advantageously utilizing several microenvironments to maintain a balance between semisedentism and permanent settlement based on agricultural considerations. The social structures that permitted this harmonious dual-economy system have yet to be researched.

Most of the material culture presented in the Morris and Burgh report pertained to the second occupation—general Basketmaker II in the authors' scheme. Some researchers would now identify that period as Late Basketmaker II, but of a type sufficiently distinctive from classic Western Basketmaker II to imply a different derivation.[71] The question remains as to whether a migration from the south initiated this particular cultural expression, as Morris suggested.[72] Such things as basketry and sandal construction, some of the lithic technology and composite range of large and small points, and elements of the rock art are more closely associated with Archaic peoples of the Uncompahgre Complex, who, in turn, had some relevance to the Gypsum Cave Archaic.[73] Perhaps by the third century before Christ, corn agriculture also came from the north (Uncompahgre) or west (Gypsum Cave). Or it could be that a common Archaic base was widely shared across the northeastern Southwest. Minor variations would have evolved as peoples adapted to differing environmental conditions. This theory would support Matson's proposed in situ early developments at Durango, wherein local indigenous tribes adopted ideas introduced from elsewhere as the need suited them.[74]

Human remains from the burial crevice, rock shelters, and Talus Village excavations were all regarded as of the same cultural group and hence were examined as a single entity.[75] The burial crevice bodies and the six skeletons found in the lower-level extramural cists might have been those of some of the first residents. But if there were physical differences between the earlier and later representatives, they were not significant enough to be recognized. For now, scholars must assume one population coming to the upper Animas at two extended intervals.

However, there may prove to be a biological distinction between the Western Basketmaker II and the Durango variants, as Morris was convinced. Turner notes important dentition differences.[76] In the future, recent DNA studies showing distinguishing characteristics between the Fremont and the Western Basketmakers may also reveal a genetic relationship between Fremont and Durango Basketmakers.[77] The study of Fremont human remains from eastern Utah done in the 1950s by Erik Reed notes, "These specimens appear to compare favorably well with early Basketmaker crania . . . from Earl Morris's cave work near Durango, Colorado, although living several centuries later."[78] A migration into the upper Animas from the northwest bringing in not only a different genetic pool but possibly linguistic variations and cultural adjuncts warrants further consideration.

Neighbors of the Falls Creek
Ancients

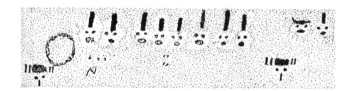

In the 1950s, large-scale private and public development that threatened the pristine landscape of the Colorado Plateau and the traces of early human activity it contained initiated a rush to the outlands in what came to be called salvage archaeology. Shovels and compasses in hand, researchers were determined to uncover the artifacts and data before the bulldozers and backhoes devoured them forever. One of these digs was the first to demonstrate that the Basketmaker II of the upper Animas district did not constitute an isolated enclave on the northeastern frontier of the prehistoric Pueblo world.

The impetus for this project was an underground transmission line planned by the El Paso Natural Gas Company that would cut across Arizona from northern New Mexico to the Colorado River, slicing through 451 miles of the vulnerable underbelly of the Anasazi heartlands. Jesse Nusbaum, Flora's nemesis, sprang into action.

As consulting archaeologist for the Department of the Interior, it was Nusbaum's job to enforce the 1906 Antiquities Act. He notified the El Paso Natural Gas Company that work across federal lands would not be permitted without proper clearance. Further, he strongly hinted that it would be in the company's best interests to support archaeological investigation along the pipeline right-of-way. Desiring either to protect altruistically the antiquities disturbed by its trenches or to reap the benefits of a public relations bonanza, the company generously funded archaeological fieldwork and reporting. Its massive undertaking set a precedent among would-be developers.

In the course of leveling land for a gas-line field station at Ignacio, Colorado, on the Pine River (Los Pinos) thirty miles southeast of the upper Animas district, heavy machinery exposed a possible archaeological site (LA2605). A team of Museum of New Mexico scientists under contract to the El Paso Natural Gas Company was called to examine the locale.[79] What the men found were some twenty scattered use-hardened circular earth floors slightly below the surface of a mesa crest. There were no hearths, post holes, or other features on these floors. Random chunks of burned clay daub that the diggers presumed to have been part of aboveground wall construction sprinkled the floors and surrounding terrain. Some pieces still held the impressions of the wood they encased. Twenty-five oval or bell-shaped cists were set down into an underlying gravel stratum. Most had been fire hardened to discourage rodent intrusion and to make the cists somewhat moisture-proof. Four contained human burials. The small collection of artifacts lacked pottery but did include basin and trough metates, one- and two-hand manos, olivella shell beads, and a notched deer scapula that the scientists inexplicably called a grass saw.

The site report does not indicate that floors overlapped, the result of remodeling. Therefore, without tree-ring dates, readers might assume long simultaneous use of all structures. The only nagging drawbacks to this scenario were the absence of a trash midden and the paucity of objects recovered. Of course, shallowness of the overburden unquestionably allowed rotting of perishables, and it would be no surprise if the construction work had scraped away exterior refuse. Another interpretation may be that on this bluff above the Pine River, there was a small sequential occupation rather than a large concurrent one. In either case, the time period involved was brief.

At the time the 1953 Ignacio job was finished, the excavators probably had no inkling of how completely their findings jibed with those made by the Carnegie crews a decade and a half earlier. With the publication the following year of the Morris and Burgh report, they knew that on the Pine River they had the second known complex of Eastern Basketmaker II houses, the first on relatively flat terrain. Their findings negatively answered Morris's question as to whether those Basketmaker II people living away from the mountain slopes dug pithouses rather than erecting surface dwellings. Examination of the skeletal material showed the Ignacio villagers to be physically similar to their fellow Basketmakers at Falls Creek and thus not unlike some Fremont folks in eastern Utah.

Site LA2605 was not an isolated Basketmaker II hamlet. Pipeline archaeologists excavated two others, one near Ignacio and the other on the Florida Mesa northwest toward Durango. They failed to file reports, rendering their efforts as useless scientifically as those of the local pothunters. Professional and nonprofessional excavators alike continued to savage an irreplaceable legacy.

Six years later, in 1959, archaeologists again met up with the Basketmaker II on the Pine River. Once more, work was initiated because of a large-scale engineering project: construction of a dam on the San Juan River that would create the Navajo Reservoir. Those waters were expected to back up into many upriver tributaries, the Pine River included. Again, it was the scientific staff of the Museum of New Mexico that undertook the then legally required archaeological preliminaries.

The broken terrain of canyons and stony bluffs that would be forever changed by the Navajo Reservoir project was approximately a thousand feet lower in elevation than the upper Animas and bordered on the dry high desert of the eastern San Juan Basin. A typical plant community of juniper, pinyon, and sage grew above broad terraces along entrenched watercourses. Although the region lacked some of the natural riches of the perennially green foothills to the north, it was warmer, with longer growing seasons, making it more suitable for both dry and floodwater farming. Centuries ago, some of the early peoples increasingly charmed by storage cists full of shelled corn moved in.

Surveyors canvassing the Navajo Reservoir district learned that the lower Pine Valley just north of its junction with the San Juan Valley had been a locus for these Basketmaker II groups. On their survey sheets, they noted twenty-four settlements and chose five to study in detail.[80] The total population of the Basketmaker II period on the lower Pine River probably never exceeded a few hundred individuals. Unlike their contemporaries on the upper Animas River, they seemed to be banding together into hamlets. It is not certain, however, that all structures in any one grouping were in use at the same time.

The material culture of what Vivian terms the Los Pinos variant of Basketmaker II was not much different from that of the Basketmaker II of the upper Animas.[81] As did their northern neighbors, the Pine River Basketmaker II erected circular ground-level houses having plastered clay floors, walls of horizontal timbers sandwiched in thick layers of mud, probable cribbed roofs that occasionally had to be bolstered by vertical post braces, and many interior and exterior subterranean storage pits of basin, straight-sided, or undercut profiles. Some cists were enlarged with surface domes created by encircling ropes of clay that for posterity retained the indelible fingerprints of their makers. This clay was strengthened by inclusions of leaves, grass, and corn tassels. Rather like modern Midwestern silos, there were small basal holes in some cist domes, permitting removal of the contents without opening the upper lids.

Several significant architectural differences between the Pine River shelters and those unearthed by Morris and Burgh on the upper Animas were due either to localisms or to improvements on a basic format over time. Some Pine River shelters were surrounded by cobblestone paving, the reason unknown. The cobbles may have been an intentionally installed hard walking surface, or they may be the remains of collapsed outer walls. Regardless, this exterior stone embellishment was more long-lasting than the houses themselves. Nor was it unique to the lower Pine; Flora partially cleared a similar feature in Falls Creek Flats in what was later regarded as a Basketmaker III structure.[82]

Other Pine River habitations had two adjoining rooms arranged in a figure-eight scheme. The excavators thought that the smaller of the two served as an antechamber through which the larger living room was accessed, a plan reminiscent of twentieth-century mud-rooms. This design also anticipated a ventilation system that would be essential to living quarters sunk ever deeper into the ground.

A provocative aspect of the architectural changes apparent in these Pine River hamlets as opposed to those of the upper Animas district was an occasional larger unit that sometimes featured artificially reddened plastered walls. Frank Eddy, who directed their excavation, felt that in them was the germ of a special sanctuary that over the ensuing centuries became central to ancient Pueblo social and religious life.[83] Other scientists are skeptical of this view.

Portable items recovered in the Pine River Basketmaker II sites were primarily familiar chipped and ground stone objects. The researchers took the relative scarcity of projectile points and bone tools to be a sign of decreased emphasis on hunting and increased focus on agriculture.[84] Impressions of basketry, cordage, and textiles remained on adobe chinking hardened when the houses burned. Because this society utilized all its resources to their maximum potential, the Pine River Basketmakers recycled fragments of these materials as tempering in construction mortar. Analyses of latex molds made from these impressions indicated that the basketry technique that Morris regarded as unique at the Falls Creek rock shelters was not practiced at the Pine River villages.

As if to defy archaeological pigeonholing, some Basketmaker II on the lower Pine River did use pottery. It was a crudely fashioned type now called Sambrito Brown. Whether it was acquired by trade with Mogollon potters to the south or made by local novices has yet to be studied. Its use reflects a more sedentary lifestyle than perhaps prevailed among their northern neighbors.

Whole corn did not survive in the Pine River Basketmaker II deposits, but the imprints of its cobs decorated numerous hardened mud clods. Builders poked stripped cobs into interstices of wattle-and-daub walls, then fixed them in place with mud. The cobs readily burned when structures caught fire, but their everlasting imprints show that in some cases planting of fields preceded planting of houses.

Cists created primarily to store corn were, on three occasions, used secondarily to store the dead. Bodies were tightly flexed to fit space available. One person was accompanied into the hereafter by a sacrificed dog. Less fortunate than his master, the dog's body was cut in half to fit the enclosure.

No tree-ring dates were read from wood samples collected from the Pine River sites. Some of the first applications of solid-carbon dating techniques yielded dates from A.D. 105 to A.D. 310, with a margin of error of 90 to 150 years.[85] Although some of these first radiocarbon calculations have been proven erroneous, Pine River Basketmaker II obviously overlapped Animas Valley Late Basketmaker II. Although the Pine River Basketmaker II may not have evolved into an identifiable entity quite as early, they now generally are lumped with their Animas colleagues into a distinct Eastern Basketmaker II grouping. Following the Navajo Reservoir excavations, a parallel eastern Late Archaic-Basketmaker II variant, En Medio, was noted to the southeast in New Mexico.[86]

Several decades passed before other comparable Eastern Basketmaker II remains were identified north of the San Juan River by contract archaeologists, modern heirs of the earlier salvage archaeologists. These contract archaeologists conducted surveys in the Ridges Basin and Bodo Canyon areas south of Durango.[87] Twenty years earlier they had been preceded by Flora, who dug in several sites but never reported the results (Figs. 2.1a-2.1c). Although surface indications were faint, the more recent surveyors thought seven sites might indicate Eastern Basketmaker II presence (see Map 3.1, page 166). Most of this evidence was habitational.

That former human presence was noted at all in this broad sweep of grassy empty land is a testimony to the diligence and sharp eyes of the field crews. Once they had learned to recognize the elusive clues, which they listed as a few flakes of worked stone, some popcorn-size chunks of burned adobe that had held pole or log walls together, and small fire-reddened igneous rocks once used in radiant heat cooking, they increased to twenty the number of possible Basketmaker II sites in their Ridges Basin–Bodo Canyon study area.[88] They considered fourteen of them to be habitations, three of which

Figs. 2.1a-c. Site Ign 12:79, believed to be in Ridges Basin, was partially excavated by Flora in 1966 to demonstrate the widespread distribution of Basketmaker II sites in the Durango area. Fig. 2.1a shows an extensive floor estimated to be approximately forty-five feet in diameter. *Lister Collection.*

they cleared. The crews were aided by magnetometer surveys indicating anomalies that might have been subsurface structures. Pioneers in the discipline of Southwestern archaeology would have been stunned by such futuristic means to read the past.

What the diggers found were a few patches of well-trodden earth scarcely beneath the present ground surface. Typically, the floors of what had been roundish single-unit houses were on inclines or ridge crests around the basin edges that enjoyed southerly exposures. Evidence of terracing secured by rock revetments was lacking because slopes were not steep enough to require them. The shallow floors sloped up at their outer edges. Although no footing logs or wall residues were unearthed, the crews assumed construction was similar to that at the Falls Creek rock shelters and Talus Village. They estimated that units ranged from eighteen to twenty-four feet in diameter. All had burned. Interior features were minimal. Charcoal flecks

Fig. 2.1b shows the channel left by a burned footing log, with the butt of an upright juniper post at one end. *Lister Collection.*

in the fill of circular floor hearths suggested fire beds rather than heating pits. Some bell-shaped or round cists were dug into floors.

Excavators working the Ridges Basin–Bodo Canyon sites recovered a few ground and flaked stone implements typical of Basketmaker II assemblages. Pottery was absent, as were human remains. Some corn specimens confirmed horticulture, but its importance in this society remains unknown. Radiocarbon dates primarily in the fourth century A.D. fixed occupation in Ridges Basin–Bodo Canyon as roughly contemporary with that of the last Basketmaker II peoples in the upper Animas.

Aside from substantiating Basketmaker II use of Ridges Basin and Bodo Canyon, the excavations yielded little new information about the people themselves. Their general living pattern and everyday goods fit well with the far richer upper Animas records and doubtless were part of the same cultural expression. Because their environment was not as tightly enclosed in a mountain setting, vegetation was lower and sparser, there were more hours of winter sun,

Fig. 2.1c shows the mouth of a subfloor, jug-shaped cist. *Lister Collection.*

and their dwellings were near arable lands, groups in the southerly Durango environs may have been more inclined to linger year-round. Still, pollen analyses reveal that native plants were utilized, indicating a possible continued reliance on foraging.

More recently, additional contract archaeological work has been conducted southeast of the Animas River toward the lower Pine River area in connection with explorations for methane gas. Scientists have encountered the same general scattered distribution of Late Archaic and early Basketmaker sites as exist west of the Animas, confirming what was probably an early utilization of this San Juan upslope area by a small population over a considerable span of time.[89] Eddy originally suspected this distribution during work in the Navajo Reservoir area. The upper Animas district people known to Morris and Burgh obviously did not live in the isolation once believed.

The Archaic remains identified through surveys of this region east of the Animas are primarily scatters of lithic flakes and tools and burned campfire rocks. No further details presently are available.

The Basketmaker II habitations in the same area east of the Animas River are shallow, oval, earthen floors on open, relatively flat land. No wall stubs remain, but excavators assume a horizontal log construction such as that defined by Morris and Burgh. The presence of trough metates and two-hand manos suggest corn agriculture was practiced. The more southerly of these eastern Animas sites produced small amounts of the same crude brown pottery as that found during the early 1960s in the Navajo Reservoir project. It now appears likely that these relatively sedentary people, stimulated by Mogollon artisans just to their south, were among the first Basketmakers to attempt the new craft. Because results are highly variable, radiocarbon dates for the eastern Animas Basketmaker II sites are not considered very reliable, but they seem to fall within the fourth or fifth centuries A.D. If this is correct, the occupation of the upper Animas district preceded it by a number of generations.

Exodus

Whether of the classic or variant type, the Basketmaker II people took fundamental steps that would define their futures. Because no lone individual or single-family group could survive for long in the wilderness, the Basketmakers responded to their challenging environment by developing a society based on shared natural resources, cooperative labors, and communal living. From whatever was at hand, they provided themselves with food, shelter, and clothing. And, in time, they saw their destiny shaped to a large extent by working the soil.

In the late fourth century A.D., this commitment to agriculture precipitated a crisis among the Basketmakers of the upper Animas. As paleoclimatic studies indicate, farming, difficult at the best of times in this inhospitable region became impossible as a prolonged period of unfavorable weather conditions engulfed much of the northern Southwest.[90] With above average precipitation and numbing cold, devastation of gardens ensued.[91] Lacking substantial reserves to tide them over for more than several seasons, these Basketmakers had few options; once the seed corn and squash went into the parching trays, the spring was barren, and it was time to move on. In an environment typified by erratic climate and the ensuing abrupt changes in biotic resources, it was a pattern repeated many times. As far as is presently known, no Basketmaker II habitations were erected in the upper Animas district after A.D. 372.[92] The ridge tops were emptied and became silent. Farther south along the lower Animas uplands, conditions allowed Basketmaker habitation to linger into the next century.

One explanation for the lack of Basketmaker II building on the upper Animas after the late fourth century may be that in the face of sustained crop failures, the people reverted more wholeheartedly to their traditional hunting and collecting economy.[93] This scenario assumes that the native plants and the animals who fed upon them did not similarly suffer because of inclement weather. The hunting-gathering mode may have been only a short-term solution, for it is unlikely that those accustomed to the security that agriculture could provide would cease to farm entirely.

Migration to a more hospitable location is more plausible. Those Basketmakers in the upper Animas Valley having strong ties to the northwest may have drifted back to these old roots, ultimately to metamorphose into what archaeologists now call the San Rafael Fremont. Those along the southern boundaries, already using pottery and presumably in contact with Mogollon settlements, likely shifted southward into the San Juan Basin. Others may have moved farther up the San Juan drainage toward the Piedra River Valley.

When the dislocated parties departed, did they perhaps turn back to see a gray cloud of smoke hanging heavily over the Animas Valley from the homes they had sacrificed to Mother Earth? Perhaps the smoke trailing softly upward from the burning houses carried a sacred prayer for better days ahead.

A punctuated stay in the northlands by early peoples is not an interpretation shared by the first scholars of regional prehistory. Earl Morris and Roy Carlson, author of a 1963 report on the 1939 Falls Creek Flats excavations, believed that the local Basketmaker II slowly evolved into the local Basketmaker III with the acquisition of new material culture.[94] This viewpoint, now termed gradualism, was a tenet of the phased Pecos Classification whereby native peoples progressed in orderly fashion from one evolutionary stage to the next. Flora thought the two groups lived side by side.[95]

Neither situation seems to have been the case. Later work has not revealed any transitional sites in the upper Animas district linking Basketmaker II to Basketmaker III. The original tree-ring dates suggesting contemporaneity were erroneous. Therefore, it now appears that there was a decisive break between the two developmental phases, a break triggered by a severe wet/cold cycle that forced a wholesale movement away from the Durango highlands. The upper Animas district may have remained uninhabited for as much as three hundred to four hundred years.

Surely an atmosphere of eeriness settled down over the abandoned places. The hum of perhaps a thousand years of activity was stilled, and what Morris once referred to as "the effacing hand of time" soon obscured physical evidence.[96] To some of the more sensitive modern observers, an aura of otherworldliness lingered. To all, the transitory nature of earthly existence was reaffirmed.

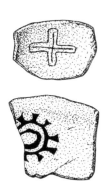

Notes

1. Morris letter to A. V. Kidder, November 4, 1937, Archives, University of Colorado Museum.
2. Seltzer, 1944, 1–33, 37.
3. Seltzer, 1944, 26.
4. Snow and Sanders, 1954, 89.
5. Christy Turner, pers. comm., October 25, 1994.
6. For comparison, Basketmaker skulls generally are described as long and narrow, of medium height, and with faces of medium length. Cranial index, skull breadth, and nasal breadth measurements of the upper Animas district Basketmaker II specimens were greater than those of a comparative sample of other Basketmakers. Snow and Sanders, 1954, 91.
7. For this and all other artifacts from the Falls Creek rock shelters and Talus Village, consult Morris and Burgh, 1954.
8. Jones and Fonner, 1954, 106–115.
9. Adams, K. R., 1994, 273–302, and pers. comm., January 11, 1994.
10. Morris letter to A. V. Kidder, November 4, 1937, Archives, University of Colorado Museum.
11. Morris and Burgh, 1954, 67, Fig. 42 (unnumbered page); see also Madsen, 1989, 9 (Fig. 10).
12. Berry, 1980, 100.
13. Flora letter to Barry Fell, June 15–October 16, 1977, Archives, Center of Southwest Studies, Fort Lewis College.
14. Morris, 1949, 33–34.
15. Flora letter to A. E. Douglass, June 4, 1941, and Flora letter to Edmund Schulman, April 7, 1953, Archives, Laboratory of Tree–Ring Research, University of Arizona.
16. Matson, 1991, 41.
17. Morris letter to Edmund Schulman, February 18, 1952, Archives, University of Colorado Museum.
18. Daniels, 1976, 21.
19. Morris and Burgh, 1954, 41.
20. Morris and Burgh, 1954, 71.
21. Fenenga and Wendorf, 1956, 207–214.
22. Morris and Burgh, 1954, 63.

23. Tessie Naranjo, Santa Clara Pueblo, pers. comm.

24. Schaafsma, 1980, 128–129.

25. Wormington and Lister, 1956, 76–77 (Figs. 56–57).

26. Cole, 1990, 118 (Fig. 43), 128; and 1993, 198 (Fig. 9.3), 201.

27. Schaafsma and Young, 1983, 13.

28. Douglass, 1943, 18–24.

29. Morris letters to A. E. Douglass, July 17, 1939; August 10, 1940; December 17, 1942; and January 28, 1943, Archives, University of Colorado Museum.

30. Morris and Burgh, 1954, 85.

31. Kearns, 1992, 18; Ware, 1986A, 98; York, 1991, 5–22.

32. W. James Judge, pers. comm.; Krieger, 1964, 61.

33. York, 1991, 5–22.

34. Minnis, 1985, 312.

35. Morris and Burgh, 1954, 80.

36. Cassells, 1983, 230.

37. Wormington and Lister, 1956.

38. Jennings, 1964, 149–174.

39. Fuller et al., 1988; Kearns, 1992, 20, 25; Nickens, 1981; Powell, 1992; Ware, 1986B, 147–194.

40. Fuller et al., 1988; Irwin–Williams, 1973, 4–5; Kearns, 1992, 20–22; Nickens, 1981; Ware, 1986C, 226.

41. Sharon Hatch, pers. comm.

42. Fuller et al., 1988, 393.

43. Dean, 1975, 30.

44. Dean, 1975, 30.

45. Beta Analytic, Inc., samples 75863–75865. Calendar year calibrations were calculated by Francis E. Smiley following a 1993 article by Minze Stuiver and Gordon W. Pearson entitled High Precision Calibration of the Radiocarbon Time Scale, A.D. 1950–500 B.C., found in *Radiocarbon,* vol. 28, no. 28, 805–838.

46. Karen Adams, pers. comm., January 11, 1994; Jones and Fonner, 1954, 111.

47. Matson and Chisholm, 1991, 444–459.

48. Wills, 1988, 65–69.

49. Matson, 1991; Minnis, 1985, 338; Simmons, 1986, 73–88; Smiley, 1993, 251–252, and 1994, 165–189.

50. Stiger and Larson, 1992, 26–36.

51. Janetski, 1993, 236, 238; Mark Stiger, pers. comm., January 26, 1995.

52. Berry, 1985, 306; Matson, 1991, 45–46.

53. Morris and Burgh, 1954, 48.

54. Morris letter to Edmund Schulman, February 18, 1952, Archives, University of Colorado Museum.

55. Vivian, 1990, 92 (Fig. 4.5).

56. Buckles, 1971, vol. 3, 1312–1320.

57. Mark Stiger, pers. comm., January 26, 1995.

58. Berry, 1980, 189–192; Lipe, 1993, 1–12.

59. William Lipe, pers. comm., March, 1995.

60. Flora letter to Edmund Schulman, April 7, 1953, Archives, Center of Southwest Studies, Fort Lewis College.

61. Dean, 1975, 29–30.

62. Berry, 1980, 189–192, 194 (Fig. 11).

63. Morris and Burgh, 1954, 75–78.

64. Dean, 1975, 29–31.

65. Vivian, 1990, 450.

66. Dean, 1975, 30.

67. Lipe, 1994, 338; Smiley, 1993, 253, and 1994, 182.

68. Biggs, 1966.

69. Reed and Kainer, 1978, 1–47.

70. See Gilman, 1987, 534–564, for discussion of cold-weather sedentism.

71. Vivian, 1990, 123–124.

72. Morris and Burgh, 1954, 80.

73. Buckles, 1971; Matson, 1991, 311; Mark Stiger, pers. comm., January 26, 1995.

74. Matson, 1991, 311–315; Vivian, 1990, 124.

75. Snow and Sanders, 1954, 89.

76. Christy Turner, pers. comm., October 25, 1994.

77. Dennis O'Rourke, pers. comm., October 25, 1994.

78. Reed, 1955, 43.

79. Fenenga and Wendorf, 1956, 207–214.

80. Eddy, 1961; Vivian, 1990.

81. Eddy, 1961; Vivian, 1990.

82. Carlson, 1963, 4 (Fig. 2), 17 (Fig. 6).

83. Eddy, 1966, vol. 2, 478.

84. Eddy, 1966, vol. 2, 477.

85. Berry, 1980, 183; Kearns, 1992, 23.

86. Matson, 1991, 315; Vivian, 1990, 123, 450–454.

87. Fuller et al., 1988; Kearns, 1992, 22, 27, 29; Ware, 1986A, 97.

88. Fuller et al., 1988, 353–354; Ware, 1986A, 100.

89. Stephen Fuller, pers. comm., August 1994.

90. Berry, 1980, 229, 255.

91. Ware, 1986C, 229.

92. Dean, 1975, 60–61.

93. Ware, 1986C, 227.

94. Carlson, 1963, 51; Morris, 1952, 36.

95. Morris letter to I. F. Flora, August 2, 1937, Archives, University of Colorado Museum; Flora letter to A. E. Douglass, June 4, 1941, Archives, Center of Southwest Studies, Fort Lewis College.

96. Morris, 1928, 420.

PART III
Pueblos Aborning

Pueblos Aborning

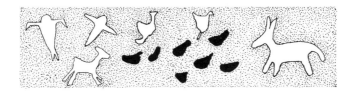

The trickle of people returning to the high country around Durango in the mid A.D. 600s became a veritable storm a century later. Settlers thickly crowded the first and second terraces along the Animas River and pushed on to mesa tops and basin slopes. This was a remarkable diaspora stimulated by undetermined disturbances in the prehistoric world. Perhaps these people were fleeing the pressures of overpopulation or the ravages of a natural catastrophe. Whatever the catalyst was, it must have been widespread to uproot so many and disperse them to the higher elevations, vacant for some three hundred to four hundred years. Scientists suspect the onslaught of another warm/dry cycle in the lowlands that made the moister highlands attractive once again.[1]

Even more extraordinary than this apparently sudden immigration was the fact that the refugees, if that is what they were, arrived with cultural orientation and outfittings that have prompted some students to regard them as the first true ancestral Pueblos in the district. Whereas their Basketmaker II predecessors were more closely tied to the Archaic past, these Basketmaker III looked to the Pueblo future. There is a fair chance they were biologically and linguistically distinct from the Basketmaker II in the same area.

The new social attitudes and material possessions the newcomers brought with them had been acquired after a previous displacement a few centuries earlier brought different groups together in favorable microenvironments where cultural traditions could blend.[2]

According to Michael Berry, transfer of ideals and ideas was inherent in this kind of yeasty contact. The Basketmaker III culture in this part of the Colorado Plateau may have resulted from interaction between Western and Eastern Basketmaker II or between Eastern Basketmaker II and Mogollon. Regardless, elements from these various spheres were assimilated over a large swath of the Colorado Plateau, then dispersed to outlying districts in the wake of expansion.

One locality the incoming settlers favored was the north end of Falls Creek Valley. There, where the valley narrows to half a mile in width, they created a tight neighborhood of at least twenty households.[3] Instead of selecting ledges or steep hillsides as building spots as had their Basketmaker II precursors, these folks preferred low knolls just above the valley bottom. At least in this area, they did not build over the vestiges of earlier habitations. These knolls afforded drainage—critical for subterranean construction—and did not encroach upon land that could be converted into garden plots.

As to the dwellings themselves, they were true pithouses, generally roughly circular with a narrow lateral extension, sunk five or six feet below ground level. Their framework is thought to have been a series of close-set vertical poles that sometimes were placed on a three-foot-high encircling bench cut above the pit base and sometimes sat directly on the floor. The poles were felled with the aid of ground stone axes that were hafted onto wooden handles, one of the advances in toolmaking over the Basketmaker II. These posts were covered on the exterior with horizontal bundles of tules gathered along the stream that cut through the valley. The tules were plastered into place with mud.

In instances where four vertical logs supported a flat roof, excavators assume that cross-beams were laid over a square frame connecting the posts, leaving a smoke hole at the center. A six-post support system probably required a domed roof of cribbed logs in order to close the space.[4] The units were completely smothered with earth to make them look like low, brown humps. Lower interior pit walls and floors were plastered with liquid mud that hardened into a smooth surface. A central hearth provided heat. The side extension, oriented to the east or southeast and dug at a slightly higher level, was connected to the living area by a narrow crawl hole and to the exterior by a vertical shaft into which a ladder was placed.

With a fire glowing in the hearth, the insulation tendered by the earth, and the combined body heat of the residents, these pithouses must have been snug retreats, even when snow was banked many feet high outside. They appear to have been permanent shelters and probably could have been used for ten or fifteen years before a major refurbishing was required.

The storage cists typical of Animas district Basketmaker II habitations were replaced by groups of up to eight contiguous small rooms arranged in an arc on the ground, generally a few feet northwest of the pit structures. A crude foundation of cobbles and vertical stone slabs probably was topped by a construction of poles and mud that is known in the Southwest by the Spanish term jacal. The rooms served as pantries and toolsheds.

Partially outlining some of the dwelling areas was a ring of cobbles gathered from the glacial moraines in the valley. The stones may have been property boundaries, or they simply may have been thrown aside in clearing the building spot. Although these rings are sometimes called stockades, the piled cobbles would not have been high enough for defensive purposes.

Each household had its own midden to one side of the yard. It was a convenient place to deposit the bodies of departed family members and therefore symbolized a connection between the worlds of the living and the dead. One excavated midden produced seventeen burials overlooked by Flora in his previous probings.[5]

The first excavations into the drift of fill in front of the Falls Creek South Shelter hit what was later identified as a Basketmaker III pithouse. Other than a few recovered artifacts, including a wood sample dated to A.D. 650, no other details about it are known. Several fragments of Basketmaker III pottery were picked up from the surface of the North Shelter.[6]

Another locality attracting many eighth-century ancestral Pueblos lay at the southern outskirts of Durango in the heights west of the Animas River. Recent archaeological investigations in the Bodo Canyon and Ridges Basin regions have covered a large area in efforts to provide a more comprehensive view of Basketmaker III and early Pueblo I settlement patterns.[7]

The settlers chose house sites primarily along the north slopes of the basin or on an alluvial fan that descended from the southwestern edge of Carbon Mountain and closed off the basin's east end (Map 3.1). Site selection clearly took into account nocturnal flow of cold air, southern exposure not blocked by terrain, and soil fertility. Each of these factors forestalled appreciable use of the bottomlands or the southern basin. There was some reuse of places chosen by earlier peoples who faced the same considerations (compare Map 3.1 with Map 3.2).

The basic household unit in Ridges Basin and Bodo Canyon at this period was comparable to that of Falls Creek Flats. A pithouse was backed by a crescentic row of jacal-surfaced rooms with a refuse deposit to one side. However, there were significant differences in details.

Pithouses were dug in rough rectangular configurations with narrow lateral antechambers. Some internal work areas were defined by low walls projecting from the side of the pit. Vertical ventilator shafts in side walls afforded air-conditioning. Wall cists were used for storing small objects. Benches cut into the surrounding ground only partially encircled the living floor. *Sipapus,* floor holes symbolizing the point where humans emerged from the lower spirit world, were present. This feature, associated with ritual, shows that the pithouse had gained an importance beyond providing eating, working, and sleeping quarters and, according to some scientists, was being converted into a specialized ceremonial chamber deep in the womb of Mother Earth. It would be a long time, however, before this structure would cease to have domestic functions.

Surface rooms likewise had new characteristics. There were many more of them than in the Falls Creek Flats hamlets and they were built in adjoining units of double, or even triple, rows. Common walls conserved both resources and construction energy but at the same time were indicative of the communal thinking that was to characterize Pueblo culture. The back row of rooms was of substantial construction. These spaces were meant primarily for storing

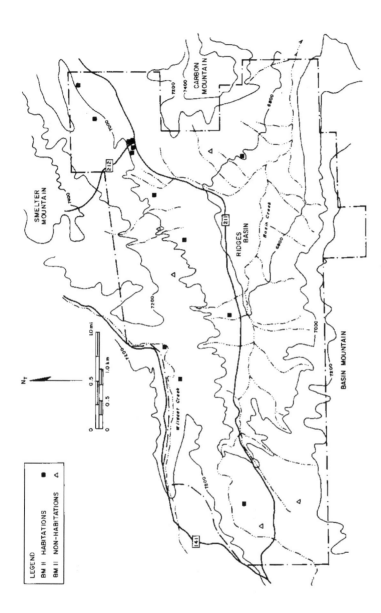

Map 3.1. Distribution of possible Basketmaker II habitation and nonhabitation sites in Ridges Basin and Bodo Canyon. *Redrawn with permission of Complete Archaeological Service Associates (CASA) from Fuller et al., 1988, Fig. 183.*

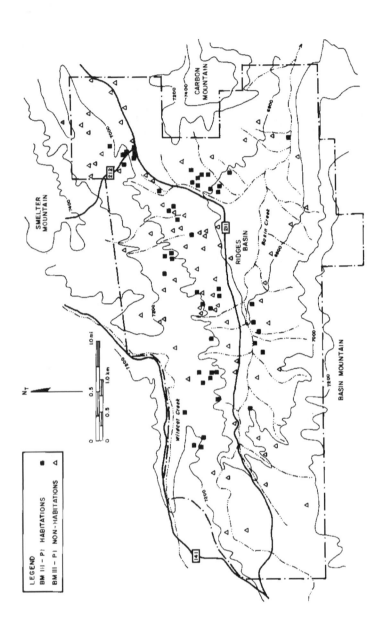

Map 3.2. Distribution of Basketmaker III-Pueblo I habitation and nonhabitation sites in Ridges Basin and Bodo Canyon. *Redrawn with permission of Complete Archaeological Service Associates (CASA) from Fuller et al., 1988, Fig. 184.*

stockpiled foodstuffs and crop seeds, without which survival would have been uncertain. The front row facing the pithouse may have resembled a series of arbors, or *ramadas*. These were work rooms or, as the presence of a few hearths would suggest, warm-weather living spaces. A move out of the ground into houseblocks that would typify subsequent Pueblo architecture seems to have been progressing.

The clustering of the pithouse-surface room complexes noted at Falls Creek Flats was even more apparent in Ridges Basin because of a larger occupation. Researchers there defined eight such groupings of up to nine complexes. It is not known that all were occupied at the same time. To some extent, the cluster accretion may have been the result of expanding families or general population growth. Associated with each cluster were from three to twenty-one outlying nonhabitational units thought to have been field camps for agricultural purposes or for collecting and processing resources on a short-term basis. It is possible such arrangements existed in Falls Creek Flats but were unrecognized at the time of excavation.

One of the occupational clusters in Ridges Basin may have served as more than a farming settlement. The soils there must have been relatively unproductive. Surveyors speculated that what appears to be the depression of a larger than usual pithouse might prove to be an early form of ceremonial construction known as a Great Kiva. If so, this cluster may have served as a center for ritual observances for the Ridges Basin Basketmaker III-Pueblo I populace. Only excavation will tell.

No such communal Great Kivas, or for that matter lineage kivas, have been found in the Durango environs. A careless comment by Harold Gladwin published in 1957 about a suspected Great Kiva in these northlands elicited interest but has failed to be substantiated. His remarks were further muddled by his and Flora's confused identification of sites.[8] A supposed Great Kiva on Blue Mesa has not been located and continues to bedevil contemporary researchers.

The practice of grouping individual habitations and sharing work and work spaces maximized exploitation of the environment for the good of all. Although rooted in a hunting-gathering collective subsistence mentality, the processes by which this communal organization elaborated to the extent it apparently did must be sought out elsewhere because evidently they already were fixed in the minds of the Basketmaker III coming into the Durango environs.

The amount of exposed wood in these Basketmaker III-Pueblo I houses, combined with open cooking and heating fires, may have made conflagrations a common fact of life. Not all house fires were deadly, but some were. If a dwelling's single exit were engulfed in flames, people could easily have been trapped, as is demonstrated by the calcined remains of a ten-year-old child found sprawled in a Ridges Basin house. The bones of an adult male were wedged into the dwelling's ventilator shaft when he apparently tried to save the doomed youngster.[9]

That the new arrivals grew corn is evident in a handful of burned kernels recovered from six pithouses in Falls Creek Flats and from soil and pollen samples taken in Ridges Basin. The kernels, although similar in some respects to corn from the rock shelters, were of the Pima-Papago eight-row type.[10] Open-ended trough metates and two-hand manos were used to grind the dried corn into meal. Dental data suggest that corn was consumed but that the diet was generally varied.[11]

The common bean, *Phaseolus vulgaris,* and the tepary bean, *Phaseolus acutifolius,* were added to the stock of domesticated plants. It is no accident that their cultivation coincided with the adoption of pottery. Fresh beans could be eaten raw or lightly simmered, and dry beans could have been ground into a mush. To boil beans at an elevation of seven thousand feet, however, took more prolonged cooking in liquid than was possible in a basket filled with hot rocks.

Given the nearness of the high mountains and their faunal richness, hunting must have supplied at least an occasional taste of meat. Deer, mountain sheep, red fox, marmot, bear, rabbit, prairie dog, and turkey bones have been taken from various trash accumulations. Although most of the pressure-flaked projectile points were small enough to have been attached to reed arrow shafts, others were obviously dart points. These differences in size indicate that at the Falls Creek Flats settlement, the bow and atlatl were both in use.[12]

Recent biological study of sixty-seven burial remains from Ridges Basin Basketmaker III-Pueblo I sites shows that the population enjoyed relatively good health. Undernutrition and infectious diseases were not as pernicious as in some neighboring areas. The children here apparently fared better than some others elsewhere. However, four of the thirteen females examined appear to have been victims of violence, for example, blows to the head with a blunt instrument. Whether these injuries resulted from witchcraft, cannibalism, slavery, warfare, spousal abuse, or some form of institutional or religious behavior cannot now be determined, but it is obvious that life was not totally pacific.[13]

Based on analogy with some modern Southwestern native tribes, ancestral Pueblo women turned to pottery making once their people gave up their wandering ways. Artisans of this culture had been making earthenware several centuries before the second wave of prehistoric peoples flooded the upper Animas district, yet the efforts of these Basketmaker III potters were still primitive. Typical examples are the tiny, misshapen, earthy brown jar forms that were punched out of wads of coarsely prepared clay. Some were unfired. Others were hardened, probably accidentally in the burning of structures. Some may have represented the efforts of young girls learning a necessary craft at their mothers' knees.

Although the dark gray pottery was hard and well fired, it remained rough-surfaced and aesthetically unattractive. Forms were diverse, as though the women were experimenting to see which shapes best served their purposes. Items were small, because neither the greenware production nor the delicate firing process had been mastered. Necked jars meant for use over cook fires or for modest storage of dry items were the most common vessels. Crude as they were, obvious thought had been given to their design. Jar bottoms were rounded so that they could be nestled into coals, with most of the basal surface exposed to the heat. Jar mouths were somewhat narrow to reduce evaporation, while at the same time being wide enough to permit easy removal of the contents. Handles were attached to some.

Small, deep bowls, not used over fire, were the typical serving receptacles. Generally, because they were used at ground level, these bowls were decorated on the inside, the vessels' most visible surface. Clusters of yucca fibers served as the paintbrush. Paint pigment was made from lead ore crushed to a powder and dissolved in an organic substance that helped bind it to the moist clay body. Some mineral pigments fired to a flat black color. In other instances, the lead weakly vitrified to create faint, glossy green-to-black colored glaze lines. The binder appears to have been ineffective in many cases, leaving only shadows of partial decoration. Execution of the small-scale, relatively sparse designs was inept, their layout imprecise. Some elements were borrowed from basketry stitching.[14] A circle frequently painted in the bottom of bowls may have been inspired by the beginning coil of a basket; some Native Americans interpret it as a representation of the sipapu.

Primitive pottery of this sort was not as durable as basketry, but it could be made with greater speed to serve a host of purposes, from keeping foods away from the mice who shared the premises, to braising a rabbit carcass, to saying farewell to a dead relative. The output of pottery by the women of the Durango sector was so great that even Flora's and Root's collecting did not put a dent in the volume of surviving vessels and fragments. The production of pottery had to be an ongoing activity for two reasons. First, it was extremely friable due to low firing temperatures. Second, because it was used at ground level, it was susceptible to being stepped on or knocked over by boisterous children and dogs.

Excavators consider the bulk of the pottery to be of Basketmaker III age. A few gray jars with coils reinforcing the neck, as well as decorated vessels bearing a splotchy white slip over the dark gray body, anticipate early Pueblo I workmanship. The scarcity of trade pottery underscores limited exchange with neighboring groups.

Construction of the Falls Creek Flats pithouse cluster is dated between A.D. 750 and A.D. 765, although outer rings of the wood samples often are missing.[15] Occupation may have continued until the end of the century but probably not much beyond. Elsewhere on the Colorado Plateau, this was the time of Pueblo I, but these Falls Creek settlers, in a refuge removed from mainstream interaction, were not quite as advanced. Dating of the Ridges Basin–Bodo Canyon pithouse sites is less well established because few wood samples suitable for dendrochronological determinations have been encountered. The span of archaeomagnetic and radiocarbon dating is thought to be too great to be absolute. Nonetheless, using cross-dating of ceramics and architecture in general, a block of time from about A.D. 750 to A.D. 830 is reasonably accurate for this horizon.[16] The cultural stage represented is transitional, one foot dragging behind in Basketmaker III, the other confidently striding into Pueblo I. The greater dependence upon cultigens, the aggregation into villages, the use of the sipapu in pit structures, and the coalescing of surface rooms into houseblocks anticipate the Pueblo lifeway.[17]

Early in the ninth century A.D., calamity struck. A combination of environmental negatives, including exhaustion of nutrients in thin soils, possible denudation, and drought, forced another evacuation after a brief but intense fifty- to seventy-five-year effort to master an undependable ecosystem. The pole-and-mud houses were left to drift over, the dry cornstalks to wither in the wind and snag roving tumbleweeds, the bruised land to heal itself once again. For hundreds of years thereafter, these heights welcomed occasional Pueblo and then Ute and Navajo hunting parties. Farmers stayed away until the whites arrived in the late nineteenth century.

Archaeological efforts to recapture the prehistory of the ancestral Pueblos of the upper Animas district have extended over sixty years. In the beginning, that prehistory was endangered because of well-meaning but reckless searchers for old Indian objects. Today, it is imperiled still, not, this time, by pothunters, but by the restrictions imposed upon scientific inquiry by changing social and economic values.

It was the Basketmaker III-Pueblo I remains in the following three locations—two of which are no longer available for in-depth archaeological study—that first opened up the proverbial can of worms. Following the 1939 Morris and Burgh excavations in Falls Creek Flats, which were not published until twenty-four years later, there have been no further professional explorations of eighth-century sites there. The post–World War II northward spread of Durango, with its massing of businesses, condominiums, houses, golf courses, and access roads, has not only put prehistory in jeopardy but surely eliminated most of it. This makes the San Juan–Rio Grande National Forest preserve of the Falls Creek Archaeological Area all the more important as a site for potential explorations.

A second focal point for signs of Basketmaker III-Pueblo I occupation is beneath the town of Durango itself. The Promised Land of Flora and his company of eager trenchers now lies under concrete and lawns, another example of prehistory lost.

The third concentration of Basketmaker III-Pueblo I remains is on the benches above the Animas River south of town. Although most of the larger archaeological zones have been repeatedly gouged for relics, modern developments did not move in that direction until the 1970s. By that time, public interest and legislation against altering federal lands without first exploring their prehistory permitted archaeologists to come to the rescue.

Among a flurry of related endeavors was a site survey by Susan Applegarth and ten Fort Lewis College students of a broad strip of land on the west side of the Animas River destined to become an industrial and business park. A student, Barry Hibbets, dug several structures there. A realignment of the southerly approach to Durango to the Animas west bank involved a team of scientists working for the state highway department. A Fort Lewis College field school group, led by John Ives, cleared two pithouse complexes on Blue Mesa.[18]

In the summer of 1975 Hibbets and two other students conducted a survey on Blue Mesa. They noted the ground so strewn with potsherds and flakes of worked stone that it was difficult to ascertain where one site stopped and another began. During that reconnaissance, the site that so impressed Morris fifty years earlier and later was probed by Gladwin could not be positively identified. It probably was Hibbets's site number fifteen, a large cultural area toward the northeast of the mesa near the cut of an old road. Hibbets described it as having a pithouse depression some thirty-five feet in diameter, with an extensive three-foot-high mound of cobbles and adobe to one side and a trash heap to the other, all of which still bore signs of extensive disturbance. The four rows of double rooms described by Gladwin could not be discerned, perhaps because of rapid erosion.[19]

A copy of a photograph described in *Sherds and Points* as a pit-house east of the Animas a few yards north of the present Red Barn Lumber Company (Ign 12:27) and later identified in a book by Gladwin as "an earth-lodge near Durango" is found in the archives of the Laboratory of Tree-Ring Research, with an attached hand-drawn sketch of sites on Blue Mesa.[20] Some fifty-five numbers dot the crude map, with number eleven at the west end of the second ridge (counted from north to south) circled as if to suggest identification of this ruin. Such confusion of data emphasizes the havoc wrought by the interference of the untrained.

Other than the publication of the excavation of several pithouses that were later demolished by road construction, all the early 1970s work went unreported or was buried in student papers or government documents. It was a disappointing beginning for a new era, because all that was learned was that Basketmaker III-Pueblo I peoples had indeed been in the vicinity in considerable numbers and that they made use of pithouses. An airstrip and houses on Blue Mesa threatened what was left of the ravaged sites there.

Meanwhile, the age of cultural resource management, or CRM, had arrived. A mounting interest in Ridges Basin as the site of a projected reservoir-and-canal system, part of the mammoth Animas-La Plata water diversionary project, stimulated reconnaissance for antiquities and some limited excavation. The Mesa Verde Research Center put a student, L. Kent Leidy, in the field in 1975 to survey the probable pool area of 2,270 acres. Two years later he was followed by another University of Colorado student, Paul Nickens, who did an overview of the cultural resources of a larger project area. The two efforts recorded three dozen Basketmaker III-Pueblo I settlements below the high-water mark, the majority of the larger ones having been previously disturbed.[21]

These two initial surveys were followed in 1980 by a contract between the Bureau of Reclamation and ESCA-Tech, a private firm in Albuquerque. The Office of Contract Archaeology at the University of New Mexico was the project's prime subcontractor. This project marked the first time that modern archaeology, with its advanced technology and interpretive focus, finally examined local prehistory with a critical eye. The contract's terms were to carry out a relevant literature and archival search, to find and plot all possible prehistoric and historic resources in the larger Animas-La Plata project area, to plan a research design, to complete the necessary governmental paperwork, and to prepare a final report. A year later the last three stipulations were dropped, but completion of the first two was a major step forward. One hundred ninety-six sites covering a possible ten thousand years of human presence were noted. In 1986 through another contract between Complete Archaeological Service Associates (CASA) and the University of New Mexico Office of Contract Archaeology, one hundred copies of the 530-page report by fourteen collaborators finally was published.[22] Representing the first important all-encompassing research tool on the area, this report looked not just at one site or one phase of development, but at a broad sweep of humankind's presence in this particular place.

The early 1980s also saw a revival of the Ridges Basin Fort Lewis College field school under P. G. Duke. During the field seasons of 1981 and 1982, five sites that suggested both habitational and nonhabitational functions were excavated. In his subsequent report, Duke incorporated the Root and Ives data that could be salvaged and presented his ideas of the subsistence and settlement patterns of the Basketmaker III-Pueblo I Ridges Basin occupations.[23]

At the same time these Ridges Basin studies were being done, the Department of Energy, in compliance with the Uranium Mill Tailings Remedial Action legislation, selected a disposal site in Bodo Canyon for the hazardous waste from Durango's former smelter. CASA was given a contract to excavate the eleven sites there destined to be impacted. They represented a cross section of aboriginal life from the Late Archaic through the Basketmaker III-Pueblo I periods, covering an estimated thirteen hundred years. Fieldwork and multidisciplinary laboratory analyses, which incorporated data gathered by the earlier ESCA-Tech Office of Contract Archaeology studies and an initial Bodo Canyon survey by Nickens, were done in

1985 and 1986.[24] They resulted in an exemplary contract report that is sure to be the basis for all future research in the northern uplands.[25]

On the heels of this auspicious start, research stalled. Almost twenty years after government engineers conceived and drew plans for the Animas-La Plata water diversion proposal, the Bureau of Reclamation awarded a multimillion-dollar contract to the archaeological laboratory of the Department of Anthropology at Northern Arizona University in Flagstaff. The contract outlined what was anticipated to be the most comprehensive look to date at affected regional antiquity. The area to be covered eventually would extend beyond Ridges Basin down the La Plata drainage, a sweep of territory known for many ruins and so extensive as to be beyond the exploration resources of a private institution. Building upon research already accomplished, fundamental questions about the relationship of ecological conditions through time on the human populations present, the processes of shifting from one basic subsistence strategy to another, cultural variability over time and space, biological continuity, economic networks, population aggregations, and many others were to be addressed. Following initial detailed surveys but before these more ambitious studies began, however, the Sierra Club filed an injunction halting the water project. The proposed archaeological studies that accompanied it are now on hold, hostages to the larger economic and political decisions that govern water development in the West.

Even if the project is eventually built, the costs of fieldwork, laboratory analyses, and publication will have escalated. In these times of cutbacks, when serious social ills cry out for funding, legislators, pressured by budgetary constraints, and overburdened taxpayers may decide that understanding the past is not as vital as facing the future. If the project is not built, the land will remain under federal control, and prehistory there will not be destroyed. Still, its scope and essence will remain unknown for years to come.

Notes

1. Vivian, 1990, 164.
2. Berry, 1980, 252–259.
3. Carlson, 1963, 2.
4. Carlson, 1963, 14 (Fig. 5), 18 (Fig. 7).
5. Carlson, 1963, 10.
6. Morris and Burgh, 1954, 73.
7. Fuller et al., 1988; Winter et al., 1986.
8. Gladwin, 1957, 55; Vivian and Reiter, 1960, 101.
9. Nickens, 1988, 441, 447.
10. Carlson, 1963, 46.
11. Martin and Goodman, 1995, 44, 60.
12. Carlson, 1963, 75–76.
13. Martin and Goodman, 1995, 46–58.
14. Carlson, 1963, 36; Wilson, 1988, 323–324 (Figs. 177–179).
15. Dean, 1975, 36–45.
16. Fuller et al., 1988, 358–359.
17. Wilshusen, 1991.
18. Applegarth, 1974; Gooding, 1980.
19. Gladwin, 1957, 56; Hibbets, 1975.
20. Flora, 1940B; Gladwin, 1957, 55.
21. Leidy, 1976; Nickens, 1978.
22. Winter et al., 1986.
23. Duke, 1985.
24. Nickens, 1981.
25. Fuller et al., 1988.

References

BOOKS, PERIODICALS, DOCUMENTS, PAPERS, AND REPORTS

Adams, Jenny L.
>1994 *Pinto Beans and Prehistoric Pots: The Legacy of Al and Alice Lancaster.* Arizona State Museum Archaeological Series 183, Tucson.

Adams, Karen R.
>1994 A Regional Synthesis of *Zea mays* in the Prehistoric Southwest. In *Corn and Culture in the New World,* edited by Sissel Johannessen and Christine Hastorf, 273–302. Westview Press, Boulder, Colorado.

Applegarth, Susan
>1974 Archaeological Survey, Bodo Business Ranches, Durango Industrial Park, La Plata County, Colorado. Unpub. MS, Fort Lewis College, Durango, Colorado.

Atkins, Victoria M., ed.
>1993 *Anasazi Basketmaker: Papers From the 1990 Wetherill–Grand Gulch Symposium.* Cultural Resource Series, no. 24. Bureau of Land Management, Salt Lake City, Utah.

Berry, Michael S.
>1980 Time, Space, and Transition in Anasazi Prehistory. Ph.D. diss., University of Utah, Salt Lake City.
>1985 The Age of Maize in the Greater Southwest: a Critical Review. In *Prehistoric Food Production in North America,* edited by Richard I. Ford, 279–308. Anthropological Papers, no. 75, Museum of Anthropology, University of Michigan, Ann Arbor.

Biggs, Robert W.
>1966 Progress Report, 1966 Investigations of Basket Maker II Sites North of Durango, Colorado. Unpub. MS, University of Colorado, Boulder.

Buckles, William
>1971 The Uncompahgre Complex: Historic Ute Archaeology and Prehistoric Archaeology. Ph.D. diss., University of Colorado, Boulder.

References

Byers, Douglas
  1941   Whose Pie Is It, Anyway? *Sherds and Points,* vol. 2, no. 2. Durango, Colorado.

Carlson, Roy L.
  1963   *Basket Maker III Sites Near Durango, Colorado.* University of Colorado Studies, Series in Anthropology, no. 8. Boulder.

Cassells, E. Steve
  1983   *The Archaeology of Colorado.* Johnson Books, Boulder, Colorado.

Cole, Sally
  1990   *Legacy in Stone: Rock Art of the Colorado Plateau and the Four Corners Region.* Johnson Books, Boulder, Colorado.
  1993   Basketmaker Rock Art at the Green Mask Site, Southeastern Utah. In *Anasazi Basketmaker,* edited by Victoria M. Atkins, 193–220. Cultural Resources Series, no. 24. Bureau of Land Management, Salt Lake City, Utah.

Daniels, Helen Sloan
  1936–1940 The Durango Public Library Museum Project. Unpub. MS, Durango, Colorado.
  1940A Durango Amateur Archaeologists Adventures. *Sherds and Points,* vol. 1, no. 2. Durango, Colorado.
  1940B NYA Museum Project in 1938. *Sherds and Points,* vol. 1, no. 5. Durango, Colorado.
  1940C NYA Museum Project in 1939. *Sherds and Points,* vol. 1, no. 8. Durango, Colorado.
  1940D Basket Makers of Falls Creek. *Sherds and Points,* vol. l, no. 12. Durango, Colorado.
  1954   Pictographs. In *Basket Maker II Sites Near Durango, Colorado,* by Earl H. Morris and Robert F. Burgh, Appendix A, 87–88. Publication 604. Carnegie Institution of Washington, Washington, D.C.
  1976   *Adventures With the Anasazi of Falls Creek.* Center of Southwest Studies, Occasional Paper, no. 3. Fort Lewis College, Durango, Colorado.

Dean, Jeffrey S.
  1975   *Tree-Ring Dates From Colorado W Durango Area.* Laboratory of Tree-Ring Research, University of Arizona, Tucson.

Douglass, A. E.
  1943   Advances in Dendrochronology, 1943. *Tree-Ring Bulletin,* vol. 9, no. 3, 18–24. Tucson, Arizona.
  1949   Note on the Early Durango Collections. *Tree-Ring Bulletin,* vol. 15, no. 4, 24. Tucson, Arizona.

References

Duke, P. G.

    1985   *Fort Lewis College Archaeological Investigations in Ridges Basin, Southwest Colorado, 1965–1982.* Center of Southwest Studies, Occasional Paper, no. 4. Fort Lewis College, Durango, Colorado.

Duke, P. G., and Gary Matlock

    1983   An Archaeological Policy for the City of Durango. Unpub. MS submitted to Durango City Council, Durango, Colorado.

Eddy, Frank W.

    1961   *Excavations at Los Pinos Phase Sites in the Navajo Reservoir District.* Museum of New Mexico, Papers in Anthropology, no. 4. Santa Fe.

    1966   *Prehistory in the Navajo Reservoir District, Northwestern New Mexico.* Museum of New Mexico, Papers in Anthropology, no. 15. 2 vols. Santa Fe.

Fenenga, Franklin, and Fred C. Wendorf

    1956   Excavations at the Ignacio, Colorado, Field Camp: Site LA2605. In *Pipeline Archaeology,* edited by Fred C. Wendorf, 207–214. Reports of Salvage Operations in the Southwest on the El Paso Natural Gas Company Project, 1950, no. 53. Laboratory of Anthropology, Santa Fe, New Mexico.

Flora, I. F.

    1938   Pre-Historic Cultures of the Durango, Colorado District. Unpub. MS. Revised 1939.

    1940A Amateur Vs. Professional. *Sherds and Points,* vol. 1, no. 1. Durango, Colorado.

    1940B A Durango Home in 630 A.D. *Sherds and Points,* vol. 1, no. 4. Durango, Colorado.

    1940C The Amateur Speaks. *Sherds and Points,* vol. 1, no. 6. Durango, Colorado.

    1940D Prehistoric Cultures of the Durango District. *Sherds and Points,* vol. 1, no. 9. Durango, Colorado.

    1940E Durango Tree Ring Dates. *Sherds and Points,* vol. 1, no. 16. Durango, Colorado.

    1941   Untitled. *Sherds and Points,* vol. 2, no. 12. Durango, Colorado.

Fuller, Steven L., et al.

    1988   *Archaeological Investigations in the Bodo Canyon Area, La Plata County, Colorado.* UMTRA Archaeological Report, no. 25. Albuquerque, New Mexico.

Gilman, Patricia A.

    1987   Architecture as Artifact: Pit Structures and Pueblos in the American Southwest. *American Antiquity,* vol. 52, no. 3, 538–564. Lawrence, Kansas.

References

Gladwin, Harold S.
  1947   *Men Out of Asia*. McGraw Hill, New York.
  1957   *A History of the Ancient Southwest*. Bond Wheelwright, Portland, Maine.

Gooding, John D., ed.
  1980   *The Durango South Project: Archaeological Salvage of Two Late Basketmaker III Sites in the Durango District*. Anthropological Paper, no. 34. University of Arizona, Tucson.

Haury, Emil
  1988   Gila Pueblo Archaeological Foundation: A History and Some Personal Notes. *Kiva*, vol. 54, no. 1, 1–75. Tucson, Arizona.

Haury, Emil, and I. F. Flora
  1937   Basket Maker III Dates From the Vicinity of Durango, Colorado. *Tree-Ring Bulletin*, vol. 14, no. 1, 7–8. Tucson, Arizona.

Hibbets, Barry N.
  1975   An Archaeological Survey of Blue Mesa, La Plata County, Colorado. Unpub. MS, Fort Lewis College, Durango, Colorado.

Hooton, E. A.
  1947   Foreword and Hindthoughts. In *Men Out of Asia*, by Harold S. Gladwin, ix–xii. McGraw Hill, New York.

Irwin-Williams, Cynthia
  1973   *The Oshara Tradition: Origins of Anasazi Culture*. Eastern New Mexico University Contributions in Archaeology, vol. 5, no. 1. Portales, New Mexico.

Janetski, Joel C.
  1993   The Archaic to Formative Transition North of the Anasazi: A Basketmaker Perspective. In *Anasazi Basketmaker*, edited by Victoria M. Atkins, 223–242. Cultural Resource Series, no. 24. Bureau of Land Management, Salt Lake City, Utah.

Jennings, Jesse D.
  1964   The Desert West. In *Prehistoric Man in the New World*, edited by Jesse D. Jennings and Edward Norbeck, 149–174. University of Chicago Press, Chicago.

Jones, Volney H., and Robert L. Fonner
  1954   Plant Materials From Sites in the Durango and La Plata Areas, Colorado. In *Basket Maker II Sites Near Durango, Colorado*, by Earl H. Morris and Robert F. Burgh, Appendix C, 93–115. Publication 604. Carnegie Institution of Washington, Washington, D.C.

References

Kearns, Timothy M.

1992   The Preceramic Archaeology of the Upper San Juan River in Northwestern New Mexico and Southwestern Colorado. In *Cultural Diversity and Adaptation,* edited by Lori Stephen Reed and Paul F. Reed, 9–35. Cultural Resources Series, no. 9. New Mexico Bureau of Land Management, Albuquerque.

Kidder, Alfred V., and Samuel J. Guernsey

1919   *Archaeological Explorations in Northeastern Arizona.* Bureau of American Ethnology, Bulletin no. 65. Washington, D.C.

Krieger, Alex D.

1964   Early Man in the New World. In *Prehistoric Man in the New World,* edited by Jesse D. Jennings and Edward Norbeck, 23–84. University of Chicago Press, Chicago.

Leidy, Kent

1976   Archaeological Resources of the Animas–La Plata Project: Report of the 1975 Season. Unpub. MS, University of Colorado, Boulder.

Lipe, William D.

1993   The Basketmaker II Period in the Four Corners Area. In *Anasazi Basketmaker,* edited by Victoria M. Atkins, 1–13. Cultural Resources Series, no. 24. Bureau of Land Management, Salt Lake City, Utah.

1994   Comments. *Kiva,* vol. 60, no. 2, 337–344. Tucson, Arizona.

Lister, Florence C., and Robert H. Lister

1968   *Earl Morris and Southwestern Archaeology.* University of New Mexico Press, Albuquerque. Reprinted 1993, Southwest Parks and Monuments Association, Tucson, Arizona.

Lister, Robert H., and Florence C. Lister

1978   *Anasazi Pottery.* University of New Mexico Press, Albuquerque.

1987   *Aztec Ruins on the Animas.* University of New Mexico Press, Albuquerque. Reprinted 1996, Southwest Parks and Monuments Association, Tucson, Arizona.

1990   *Aztec Ruins National Monument: Administrative History of an Archeological Preserve.* National Park Service, Southwest Cultural Resources Center, Professional Paper, no. 24. Santa Fe, New Mexico.

Madsen, David B.

1989   *Exploring the Fremont.* Utah Museum of Natural History, University of Utah, Salt Lake City.

185

References

Martin, Debra L., and Alan H. Goodman

    1995   Demography, Diet, and Disease at Ridges Basin in the Transitional Basketmaker III/Pueblo I Period. Unpub. final report, Animas–La Plata Project. Bioarchaeological Investigation. Fort Lewis College, Durango, Colorado.

Matson, R. G.

    1991   *The Origins of Southwestern Agriculture*. University of Arizona Press, Tucson, Arizona.

Matson, R. G., and Brian Chisholm

    1991   Basketmaker II Subsistence: Carbon Isotopes and Other Dietary Indicators From Cedar Mesa, Utah. *American Antiquity,* vol. 56, no. 3, 444–459. Lawrence, Kansas.

Minnis, Paul E.

    1985   Domesticating People and Plants in the Greater Southwest. In *Prehistoric Food Production in North America,* edited by Richard I. Ford, 309–340. Museum of Anthropology, Anthropological Papers, no. 75. University of Michigan, Ann Arbor.

Morris, Earl H.

    1928   *Notes on Excavations in the Aztec Ruin.* Anthropological Papers of the American Museum of Natural History, vol. 26, part 5. New York City.

    1949   Basketmaker II Dwellings Near Durango, Colorado. *Tree-Ring Bulletin,* vol. 15, no. 4, 33–34. Tucson, Arizona.

    1952   Notes on the Durango Dates. *Tree-Ring Bulletin,* vol. 18, no. 4, 36. Tucson, Arizona.

Morris, Earl H., and Robert F. Burgh

    1954   *Basket Maker II Sites Near Durango, Colorado.* Publication 604. Carnegie Institution of Washington, Washington, D.C.

Nickens, Paul R.

    1978   Archaeological Resources of the La Plata River Drainage, Colorado and New Mexico. Unpub. report prepared for Bureau of Reclamation, Salt Lake City, Utah.

    1981   Cultural Resource Evaluation of Bodo Canyon Area E, Durango, Colorado. Unpub. report prepared for contractors Dames and Moore, Golden, Colorado.

    1988   Human Skeletal Remains From Sites 5LP481 and 5LP483. In *Archaeological Investigations in the Bodo Canyon Area, La Plata County, Colorado,* edited by Steven Fuller et al., Appendix C, 435–460. UMTRA Archaeological Report, no. 25. Albuquerque, New Mexico.

References

Phillips, Ann

    1993   Archaeological Expeditions Into Southeastern Utah and Southwestern Colorado Between 1888–1898 and the Dispersal of Collections. In *Anasazi Basketmaker,* edited by Victoria M. Atkins, 103–120. Cultural Resources Series, no. 24. Bureau of Land Management, Salt lake City, Utah.

Powell, Shirley, prep.

    1992   Cultural Resources Data Recovery, Animas–La Plata Project. Technical Proposal, vol. 1. Solicitation no. 1425-2-SP-40-11730. Department of Anthropology Archaeological Laboratory, Northern Arizona University, Flagstaff, Arizona.

Reed, Alan D., and Ronald E. Kainer

    1978   The Tamarron Site, 5LP326. *Southwestern Lore,* vol. 44, nos. 1–2, 1–47. Boulder, Colorado.

Reed, Erik K.

    1949   The Significance of Skull Deformation in the Southwest. *El Palacio,* vol. 56, no. 4, 106–119. Santa Fe, New Mexico.

    1955   Human Skeletal Remains From the Turner-Look Site. In *A Reappraisal of the Fremont Culture,* by H. M. Wormington, 38–43. Proceedings, no. 1. Denver Museum of Natural History, Denver, Colorado.

Schaafsma, Polly

    1980   *Indian Rock Art of the Southwest.* School of American Research-University of New Mexico Press, Albuquerque, New Mexico.

Schaafsma, Polly, and M. Jane Young

    1983   *Early Masks and Faces in Southwestern Rock Art.* Papers of the New Mexico Archaeological Society, no. 8, 11–33. Albuquerque, New Mexico.

Seltzer, Carl C.

    1944   *Racial Prehistory in the Southwest and the Hawikuh Zunis.* Papers of the Peabody Museum of American Archaeology and Ethnology, vol. 23, no. 1. Cambridge, Massachusetts.

Simmons, Alan H.

    1986   New Evidence for the Early Use of Cultigens in the American Southwest. *American Antiquity,* vol. 51, no. 1, 73–88. Lawrence, Kansas.

Smiley, Francis E.

    1993   Early Farmers in the Northern Southwest: A View From Marsh Pass. In *Anasazi Basketmaker,* edited by Victoria M. Atkins, 243–254. Cultural Resources Series, no. 24. Bureau of Land Management, Salt Lake City, Utah.

1994   The Agricultural Transition in the Northern Southwest. *Kiva,* vol. 60, no. 2, 165–189. Tucson, Arizona.

Smith, Duane A.
1981   *A Love Affair That Almost Wasn't–Durango and Mesa Verde National Park.* Mesa Verde Museum Association, vol. 1, nos. 1–2, 1–7.
1986   *Rocky Mountain Boom Town: A History of Durango, Colorado.* Pruett Press, Boulder, Colorado.

Snow, Charles E., and William T. Sanders
1954   The Durango Skeletons. In *Basket Maker II Sites Near Durango, Colorado,* by Earl H. Morris and Robert F. Burgh, Appendix B, 89–92. Publication 604. Carnegie Institution of Washington, Washington, D.C.

Stiger, Mark, and Mark Larson
1992   A Radiocarbon Date From the Cottonwood Cave Corn Cache and Problems Interpreting the Origins of Farming in Western Colorado. *Southwestern Lore,* vol. 58, no. 2, 26–36. Boulder, Colorado.

Vivian, R. Gordon, and Paul Reiter
1960   *The Great Kivas of Chaco Canyon and Their Relationships.* School of American Research and Museum of New Mexico, Monograph, no. 22. Santa Fe, New Mexico.

Vivian, R. Gwinn
1990   The *Chacoan Prehistory of the San Juan Basin.* Academic Press, New York City.

Ware, John A.
1986A   Culture Change, Patterns and Process. In *The Cultural Resources of Ridges Basin and Upper Wildcat Canyon,* edited by Joseph C. Winter et al., 95–103. Office of Contract Archaeology, University of New Mexico, Albuquerque.
1986B   The Prehistoric Sites. In *The Cultural Resources of Ridges Basin and Upper Wildcat Canyon,* edited by Joseph C. Winter et al., 147–194. Office of Contract Archaeology, University of New Mexico, Albuquerque.
1986C   The Reevaluation of Durango Area Prehistory. In *The Cultural Resources of Ridges Basin and Upper Wildcat Canyon,* edited by Joseph C. Winter et al., 225–229. Office of Contract Archaeology, University of New Mexico, Albuquerque, New Mexico.

Wills, W. H.
1988   *Early Prehistoric Agriculture in the American Southwest.* School of American Research Press, Santa Fe, New Mexico.

References

Wilshusen, Richard H.

    1991   Early Villages in the American Southwest: Cross-Cultural and Archaeological Perspectives. Ph.D. diss., University of Colorado, Boulder.

Wilson, C. Dean

    1988   Ceramic Studies. In *Archaeological Investigations in the Bodo Canyon Area, La Plata County, Colorado,* edited by Steven Fuller et al., 317–329. UMTRA Archaeological Report, no. 25. Albuquerque, New Mexico.

Winter, Joseph C., et al.

    1986   *The Cultural Resources of Ridges Basin and Upper Wildcat Canyon.* Office of Contract Archaeology, University of New Mexico, Albuquerque.

Wormington, H. M., and Robert H. Lister

    1956   *Archaeological Investigations on the Uncompahgre Plateau in West Central Colorado.* Proceedings, no. 2. Denver Museum of Natural History, Denver, Colorado.

York, Robert

    1991   Evidence for Paleoindians on the San Juan National Forest, Southwestern Colorado. *Southwestern Lore,* vol. 57, no. 2, 5–22. Boulder, Colorado.

ARCHIVES

In preparing this history of Durango archaeology, I have relied extensively on personal documents. For those documents listed in the Notes *sections, the reader should consult the following archives.*

Daniels papers: Center of Southwest Studies, Fort Lewis College, Durango, Colorado; Durango Public Library, Durango, Colorado.

Douglass/Flora/Morris papers: Laboratory of Tree-Ring Research, University of Arizona, Tucson, Arizona.

Flora catalogue: Arizona State Museum, Tucson, Arizona.

Flora papers: Center of Southwest Studies, Fort Lewis College, Durango, Colorado.

Flora/National Forest Service papers: San Juan National Forest, Durango, Colorado.

Flora/National Park Service papers: Mesa Verde National Park, Colorado.

Gladwin/Gila Pueblo papers: Arizona State Museum, Tucson, Arizona.

Morris papers: University of Colorado Museum, Boulder, Colorado.

Root catalogue: Arizona State Museum, Tucson; Center of Southwest Studies, Fort Lewis College, Durango, Colorado.

References

NEWSPAPERS

Denver Post, November 4, 1973, article by Howard Kaplan in "Empire Magazine," a
   Sunday section.
Durango Herald, March 23, 1979; March 25, 1979.
Durango Herald Democrat, April 30, 1939; October 1, 1945; October 12, 1945.
Durango News, January 13, 1939; February 3, 1939; July 28, 1939; March 10, 1941;
   October 12, 1945; October 3, 1947; July 13, 1949; September 6, 1950.
Great Southwest, April 18, 1893. Durango, Colorado
Science News Letter, December 24, 1938.

RADIO

KDGO, *Senior Saturday,* December 1, 1976.

Index

Acoma Pueblo, 9
Allen, James G., 21
Alva Site, petroglyphs at, 122
Amateurs, xiii, 11, 29; professionals and, xii, 72–73, 80, 81
American Antiquity, Flora/Daniels and, 72
American Civil Liberties Union, 85, 86
American Indian Movement, protest by, 90
American Museum of Natural History, 15
Amsdem, Charles, 43, 72
Anasazi, 9, 125; corn and, 135; Kayenta Branch of, 138
Animas City Mountain, 19, 102
Animas River Valley, 4, 10, 163; Basketmaker II in, 148, 152; Basketmaker III–Pueblo I at, 174; contract archaeological work   at, 151; corn in, 134; formation of, 101. *See also* Upper Animas district
Antiquities Act (1906), 7, 30, 77, 143–144
Applegarth, Susan: site survey by, 174
Archaeological Resources Protection Act (1979), xii
Archaic, 131–132, 135; artifacts of, 131; dating, 136, 137, 138; Late, 138, 139, 151, 176
Archaic peoples, 130, 141–142; at Falls Creek, 136
Artifacts, finding/transporting, 26–27
Ashbaugh, Harley, Jr., 80
Atlatls, 170
Awatovi excavations, 29
Ayres, D. W., 6
Aztec Ruins, 8, 14; great houses at, 5; Great Kiva of, 15
Aztecs, 129

Bags, 26, 119
Bannister, Bryant, 86
Basketmaker I, 9, 107
Basketmaker II, 9, 29, 42, 140, 143; Archaic and, 163; Basketmaker III and, 154–155; dating, 51, 123, 136–139, 152; Early/Late, 137, 139, 141, 148; Eastern, 145, 148, 164; environmental challenges for, 153–154; fires for, 116–117;

food preparation by, 111; forerunners of, 107; housing for, 116, 117; Los Pinos variant of, 146; Mogollon and, 164; Neanderthals and, 92; pottery and, 120; staying power of, 110; Western, 141, 142, 164
Basketmaker III, 9, 15, 16, 18, 20, 42, 50, 92, 176; Basketmaker II and, 154–155; dating, 51, 137, 138, 173; development of, 164; masks by, 123; Pueblo and, 163; settlement patterns of, 139–141, 165–166
Basketmaker III–Pueblo I, 173, 174; burial sites of, 171; development of, 169–170
Basketmaker II sites, 19, 30, 35, 43, 83; excavation of, 82; photo of, 61, 83, 84, 85, 86
Basketmaker III sites, 19, 22, 23, 90
Baskets, 26, 28, 46, 130; manufacture of, 111, 112; pottery and, 171
Bead Girl, 27, 75
Beans, domestication of, 170
Berry, Michael, 173, 164
Biggs, William, 82
Bison Antiquus, 126
Blue Mesa, 4; excavation at, 16, 18, 90; Great Kiva at, 169; pithouses at, 174; site sketches for, 175; survey at, 174
Bodo Canyon, 131, 148; Basketmaker II at, 149–151, 167 (map); Basketmaker III–Pueblo I at, 165–166, 168 (map); excavation at, 149–150; hazardous waste site in, 176; household units at, 166; pithouses at, 173
Bows and arrows, 6, 170
Brew, J. O., 12, 14, 60, 66, 72
Bureau of Reclamation, contract with, 175, 177
Burgh, Robert F., xv, 49, 131, 135, 145, 151, 152; Basketmaker II and, 59, 64, 105, 108, 123, 141; baskets and, 112; on cists, 133; criticism of, 77; at Falls Creek, 35, 112–113, 173; on floors, 116; on gambling, 119; at Talus Village, 62, 63; work of, 42, 80, 81, 125
Byers, Douglas, 72, 73

Index

Falls Creek Archaeological Area, xiv, 132, 139, 141, 174
Falls Creek Caves, 74
Falls Creek Flats: corn at, 170; explorations in, 49–53, 58, 173; household units at, 166, 169; pithouses at, 169, 172
Falls Creek rock shelters, 102, 125, 132, 149; Basketmaker III at, 165; baskets at, 111, 112, 147; corn at, 109, 135; dating occupation of, 43, 74, 136–137, 137–138; discoveries at, 26–28; excavation of, 29, 35–37, 39–44, 46–47, 49; food preparation at, 111, 112; life at, 40–41, 112–119
Falls Creek Valley, 20, 23, 105; Archaic culture in, 132; architecture at, 113–115; Basketmakers in, 64, 106–107, 123; burial crevice at, 75, 88; formation of, 101–102; photo of, 24; pictographs in, 121–122; points in, 127; settlers in, 164
Field Museum of Natural History, 60; Daniels letter to, 22, 66
Floors: making, 113–114, 116; photo of, 85, 86
Flora, Isaiah Ford "Zeke," 20, 23, 43, 47, 60; on amateurs, 80; Basketmaker II and, 30, 49, 59, 64, 67, 83, 105, 107, 114, 137, 154; Carnegie and, 32, 68–69; on clothing, 117; collection of, 12, 14, 111; controversy surrounding, xv–xvi, 67–69, 74–75, 81– 82, 85; death of, 92; establishment and, 71–72; Esther and, 3–4, 26–27, 44, 75–76, 85, 86, 90–91; at Falls Creek, 25, 26, 31, 35, 42, 74; on floors, 116; Jasper and, 79; missing artifacts and, 77–78, 79; permit for, 30, 77; photo of, 13, 38, 41, 51, 52; at Talus Village, 63–64; work of, 12, 16, 18, 19, 20, 30, 36–37, 40, 58
Florida Mesa, 145
Folsom Mesa, 127; discoveries at, 8; excavation at, 21
Foods/food production, Basketmaker, 107–109, 110–111, 112
Footing log, photo of, 150
Formative Period, 136
Fort Lewis College, xiv; field school at, 176; Root at, 88–89, 90
Franke, Paul, 37
Fremont people, 112, 145; corn and, 135; gambling by, 119; rock art of, 122; San Rafael, 154; Western Basketmakers and, 142
Friends of the Falls Creek Rock Shelters, xiv

Gambling, 119
Gardner, H. E., 37

Gila Pueblo, 18, 19, 21, 23, 42, 68, 88; Flora and, 16, 87
Gilbert, Walter, 76
Gladwin, Harold S., 18, 19, 28, 31; Basketmaker II and, 67; criticism of, 69, 72; dating and, 42, 43, 51, 136; Douglass and, 42; Flora and, 15–16, 20, 68, 69; on Great Kiva, 169; work of, 58, 63, 88, 134, 174, 175
Graham, Howard, 6
Grand Gulch, 29, 138
Grandma Niska, 28, 81, 82
Graves, 130; Basketmaker, 120–121; digging at, xiii
Great Kiva (Aztec Ruins), 15, 169
Green, C. H., 6
Griffiths Heights, 20; excavation at, 21–22
Grinding stones, 24, 108, 111, 114; photo of, 86
Grinnel, Clayton, 6
Guernsey, Samuel, 9
Guthe, Carl, 72
Gypsum Cave Archaic, 141

Haury, Emil, 20, 31, 43, 72, 74; at Falls Creek, 42; Flora and, 19
Hibbets, Barry: excavation by, 174–175
Hidden Valley, formation of, 101
Hill, W. W. "Nibs," 43
Hohokam, 60, 125
Hohokam/Basketmaker Complex, corn at, 109, 134
Holocene, glacial ice during, 101
Homo sapiens neanderthalensis, 66
Homo sapiens sapiens, 66
Hooton, E. A.: on Flora, 20
Hunter–gatherer society, 154, 169–170; studying, 129, 131, 132
Hunting, 108, 170
Hurst, Clarence T., 135; Flora/Daniels and, 72; *Southwestern Lore* and, 129; Tabaguache Cave and, 136; Uncompahgre sites and, 128–129
Huston, J. B., 75

Iconographic art, 130
Ign 7:23, photo of, 54
Ign 7:30, photo of, 52, 55
Ign 7:31, photo of, 53
Ign 7:36, photo of, 51
Ign 7:101, dating, 137
Ign 7:103, photo of, 83
Ign 12:46: corn at, 134; photo of, 84
Ign 12:79, photo of, 149
Ignacio, excavations near, 144–145
Irwin–Williams, Cynthia: Oshara Tradition and, 131

Index

PRAISE FOR

RHYME & RHYTHM: POEMS FOR STUDENT ATHLETES

Rhyme & Rhythm: Poems for Student Athletes, edited by Sarah Donovan, is so much more than an anthology of poems about sports. The talented poets use the topic of sports as a backdrop for writing poems full of self-realization and identity. They take on topics such as diversity and equality, told from the student athlete's point of view. It is a book full of poems that all teens can connect to, and that teachers will share with their classes.

Stacy Mozer, Sporty Girl Books

In this engrossing collection, Sarah J. Donovan presents a rich tapestry of poetic voices that speak to the varied experiences of youth athletes. Whether competing to win, playing for fun, or preferring to opt out of sports altogether, readers will find within these pages evocative poems that resonate.

Luke Rodesiler, Associate Professor of Education at the School of Education at Purdue University Fort Wayne
Co-author of *Developing Contemporary Literacies through Sports: A Guide for the English Classroom*

Rhyme & Rhythm exemplifies what it means to amplify all voices. While the subtitle implies this collection of poetry is an anthology for athletes, the imagery embodied within these pages encompasses a tapestry of diverse stories marginalized in not only the sports narrative, but also literature. It is refreshing to have a selection of poems that depict the intersectionality of sports and sociocultural identities. *Rhyme & Rhythm* makes tangible the reality we've all known – sports is more than sports.

Dr. Katherin Garland, Associate Professor of Education, Santa Fe College
Co-editor, *Stories of Sports: Critical Literacy in Media Production, Consumption, and Dissemination*

This collection of sports poetry offers readers the opportunity to see themselves as athletes, spectators, critics, and people as they engage with writing across a rich array of forms and styles.

Dr. Wendy Glenn, Professor of Literacy Studies at University of Colorado Boulder

The Covid-19 pandemic put a damper on youth sports, from modifying rules to outright canceling a season. One positive outcome from this is *Rhyme & Rhythm: Poems for Student Athletes*. The poets have channeled their pent-up feelings for sports into this remarkable collection of poems. Just like there is a sport for everyone, there is a poem inside this book for everyone ... from the student who celebrates the cancellation of P.E., to the dancer who finds the solace of rhythm, to the competitor who finds drama on the field, court, pitch, and more. Sports are a physical drama; poetry is a written one. This book tells the stories of individuals combining both.

Mia Wenjen, author of *Changing the Game: Asian Pacific American Female Athletes*

I'm a fan of this book on multiple levels: as a poet, educator, and former coach, as well as someone who loves the poetics of sport. Youth poets and youth athletes keep the sport of poetry and the poetry of sports alive. In this vibrant collection, poets will discover the poetry of sport and athletes will better understand the sport and pastime of poetry. It's a win-win situation for all.

Peter Markus, author of *Inside My Pencil: Teaching Poetry in Detroit Public Schools*

RHYME & RHYTHM
POEMS FOR STUDENT ATHLETES

EDITED BY SARAH J. DONOVAN, PH.D.

ARCHER PUBLISHING
WASHINGTON, DC

RHYME & RHYTHM: POEMS FOR STUDENT ATHLETES
Published by Archer Publishing
1315 Park Road NW
Washington, DC 20010

Images licensed through iStockphoto.com

ARCHER PUBLISHING is a registered trademark of Archer Media Networks LLC.

The ARCHER PUBLISHING logo is a registered trademark of Archer Media Networks LLC.

Library of Congress Control Number: 2021914714

Archer Publishing ISBN: 978-1-7352531-4-5
eBook ISBN: 978-1-7352531-5-2

PRINTED IN THE UNITED STATES OF AMERICA
10 9 8 7 6 5 4 3 2 1

Paperback and electronic copies of this book may be ordered
from the publisher through its website Mojo Marketplace.

www.mojo.amncentral.com

For Dan.

Thank you for reading poetry with me.

Poems

IN THE RHYTHM

ON SCHOOL GROUNDS

IN THE GAME

ON HOME COURT

OUT OF BOUNDS

INTERNAL RHYME

Introduction

THIS POETRY ANTHOLOGY IS FOR YOU. Whether you participate in an organized sport in school or a club, compete against no one other than yourself, or find that your court, field, road, hill, water, ring, rink, or mountain is the only place you feel safe or yourself, this anthology is for you. If you've ever avoided gym class, spent Friday nights cheering on your "more athletic" sibling, or defended video games as sport — this anthology is for you.

For me, it's all of the above. I grew up with ten siblings, so there were always comparisons and competitions. And there were plenty of times I tried to avoid the mile run in gym class. I played indoor club volleyball all through middle and high school. This was highly organized with coaches, levels, uniforms, rules, and long weekend tournaments in stuffy gyms. I never felt like I belonged. It wasn't until I was older that I found my sport: beach volleyball. No coaches or stuffy gyms – just a few girls showing up lakeside to play a game. I'd play all day, every day if I could.

Every spring I wait for the first day of fifty-five degree weather, when the snow melts from Chicago's Oak Street Beach and sand socks offer just enough warmth to let us play a few games without frozen toes. I'm a teacher, so on those fifty-five degree days (and warmer), I would race out of school after bus duty to beat the traffic, eating a granola bar and changing clothes on the way. With an old volleyball net, a few Wilsons, and three friends — I'd play until sunset, forgetting school, work, the world. When I play, I just am. Maybe you know the feeling.

But in the spring of 2020, there was no beach volleyball on Oak Street Beach or anywhere else for that matter. Instead, there were Instagram videos about quarantine exercise and pictures of peppering in backyards with face masks. Peppering is when two players pass-set-hit the ball back and forth. My partner and I resorted to playing one-on-one volleyball over our fence.

Across the world, all spring sports seasons were canceled, gyms were closed, and even public parks and fields were restricted. After some time, I started feeling something like depression but maybe it was closer to grief. I missed playing volleyball. I missed my friends. I missed who I was when I played. I think I was mourning the loss of me.

In the meantime, school continued online, and because I'm an English teacher, I began preparing poetry to celebrate National Poetry Month. I like to introduce verse novels and poetry anthologies to students. They always groan at first but end up loving poetry. One book sort of shook me from my sadness. I was struck by the cover of Kwame Alexander's *The Crossover* (2014). On it was an illustration of a boy with a basketball full of words. I opened the book to "Dribbling." The poem begins with a first-person account of a basketball scene: "At the top of the key, I'm MOVING & GROOVING,/POPping and ROCKING—". The words fly across the white space, and the caps, italics, and different font sizes make the scene come alive. It was exhilarating to read. I opened my notebook and wrote: "At the net, I wait with my hands/raised—not in surrender but in stealth/ to BLOCK or pull...". And just like that, I was there—on the court again. Alexander started a conversation with me through his poem, and I responded with my own, stepping into my game and, for a short time, out of my grief.

As an educator and athlete, I wondered how student athletes were coping. For some, school sports are about pride, loyalty, legacy, and the

opportunity to go to college, but there are student athletes who are happy to be on a team of one, lost in their stride, who are their own coach. There are some student athletes who don't see what they do as sport but rather a way of being, or they use sports as an escape from stress at home, a broken heart, a world not yet ready for them.

When I was a student athlete in high school playing club volleyball, I didn't see this range of student athlete representation in the media, and I certainly didn't see it in the books that we read in English classes. Come to think of it, the only poem I read about sports when I was in school was "Casey at the Bat." I struggled to balance school, work, practice, and long weekend tournaments while trying to date and stay connected to friends. Those experiences were nowhere to be found in the poetry we read in school.

Like sports, poems have different sets of "rules," but also like sports, poetry invites and celebrates the unexpected, the beautiful, the tragic. Poems play with words, shape, craft, and mimic actions like the punch of a boxer or the glide of an ice skater. Their sweat may be fear or doubt; the "tear" may mean cries of pain or a "tear" in an ACL. Their body is part of their identity when they are jogging in a neighborhood or when they are stereotyped by a fan. The line breaks in a poem may represent a wish to break from a family legacy or for a scholarship that may not come. And what about the bodies that don't fit into neat rhyme and meter because the sport they want to compete in isn't for girls, or because as transgender, their body is not written into the rules to compete. Free verse may be a resistance—there's still structure, but it's up to the poet to decide the "rules," disruption, and art.

Sports inspire poets. When I asked poets to send in poems about being a student athlete, they confirmed what you already know. Student athletes have to navigate so much more than showing up for the game: doing homework on the bus to stay eligible, keeping a part-time job to pay for your gear, making dinner for your siblings while parents work late, and finding time for friendship and love. And what about the impact of COVID-19, racism, and gender inequities?

This anthology of young adult sports poetry uses the white space and ink to realize the many ways of being a student athlete, reaching out, up, down, and across the pages. If you've ever felt like you didn't fit in with teammates, check out "A Monster Joins the Track Team." If you've ever had a coach that you admired or hated, check out "Cross Country Meet, October of Freshman Year," "Soccer Rules," and "Learning to Lead." There are poems about our opponents: how we honor them in "At the Summer Court" and hurt them in "The True Meaning of Football." Poems about feeling powerful like Nikki Grimes' "Runner," and Karen J. Weyant's "The Girl Who Eats Baseball Cards." There are poems about family such as Glenda Cowen-Funk's "Play by Play," J.M. Allen's "The Drive Home," and Mary E. Cronin's "A Slice of Time."

We've included poems in a variety of forms so you can see how poets create movement with the use of ink and white space. Some rhyme. Some don't. Some move down the page with short lines such as "Side Out" by Liza Moore Ramée. Some are narrative and tell a story, such as "Again and Again" by Valerie Hunter, others are lyrical such as "Seams" by Sandra Marchetti and "Athletic-Meta-Poetic" by Stefani Boutelier.

My hope is that this anthology finds its way into book stores, libraries, and classrooms for student athletes who need to be seen in the books they read. Maybe a teacher will share one in English class, maybe you will read a few on the bus after a game, maybe you'll fill a notebook of poems inspired by this anthology. *Rhyme & Rhythm: Poems for Student Athletes* is a call and a comfort to see the less visible, perhaps less celebrated ways of being a student athlete, and to tell you that we see you. We are holding space for your lines and stanzas in the margins of the poems on these pages.

Sarah J. Donovan, Ph.D.

RHYTHM

Fearless in Waking
Gae Polisner

So often, I dream I'm adrift
in
open water,
seas gray and turbulent, and
violent.

The shore vanishes, and
sky blends with harbor until it is
impossible
to tell
one from the other.

"You know how to
swim,"
I remind myself,
how to breathe,
how to press my chest
firmly down
with each
stroke.

How to Frankenstein my arms
to prevent
crossover.

But in slumber
skill eludes, and
the endless waves swell
all around
leaving me
daunted.

Awake,
the autumn sun effervesces
off the surface of the
harbor like
sparkle popcorn.

It's likely the 100th day that
I've been in
since
May.

Yards off shore,
harmless bunkerfish,
their cartoon fins poking the
surface,
swirl the water in frantic
efforts to
avoid.

Here, near me,
tiny schools of silver-gray fish
flash and dart and weave around
my calves,
clearing the
way for me to
enter.

I swim,
effortlessly,
letting my stroke adjust,
letting the saltwater
buoy me,
as
moon jellies drift and
disappear.

I acclimate quickly,
stroke toward the far beach,
a rhythm now
committed fully
to
rote.

I breathe.
I swim.
I am.

In daylight,
I am
never
afraid.

Cross Country Meet, October of Freshman Year

Kate Sjostrom

I'm pounding out the second movement
of Beethoven's seventh symphony.
It's not a pounding song,
but I'm pounding it,
picking up its pace to match my
footfalls on this forest preserve path.
There are only five pairs of feet
in front of me now.
Too many.

I'm pounding out the second movement
of Beethoven's seventh symphony.
It's not a pounding song,
but I'm pounding it,
its steady bass throb keeping me going,
its minor melody pumping my chest.

I'm pounding out the second movement
of Beethoven's seventh symphony.
It's not a pounding song,
but I'm pounding it,
stomping into mind thoughts that keep
racing away: Yesterday
Dad moved out. Today
he's not here.
Tonight he won't be home.

I'm pounding out the second movement
of Beethoven's seventh symphony.
It's not a pounding song,
but I'm pounding it.
Even so, it is so beautiful
it hurts.

I'm pounding out the second movement
of Beethoven's seventh symphony.
It's not a pounding song,
but I'm pounding it,
a pack to myself
between two groups of girls, so
alone I dare exhale a note out loud,
feel its buzz in my brain.

I'm pounding out the second movement
of Beethoven's seventh symphony.
It's not a pounding song,
but I'm pounding it,
getting closer to the runners before me,
closer to the symphony's center,
closer to its beating bass heart.

I'm pounding out the second movement
of Beethoven's seventh symphony.
It's not a pounding song,
but I'm pounding it,
passing one runner then
two, pumping to the
finish line. Pushing
through the press
of people, in search
of my mom.

There she is with my coach,
next to my team's blue and orange tent.
My ears open now to the sound around me,
the music of whistles and hollers,
my mom saying,
"Can you believe it?,"
my coach clapping
at my approach.

Curveball
Ed Meek

It was a slow curve — a big bender,
spinning against the trajectory
of the ball. It hung
at the apex
suspending
time
distorting space
like a full moon, while
I waited back on my heels
And when I went for it, it was
nowhere near where I expected it to be.

Finishing Kick
Dennis McGonagle

Off went the gun and we broke into a run
I'll keep up with the pack, let them set the pace
With the finish in sight, take command of the race
And up on the hill, I was somewhere near done
Top of the mountain, lightning splash all around
Runners shuffled to the sidewalk — all except me
But then a path opened, a parting Red Sea
and I walked on waves all the way down

They looked like statues from my own diamond lane
But my quads were exploding, and soaked by the rain
my tank was empty, burning on fumes
Yet a hundred yards left, I was a human typhoon
When I closed like a freight train, lit up the crowd
and dedicated the medal to an obliging rain cloud

Soccer Ball
Joe Bisicchia

Allow it to gather our eyes,

not to hypnotize but to galvanize

and

envelop all our breath.

The skin is a puzzle

of ourselves,

patterned with hexagons and pentagons and

this world we share is round.

It can no longer be silent

as each of us in our own way

together

rouse it around .

Turner Syndrome Court
Sarah Allen

Missing: chromosome

Missing: non-verbal team-ing

and the highest tones

of Coach's whistle.

Ms. Back back seat of the van

sing loud, hardy teams

from microscopic

schools. Ms. Heart scar on left ribs

missed those few inches

no matter the shots,

shots of growth hormone taken

daily, all the shots

taken daily. In

this far city this one chance

varsity ending

Coach doesn't dismiss

you the squeak squeak foul doesn't

miss you. Aligned on

the floors painted scar

heart to arms, shooting — verdict:

Ms. Missing Nothing

and this time you hear

all the non-verbal hope midst

the net's sound; the swish.

Deep
Natalia Sylvester

The game I love has rules:

    Stay within the lines.

    3 hits to the other side.

    Don't let the ball touch the floor.

And I have mine:

    Pretend your hip and spine are aligned.

    5 surgeries and counting.

    The ball of my left hip does not sit right inside its joint.

Sometimes I wish

the rules of my body would bend like the curvatures of

my spine. Instead I can only lunge right

because my left is

another story

I'd like to tell

no one.

I play anyway.

Because my overhand serves
butterfly into aces
and I make myself hard in the face
of a kill.
Because I dig digging
spikes out of impossible corners
and diving
as if the court were made of water.
Because I'm still an athlete and
my mom, grandma and sister
say the game is in our blood.

I close my eyes before serving and trust it's

pulsing
deep
inside
my bones.

Fierce

Ismée Williams

Cold sculpts the breath
    that blooms from my mouth
    into billows of winged shapes
        escaping.

I tip forward.
    Poles plant through crusts of white.
    Toes press against boots,
    anticipating lift off.

I think of that boy,
    who follows me in the lodge,
    and makes fun of my name.
    No girl could be as fast as me,
                he says.

My heart beats in double time to the countdown.

I launch,

        off the ledge,

        hips snap straight,

        legs coil

        and unleash.

Arms pump

      propelling me.

      I am skating,

        racing

           away from that boy and his

words.

I swoop by the first gate,

        so close it grazes my skin.

      I lean in,

      carve my path,

      again

        and again.

Wind bites at the bones of my face,

      finds the gaps in my armor,

          tears at my eyes.

      Going down each breath

                burns.

      I gulp hungrily.

I tuck,

      launch again,

      breaking contact with the icy earth.

      I plummet.

I am no longer a small bird fleeing.

    I am the hawk, the eagle,

    –no–

    a falcon,

    wings tucked,

    talons out,

    fierce.

I plunge across the finish

    to the sound of cowbells and fog horns and cheers.

    I unfurl my arms, my body and shred to a halt.

The snow I've kicked up settles.

    The boy is there.

    He is not looking at me.

    He's looking at the board,

    at the impossible time listed beside a name he cannot pronounce.

I empty my lungs,

    smiling as my exhale takes flight.

Cleatless
Heidi Mordhorst

What about my game, my sport?
The one for a curvy-soft and short
girl—doesn't own a pair of cleats,
but sure knows how to work her feet.
I'm not here to crush it, win it;
I can't run more than a minute—
but play the music: body sings!
Rumba, salsa, west coast swing,
      I can dance to anything—
cha-cha, polka and merengue,
rhythm fever like the dengue—
two-step, tango, lindy hop,
son, bachata—I don't stop.

Duck and weave? Dribble? Shoot?

I don't need a warm-up suit.

Serve or pitch? What's "defense"?

but check my kinesthetic sense:

I feel the beat, I know its tactics —

fast or slow this girl attacks it,

sees the play, your hands in mine —

no rushing towards the finish line.

I throw my weight in this dark gym,

I'm spin and flex; I'm fly and swim;

hips and heels and head and knees —

my every move is varsity.

Side Out
Lisa Moore Ramee

Side out

My inside doesn't match my

out

side.

Face cool

calm

while fear drips down

my spandex

pressing into my

ankle guards.

My inside doesn't match my

out

side.

Chest flattened

tight

no flinch betrays

my heart pounds

threatening to burst

give way.

My inside doesn't match my

out

side.

Hands curved

tense

ready to lift or strike

my energy

coiled like a snake

waiting.

My inside doesn't match

my outside

my inside out side.

Ball up

Side out

I Am the Eye
Padma Venkatraman

Rising up as the music surges,
my brown arms are the branches of a swaying tree.
I glide, I leap, I fly like a storm-tossed leaf,
the ice-rink shimmers below me...

I land. I'm centered. Mountain strong.
Mountain still.
I hold the roots of a whole forest.
I bend to no one's will.

Gamified
Stefani Boutelier

Blink, blur, breathe

Check my stats

Noise canceling gear, couch

Viewing, Trolling

Next level, Easter eggs

> *Blink, blur, breathe*
>
> *Whistle blows, stampede*
>
> *Hundreds of fans, bench*
>
> *Cheering, crowding*
>
> *End zone, goal, net*

Bask in glory

Stepping out, ready, set, play

Setting up, 3, 2, 1...face off

Explode, my senses activate

Finger muscles, eye muscles, anxiety

The sweat of emotion, not pain

Gasses my flow, my addiction

Bitcoins, credit galvanize a flame that traps me

In the alternate world, Twitch.tv

Bask in glory

Stepping out, ready, set, start

Step, run, 3, 2, 1...game on

Explode, my senses activate

My heart tugs at all my muscles, anxiety

The sweat of pain, not emotion

Gasses my flow, my addiction

Standings, scores galvanize a flame that traps me

In the anaerobic world, ESPN.go

Beg for the physical, not the digital

Addicting mirror, my reflection gazing, staring, cannot look away

Must run, yet the magnetic noises of the circuit pull me back

Multi-platform, streamer, no longer a noob

No longer rekt, I will be a Legend of this game

Beg for a digital break, not the challenge

Addicting endorphin release, pushing my body to the limits

Must run, yet the needed interval break distracts me

Remix the right reps, just go, no longer an amateur

No longer destroyed, I will be the MVP of this game

Knuckleball
Ed Meek

Before the game he files his nails flat.
His fingers, blunt talons, clutch the ball.
He throws like a child — all arm and wrist —
the wind-up nonchalant, follow-through
an afterthought: it isn't about speed.

And when he lets it go
the ball floats and flutters without spin...
batters swing in vain wild attempts
to believe their otherwise reliable eye
as the ball sinks through the strike zone
toward the baffled catcher's mitt.

Hitters shake their puzzled heads
on the way back to the bench.
It ain't natural, they mutter
glancing at the pitcher
who, in the bottom of the eighth,
doesn't even appear tired.

Yet he sweats because he too knows
the knuckleball is a mystery
that comes and goes. And when it goes...
it hangs up above the plate--
a bulls-eye, a grapefruit, a beach ball...
and it's gone—over the wall, out of the park.
That's why, as the knuckler knows,
you can never get too high, or too low.

ON SCHOOL GROUNDS

Hypothesis: athletics (x) > academics (y)
Beth Brody

Remember back in grade school,

when gym was fun and we played games,

and everybody always, *almost* always, got along.

Now I reach the end of AP Math and I'm a wreck.

Knowing gym is next my stomach ties a hangman's knot.

Cause here in Math I'm in control. My brain knows what to do.

I follow through with every step.

But –

In the gym those systems of exponents, functions, matrices,

so clear to me in Algebra,

evaporate in sweat.

On the turf or hardwood floor I slide into inertia.

It's simple for my mind to calculate the winning moves,

but my body won't perform, refusing to negotiate,

the way I need it to.

Kids rolls their eyes or laugh or even look away in pity.

The self-esteem that grew in math gets booted out of bounds

and out of play.

My breasts defy all Newton's Laws of Motion.

The mildewed smell of gym clothes makes me gag.

The locker room's a labyrinth of ego and regrets.

I won't strip down to naked,

so I sit through Chem in sweaty bra and panties.

Acid-based reactions don't make my eyes burn like some girls,

fit and lithe team players, who grace our halls in warm-up suits,

while I, an Elemental shadow,

keep invisible to all.

I pray for cramps each day till June.

Perhaps I'll sprain my ankle one day getting out of bed.

My parents say: "Your time will come.

In college you will meet your peers."

I answer that's a million years from now.

I dream of solving global warming.

Maybe I will be the one to figure how to feed the world

and find a cure for hunger.

For now, I'm just a High School hostage

bound by intramural theorems.

Math helps me solve everything,

except how to skip gym.

A Slice of Time
Mary E. Cronin

Our plastic hockey sticks clatter

in the high school gym

We jostle, scrap, attack the puck.

We sweat, we laugh, talk smack.

There are no crowds or cheers or refs

in intramural sports —

just a slice of time for us girls to play

after school,

before I pick up my brother,

before I start dinner,

before Mom gets home from work.

Before all that,

I linger to watch

the varsity field hockey team—

well, Clara.

She pounds down the sunlit field,

muscles rippling—

those cleats must cost more

than a day of Mom's pay.

I dream of sprinting alongside her,

our braids bouncing,

our cleats gleaming in the wet grass.

Our arms would touch,

the whistle chirping as the crowd cheers,

hours of play stretching ahead of us.

Again and Again
Valerie Hunter

The annual Caldwell High Powderpuff Flag Football Game
is a senior requirement, as though school spirit
can be force-fed. Cori wonders what would happen
if she refused, but she doesn't try. She knows it's pointless.

It's a lesson she's learned through experience. She's always
been an angry girl, angry at the way the world works,
the way no one listens when they should, all the little stupid things
that people do for stupid reasons. She spent countless hours
in detention, or sitting in the guidance office listening to advice
that just made her angrier, until she learned to hold in her rage,
to let it bubble and boil and brew in some deep recess of her body
where no one has to see it or acknowledge it, not even her.

So here she is putting on the stupid flagged belt, all the underclassmen
laughing and cheering from the bleachers, the senior boys parading
the sidelines with yellow pompoms. The senior girls held unofficial practices
last week, which Cori skipped. She discovers that she's been designated
as her team's kicker, which she didn't even think they had in flag football.
"You used to play soccer, right?" Brielle says, and Cori nods. She quit soccer
freshman year because she got too many red cards, and the coach hated her.

Cori figures this game will be such a mess that there won't
be much need for a kicker, but her team, the appallingly named
Glitter Girls, scores touchdown after touchdown, and she is called upon
to kick for the extra point again and again. A football is different
than a soccer ball, but she adapts, enjoying the solid contact
of her foot against the leather, the way the ball is propelled
by her anger and aggression. She thinks she might have stuck with soccer
if this was all she had to do, just kick, let it fly, again and again.
The frenzied yells of the crowd as she makes every point merge with the roar
in her head, that red buzz that she's trying to release with every kick.

Afterwards, once they've won this stupid, meaningless game,

the head football coach approaches, asking if she'd like to do this for real,

kick for the actual football team. He looks serious, but Cori can't quite tell

if he is, and anyhow, she doesn't want to, doesn't want to be an anomaly,

a story, *that girl on the football team*, so she shakes her head and hurries

away.

But afterwards, on Tuesday nights when the field is dead and dark,

she takes an old football and kicks field goals again and again,

until her toes throb. Again and again, because it releases that pent up rage

she's not supposed to feel. Again and again, because she can.

No one watches, no one cares, but it's real enough for her.

Running Stairs
Laura Shovan

At the start of practice we run stairs —
a pack of girls thundering
up and down the stairwell.
Doors closed. Windows foggy
with our heat. We're laughing.
Boom, boom, boom.
I drip in my dad's old sweatshirt
from Round Up Ranch.
The fleece is thin, perfectly broken in.

Thighs burning, stronger with each stair.
I watch our captain, legs thick with muscle —
a fencer's true weapon. "Sprints!" she calls,
and we spill into the almost-empty senior hall.
He is there with a friend. I sprint closer,
part of the stampede, but he singles me out,
eyes on my sweatshirt.
                    "Round Cup Ranch!"
he points. His friend doubles over, laughing.

"Jerk," one of my teammates mumbles.
We disappear down the stairwell,
where I feel every bounce
of my too-large breasts, feel out of breath,
stop running, stop wearing
Dad's comfortable old sweatshirt,
stop showing up for practice,
avoid stairwells, forget I was training
to be a girl with a weapon in her grasp.

Soccer Rules
Kristin Bartley Lenz

They call it a stitch, but my spleen is rupturing,

splintering my ribcage. My lungs scorch, but still

I run and run and run, chased by cleats

scraping my Achilles. Coach knows

I need a sub, but he's a bellowing bull,

"I'm counting on you!"

I count ten girls

on the bench

who never get to play.

We hug sweaty shoulders, chug plastic polluted water, unwind

tape from stress fractured ankles. We are turtles

waddling off the field, weighted

with two backpacks

and two hours of homework.

Coach's parting words every evening:

"Remember ladies, prioritize sleep,

take care of your bodies."

Back at my house, I bury my nose deep

in my dog's neck. My phone needs answering,

my white uniform needs soaking, my little sister needs

help with fractions. I cut

a sandwich in half, then quarters

for our dinner.

Our team gathers under the giant beech, the base

of its wrinkled trunk like elephant toes. Coach reminds us

that any player will be punished for missing

a practice, his eyes on me. My job at Pronto Pizza

starts tomorrow. My throat is thick, and I want

to tell him - we're all playing our best, but

none of us

will earn a soccer scholarship.

My stomach rumbles loud enough

to make my teammates laugh. A yellow leaf

falls to my shoulder; I want

to sweep it into my mouth.

Coach's eyes skitter

to his chiming phone. But we girls,

We girls grip hands

and squeeze.

Hammerhead Practice
Robin Yardi

Spring sightings of hammerheads and great whites
keep everyone at the edges of waves over break.
But at the pool there's only one swimmer
sitting alone on the bleachers.
Her mom doesn't want her practicing
when she's bleeding.

But there's this bulk box of free tampons in our locker room to use,
ones that are too long and uncomfortable
all puffed full up and poking out of you.
Still.

Bleeding, I flip at the end of the length.
Reach, swirl, push, and stroke.

That girl's mom is afraid we'll get eaten by sharks
if we decide for ourselves and throw our bodies
at the waves and into these lanes
to bleed out into the water.

Or maybe she knows

we could be the sharks if we wanted.

A quiet drumming rush of bubbles ahead of me and after me

keeps me glad I can only speak for myself.

Bleeding, I flip at the end of the length.

Reach, swirl, push, and stroke.

I could be a hammerhead.

Wear it like a suit, like my goggles, and cap.

Stretch it over my jiggly self and never take it off

even when I haul out of the chlorine sting of the pool.

I'll have that big hammer for a head,

with eyes out on the edges.

Protuberances.

Bleeding, I flip at the end of the length.

Reach, swirl, push, and stroke.

You know, the eyes of a shark never close

and a shark never stops swimming.

They dream with those edge-eyes open

and see while they're dreaming.

That's what being a girl is.

Swimming without stopping and

seeing the world from underwater.

From the edges.

All while dreaming.

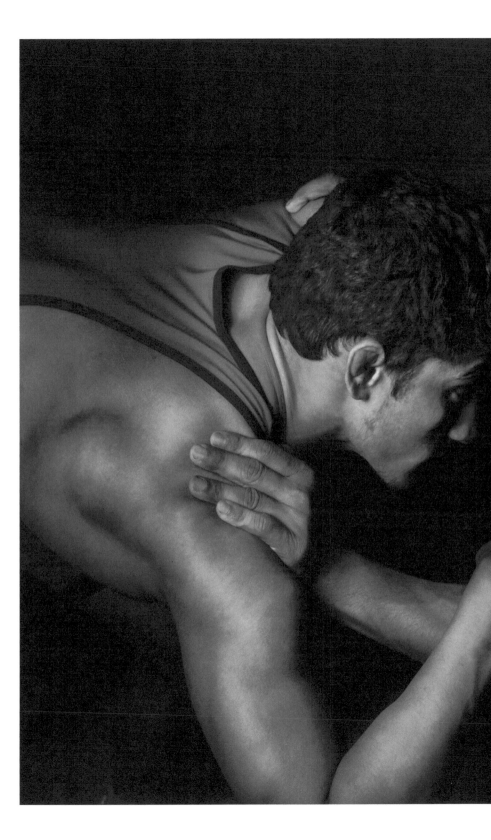

Athletics and Academics
Stacey L. Joy

Spelling any word forward and backward
Slightly slanted cursive and perfect punctuation

Legs straight with fluttered kicks
Head rolls, one ear in water, quick breath, pull

Literature broadens your world view
Mathematics expands opportunities

Count your laps in sets of twos, threes, then tens
Butterfly stroke for strength

Never begin a sentence with *because*
Follow the rules for using I and me

Arms overhead and back straight
Look behind before you jump

Homework is not optional or negotiable
College degrees are generational

Balance on the edge of the board
Bounce three times before touching tips to toes

Teach your children to love sports and school
Go to their games and read their silly stories

In flight, inhale through blue skies
Trust technique and training over fear of failure

Defining Myself
Celeste Trimble

I'm a foot taller than the other girls on my gymnastics team.

My hips, wide. My breasts, heavy. My period, a reality.

I look like a woman beside these elementary school girls,

      But I'm only 15.

Sometimes, when it's my turn, and I pull the springboard away from the vault,

so much farther than the other girls,

I notice my height.

      Maybe I'm too tall.

But when my teammates need help carrying heavy equipment,

and even three of them together can't move a big mat, but I can,

I notice my strength.

      I am powerful.

Sometimes, when I ride my bike to practice, or take a bus to a meet

without my mom driving me, or packing me a snack, or fixing my hair,

I notice my independence.

      Maybe I'm too grown up.

But when Coach asks me to lead the team in conditioning,

Mountain Climbers, Burpees, Frog Jumps, V-ups, Wall Sits,

I notice my perseverance.

 I am a leader.

Sometimes, when I'm tired from staying up late to do homework,

then rushing to the gym after school to teach a toddler class before team practice,

I notice my tiredness.

 Maybe I'm doing too much.

But when I get an A on my test, and my tiny students give me a high five,

and I get a paycheck, good grades, AND first place on the floor exercise,

I notice my determination.

 I am capable.

I am strong and powerful.

I am a determined and capable leader.

I am defining myself.

 I am a gymnast.

A Monster Joins the Track Team
Erin Becker

It's strange attending school
with those who sleep in beds,
not under them.

It's strange to catch words between sprints,
to hear how your name
means *the worst thing you could be.*

Practice was long over,
but I hid in a locker.
The hard dark space
felt swaddling and right.

They were gone,
the teammates who
twined soft curls around fingertips,
who stepped out of showers
with rings on their toes.

I slouched across linoleum.

Crushed metal padlocks.

I had to uncover their secrets.

I had to understand.

Delicate feminine

things felt small in my fingers.

(My hands were notched with knuckles

I now understood as ugly, bulbous, warped).

A pineapple-aloe face mask.

Black glitter nail polish

dark and shiny as sky.

Lacy pink briefs,

more air than clothing,

the most fragile, most perfect thing.

I wanted to learn this language.

I wanted a reason for lacy pink things.

I didn't want to be the monster anymore.

What's the Big Deal?
Anna J. Small Roseboro

Gym class for girls of brown color
Was a regular weekly challenge back then.
You may not remember ... I'll tell you when.
At the school where few of us were students.

No one understood why swim day
Was avoidance day back then.
No matter our excuses, we just couldn't win.
At that school where few coloreds were students.

Back then we wore our hair straightened.
Kinks weren't in, nor was nappy hair.
Making us get wet in pool just didn't seem fair.
At that school where few Negroes were students.

Even when we got perms and wore our hair in curls
Few teachers and classmates understood
Permed hair dried under dryers was not good.
At that school where few Blacks were students.

Our classmates thought we were weird, even brash
With hair in big bushes or shiny bead braids
They didn't understand chemicals or after swim ash.
At that school with few Afro-Am students.

"You're so courageous on the courts and fast on the fields!
Fleet on the tracks and fluid on dance floors,
So why won't you use those muscles and swim?
It can't be your weight. You're both trim and slim!"

They didn't understand when few of us were there.
It wasn't fear, fat or muscles. It was mainly our hair.

IN THE GAME

Give me victory or...

The True Meaning of Football

Play by Play

Learning to Lead

Simona the Runner

At the Summer Court

That Championship Season

Twilight

Runner

Give me victory or...
Chris Crowe

People

fear many things

pain heights flying snakes death

but what terrifies me most is

Defeat

The True Meaning of Football
Chris Crowe

Stadium lights bleed through hot, dusty air as
we kneel around our red-faced Coach.

"Be ruthless!" he bellows.

"Crush your opponent!

"This is what football's all about!"

I swallow his poison, and,

stirred by the crowd's rumble,

I line up for the kickoff like an arrow

notched on a bowstring.

My target: a scarecrow-thin kid

50 yards away.

Our kicker launches the ball deep, and

I explode down the field, locked-in on

the kid who catches it and zigs-zags upfield,

veering toward me.

The space between us shrinks, and

    I lower my shoulder, ready to crush him.

    Just before we collide, he sees me—and he smiles—but

    I

    am

    a

    missile,

    and I ram him with everything I've got.

        He flattens like he's made of straw.

    Air bleeds out of him when we land, something cracks;

    he moans and goes limp.

        What a rush!

    My teammates swirl around me, roaring:

        "BOOM!"

        "You nailed that dude!"

        "Tattoo artist!"

    I am Wired. Stoked. Sky High!

This must be what football's all about.

    Amid the frenzy, Coach yells,

        "That's how you do it! You killed him!"

    Killed him?

        My high falls flat, and a chill shivers me.

    I look, and the kid's still on the ground, unmoving.

    I will him to get up.

    Trainers load him onto a spine-board and, like pallbearers,

    carry him to an ambulance.

        A fog of silence blankets the stadium, and I feel

    no pleasure.

    No high.

    Nothing.

Is this what football's all about?

Play by Play
Glenda Cowen-Funk

We enter the basement gym in
Old Webb City High School,
My father wearing his dark sunglasses,
His red-tipped white cane extended,
Tapping his way to a seat I selected.

Even though he can't see the game,
Can't follow the shadow of my brother,
His son–whose first word was ball–
Running up and down the court in
His prepubescent body, dad insists on

Seeing the game & observing his prodigy.

I sit next to our father on the small bleacher.

Pushing my bifocals up the bridge of my nose,

Clearing my throat, I prepare to call the game.

Prepare surrogate eyes for dad's broken orbs.

I watch basketball as an armchair Fanatic

Witnesses sport from the nose-bleed section. I

Imagine seeing what every dad sees: a perfect baller.

"Ref just called a foul on Steve.

One more and he'll foul out. "

Rising like an aggrieved player cut from the team,

My father's angry remonstration booms across the gym:

"Hey ref, you wanna borrow my glasses." Only threat of

Ejection & the pull of my hand on his arm move

My father to sit & grip his cane in silent surrender.

Learning to Lead
Padma Venkatraman

We came here for you, my parents have told me, ever since – who knows? I can't quite remember. My mother carried me in her womb, my father carried me in his arms, as they got off the airplane. And now I carry their hopes. I'm the eldest. I must set an example. I must study hard. Play hard. Not just do well but excel. They don't say so, but I know so. They left all they loved behind. For me.

We're American now. But when Amma and Appa open their mouths, some people assume they're foreign. We laugh it off, but I see the subtle shift in my parents' shoulders when new coach speaks extra-slow to them. As if they're carrying an extra load. Although Amma speaks English just fine, coach assumes Amma can't understand because Amma "has an accent." New coach does too.

We all do. But I don't say a thing, though I'm boiling, because I'm the star of the soccer team. And that makes Amma and Appa happy. I need a soccer scholarship, too, so I can get to—and through—college. So I keep my mouth shut even when new coach calls my friend and teammate Kavita, whose parents also come from India, my twin, though she looks nothing like me. Nothing at all.

Her hair's straight and long. Mine's frizzy. Her skin's cinnamon. Mine's mocha. She's petite. I'm not. When they play the national anthem before our game and coach moves my hand to my heart, only mine, and Kavitha's, not any of the other girls' hands, just us two, I want to shout, that's not our way – but that's not to say we don't love our country! Did you give up anything to get here? My parents did.

But then at practice, next day, after we run laps around the field to warm up, and stretch and then practice toe touches, and dribble the ball, coach splits us up. "We're going to do something special today," coach says. Coach makes half of us play against the other half. I lead my half-team to victory.

I beat Kavita's team. She grins, though. She's a good loser. Better than me. "Now line up," coach tells the girls who lost, including Kavita. "Bend down." Then coach orders us to "Kick their loser butts." What? I hear a team-mate giggle. No way. This can't be serious. Kavita stares at me. Shocked. "Turn around and bend down," coach tells her. Kavita obeys. Coach tosses me the ball and grins.

What will happen if I say no, I think this is wrong? Will coach kick me off the team? Will this be the end of soccer for me? Will it destroy my chances even of getting to college? I can't let down my parents who came all the way to the land of the free for me. But then I see. If I don't speak up, I'm not being American, like they wanted me to be. So I stand tall. I say, "No." And my team-mates follow me.

Simona The Runner
Valerie Hunter

Simona joins cross country because Kaylee makes her,
insisting they need to expand their horizons, and that a sport
will look impressive on their college applications. Simona agrees
even though she's always low-key hated running. Simona always agrees,
and besides, she's worried that her college application will be lackluster.

On the first day of practice, Coach Montoya says cross country
isn't about being fast, it's about endurance and stamina, about intuition
and knowing the terrain, and, most of all, about knowing yourself.
Simona thinks she knows herself just fine — she's Simona Wainwright,
youngest daughter, straight A student, always doing what she's told,
following other people's rules. Always trying to keep
her anxiety at bay, always pretending she's succeeding.

Kaylee twists her ankle during their second practice and never returns,
even though she's fine by the end of the week. Simona thinks
about quitting, too, but the humiliation of doing that outweighs
the panic she feels at carrying on without Kaylee. Simona's life
is often made up of such choices, of turning her anxiety
into some kind of algebraic equation and figuring out which answer
she can more easily live with, which one will cause her less stress.

In the end, the meets aren't so bad, even the one where
she takes a wrong turn. She doesn't even realize she's lost
until Coach and Elijah come find her, long after the meet ended;
she just thought the course was extra-challenging, had been enjoying it,
actually. Elijah teases her, calling her Wrong-Way Wainwright,
but she just laughs. Afterwards she's more careful, and usually finishes
middle of the pack, respectable, invisible, just the way she likes it.

It's practice, though, that she truly loves. On days they run through
the neighborhoods around the high school, she hangs with Elijah
and Asher. She's had classes with them forever, but now she feels
like she knows them both better. Talking while running is impossible,
but their feet pound against the pavement in unison, a steady, familiar beat.

On days they run in the woods, though, she veers off alone, enjoying
the mud and muck and slippery moss, leaping over fallen trees
and looping around rocks, pretending she can outrun all the stresses
of the day, all the small disappointments and worries, returning
to the school breathless but triumphant, having managed to lose
her pursuer, to escape the pressing anxiety for a while. She likes
getting to know this new Simona, Simona-the-runner,
Wrong-Way Wainwright, and wishes she could be her all the time.

At the Summer Court
Pastel Schway

The sky unfurls strong sunlight hustling

through the loose-ends of my ponytail.

Honey and lemon rays storm the hideout

of my cap's fighting visor.

Bold stark white lines prowl the court

splintering its sovereignty horizontally and vertically.

I run. They stretch slithering as if alive

around my ankles as I move.

My mind darts in and out of smeared strategies

heaved and slapped upon my shoulders

by coaches, assistant coaches, and want-to-be Dad-coach

as I awake to sweat on my bedroom floor,

thinking of all the ways I've sinned

from skipping two practices this month to

pushing planks and ab crunches on a devoured chocolate bar.

I'm still clinging onto my bare back to hold me tall

under the team's lock and cheer,

disappearing into my breath, sparing the spewed smoothie

hidden behind my tennis bag.

I look down one more time from the baseline on the court.

My hand squeezes the dimensional ball —

thinking life could not go on even if

the ball fated to rip the turf of space between us,

the Player and the played,

slamming against two precipitous walls of blurred polyester strings,

could untie the glare between Dad and me, as I

hunger for Instagram and Snapchat, the ways of a normal teenager,

over the molded athlete wavering momentarily

under the season's top ranking.

I lunge forward to return the shot that I honed before I could spell.

My calves burn, those same calves that sacrificed

on the altar of the floorboards repenting

with squats so deep they bent hidden dreams of becoming somebody —

someone Daddy master-minded since I was crated

babbling inside the crib with a foam ping-pong racquet

tied to one small hand,

under a five-pronged,

musical tennis-ball mobile revolving his egos and dreams

that no longer sings.

Then I remember

blood gushing to my head in the mercy of the court's baking sheet

as I chase down my opponent's heated offense.

My ball lands indolently short, and my gut churns like rancid butter.

A roar of applause from the side audience, nothing less entirely,

and it was over.

I turn against the blaring sunlight,

as a morsel of chocolate chip washes bittersweet down my throat.

I count the moments sloshing towards repentance.

My hand raises across the net into the lonely lore

on the other side to congratulate the Player.

The high sun still sits on the afterthought of that vacant sky

wondering if Mom and Dad would still be proud of me.

Walking away from the court

I see now

my chance was never there.

That Championship Season
Lisa Timpf

As one of the rookies on the senior girls' basketball team
I can't take credit for the pennant we've just won —
in the tournament final, I almost blew our lead
with errant passes, the few minutes I played.

My teammates don't hold it against me though,
and to be fair, I made a contribution,
scored some buckets here and there in the early games.
Earning the title is cool, but even more fun

is the bus ride home. Our first-string centre
can belt out the tunes, and our star point guard
has a talent for harmony, and led by their resonant voices,
the rest of us join in as the miles roll by, rendering

a capella versions of "You Are My Sunshine"
and "Hooked on a Feeling" and we are, in fact,
hooked on that feeling of sisterhood,
the sense of teamwork forged by our joined voices

having played as much a role in on-court success
as our coach's strategies. If I could hold back
time's relentless march, I wouldn't choose that moment
when the final buzzer sounded —

stunned disbelief followed by jubilation —
fine as it was. Instead, I'd stay here on this yellow bus
and ride through rolling country roads
immersed in that sweet music.

Twilight
Sandra Marchetti

Some young men play catch
in a field, call each other
on balls and strikes. How
can they possibly know? Dancing
through the grass, one high,
then low, and up again—
just outside! The seams slap
old leather. How can we know
where the strike zone is—imaginary
cube, filament I could not hold
in my hand? I asked, "How can
you tell?" and my father said,
"Watch—you'll learn. You'll know."
They play, rhythmic and swift,
until the young men are gone.

Runner
Nikki Grimes

Side-eyed
I see you in the bleachers
licking your lips
at the sight of my thighs
stunning in their musculature.
I shake out my limbs
at the starting line and smile
knowing you are mistaken
in my body's purpose.
Head smartly on the swivel,
my neck and shoulders
display perfect posture.
The mounds rising from my chest
soft as pillows
camouflage the sturdy heart beneath.
My waist cinches in all the energy
needed to fuel my stride.

I lunge and stretch quadriceps

and calves curved and toned from

routinely carving a line

around this track,

discipline being

the only middle name

I answer to.

My chiseled black arms

are motors of movement

ready to swing in counterbalance

to help lift me off the ground.

My impressive *gluteous maximus*

is more mighty engine than cute caboose.

You've got no clue.

I dig my toes in the dirt

wait for the starter gun,

and explode off the blocks

my destination in clear sight.

Later, boys.

ON HOME COURT

The Player Walking Home from School

Krista Surprenant

Thump,

        thump,

                thump,

an orange basketball

dirtied with its dribbling.

Its travels

that seem to know

its way up to his hand

        like a yoyo tied to a string.

He jogs

down the sidewalk,

dodging defenders.

A quick

        switch,

                swoosh,

                        shift,

left then right

crossover,

pivot,

UP

to his shooting hand.

It rolls off

his fingertips at an imaginary net.

He pauses,

tilts

his ear to hear

the silence

of nothing but net. Then

it drops back

into his palm and the rhythm

beats out the game playing in his head.

Imagined opponents all around,

the sun a yellowy glow like the gym's

floors and fluorescent lights.

The scoreboard counting down

to the final buzzer.

A baller,

his ball,

a concrete sidewalk,

the walk home.

What People See

Ismée Williams

What do people see when they take in
all 6 ft 2 of me,

the bulk of muscles that even a
winter coat
        can't hide,

my skin
closer to Pirates black
than home team white?

When I stand on a mound,
a ball about to fly 95 mph
from my hand,

or over a strip of base,
fists clutching 3 lbs of hard ash,

they cheer.

But on the subway,
even if I'm wearing my baseball cap,
strangers' eyes skitter

to the floor

to the seats

to the graffitied walls,

anywhere

but on me.

Except for you.

You were a stranger

once

on a train

yet you saw

more.

You saw beyond the

menace of this body.

You saw beyond the

promise of my uniform.

You smiled at my words

and cracked open my heart

like a bat striking a ball from the park.

Your small dancer's hand took mine

and you stayed

because you saw

me.

Sixteen
Erin Becker

The story you tell
is you don't like driving.
But really you don't like
him telling you how to drive.

This is why, most nights,
you ride home from track
in the passenger's seat
of your own damn car.

But he's not here
and it's Saturday
and for once
there's no meet,
no team pasta dinner,
no reps in the weight room

and no one to tell you what to do.

You're cruising ten over
just because you feel like it.

You're playing your music
and don't care whether
"the bands on his list are better."

You've got the windows down
because free people don't worry
about messing up their hair.
Highway slopes with horizon,
up and up and up,
rows of green cornfields
as new and alive as you.

Fight
Natalia Sylvester

The day I found my sister's friend
reading my journal on my bed,
I hit him on the head with it
then nailed my overhand serve
by picturing his face on the ball.

After we won
Coach said my follow-through
was perfect,
my strength finally showed.

But I wondered how many times
a girl has to protect herself
just to claim
a victory.

The Drive Home
J.M. Allen

The game just ended, and I did a few things bad.
Now for the drive home, and hearing from my dad.
While he drives the car, he goes over every misstep.
And do I agree with an analysis? I just say "Yep".

On each mistake, I'm told what I should have done.
And it doesn't matter whether our team lost or won!
He hopes he can teach me, and maybe he might?
Just agreeing with him is better than putting up a fight.

It matters so much more to him than it does to me.
He records my game stats for something for him to see.
He has expectations for where my game skills are headed.
But if only dad knew: how much the drive home is dreaded.

Numbers
Sarah J. Donovan

Jersey wet on the basement clothesline,
I yank it so hard the cord snaps; bras,
jeans, and tees fall like leaves and limbs
from a dying tree. Stairs by two, I pull
Number Nine over my sleep-messed bun
calling out for Dad, hoping he's
sipping tea waiting for me--but he's not.
He was my ride to the tourney, I say.
My sister, eating cereal, watching
Saturday morning cartoons, is silent
until the stainless steel of her spoon
clangs in the kitchen sink and she says,
I'll be your ride.

February snow covers the crown of
our American Elm; its twigs bowing from
the weight they carry leave debris to scrape
and she does, as I wait in the passenger seat
wondering if I am missing warm-ups,
wondering if Dad will come,
wondering if she'll ask for gas money.
Slush puddles on the rusted floor of her TC3
as she turns the key and we ride.

Teeth chattering, lips purple. She shakes her
head. A smirk. Turns up the heat, reaches
for a blanket from the back seat. Makes me
take off my jersey, wraps my bare shoulders
in her cloaked branch, a no-sew fleece in
orange and blue. School colors, our roots.
As she covers the vents with Number Nine,
she says, *I thought I'd stay to watch* and
reaching inside her jacket says,
Maybe Coach will let you wear this.
She offers me her dry Number Eight.

Snow days
Laura Shovan

are the best.

No school. Sleep late.

Breakfast in pajamas,

downing Nestea,

hoping practice is cancelled.

Text friends. Play Switch.

How do I get past this level?

Mom calls, "The snow!

Did you forget how to shovel?"

No news about practice.

Catch up on homework.

Help my sister dress up.

In the kitchen with Dad

baking my favorite,

banana chocolate chip cake.

No word from coach.

Hold my breath. Hope
and hope and hope this day
will end with family movie night,
popcorn on the couch,
instead of drilling moves
on a sweaty wrestling mat —
ankle picks, cradles, my arms
and legs trapped in a lock
I have to break. I eat
another slice of cake,
no weigh-ins tonight.
When snowplows rumble by,
Mom checks her email
one last time. "Practice is on.
We've gotta fly!"
Sigh.

A Fencer's Lament
Tamara Belko

In my mind's eye

> A debut nothing short of genius
> Like my brother, gliding across the floor
> Remember me, like Musketeer lore
> Parry, parry repost then a feint
> Electric lunges, thrusts, no restraint
> I'm on fire, just like Zorro

In reality

> A fencing debut disaster,
> nothing like my brother
> Footwork, slow, a lumbering boar
> They will remember me tripping across the floor

and nothing more

Downtown Boxing Gym
John G. Rodwan, Jr.

The canvas covering

the ring tight

in the former car-repair shop's corner

absorbs much more

than blood and sweat.

It thirstily soaks up

anger and angst

fear and funk

desperation and dread

hatred and hurt.

The spiritual descendants

of Joe Louis

(who years earlier

lived and learned

not far from here)

leave it all on the floor

before bowing

between the slack ropes

and walking

beneath the sign advising

"Train Hard"

to glide serenely

down St. Aubin Street –

bobbing and weaving

through the city's uncertainties.

A Girl Like Me
Zetta Elliott

Daddy says boxing is a man's sport

if he thought that would stop me

from getting in the ring then

he don't know me too well

how could he?

Daddy got locked up when I was still

running round the house in diapers

Mama raised us best she could

but these days she needs a drink

the same way I need to throw

a punch sometimes

just to feel alive

boxing is all about control

that's what Coach taught me

I been out here fighting

every damn day

a girl like me

ain't got no choice

but to swing on somebody

just to earn a little respect

can't be soft in these streets

Bre's got a tongue sharp
as a razor and so far that's
kept my little sister safe
but Mama needs somebody
to help keep the lights on and that's
why Jamar got a key to our house
he don't mess with me 'cause he
knows I'll knock out the few teeth
he got left but I think about him and
Bre when I'm beating up that bag
I stay at the gym as long as I can
train hard train smart just like
Coach taught me 'cause I
gotta get my family up
outta this place

Coach been out here for years
looking for a champion
said he never thought
it'd be a girl like me
I'm the only female here
so I spar with the fellas
some of 'em don't wanna dance
but Coach tells 'em to treat me
just like any other fighter

Darnell's different
he ain't scared of getting
knocked down by a girl
and I don't hold back
or try to act dainty
I'm in the ring to win and
don't have a problem
beating up a boy
even one as cute
as Darnell

Coach is determined
to keep us apart
saying I ain't got time
to be messing round
with no boys
he thinks I got a real shot
at making it to the Olympics
I can already feel that gold
medal hanging round my neck
I know I got a date with destiny
but a girl like me still needs a
little love now and then
folks think I'm hard 'cause
I've had to be tough just
to make it this far but
my heart beats and breaks
just like everybody else

for now I just focus

on being unbothered

staying undefeated knowing

that someday all these haters

gonna have to call me the GOAT

I tell Daddy

not to worry 'bout me

after all even Ali

got a daughter

in the ring

OUT OF

BOUNDS

That One Guy
Lisa Timpf

it's the 1970s, and girls' hockey
is unheard of in my home town,
as though the sport by its nature
belongs behind the closed doors
of some exclusive boys' club

undeterred, my female friends and I
don the sweaters of our NHL heroes
and play road hockey, firing tennis balls
at a makeshift goal one of our dads
jury-rigged from two-by-fours
and netting

now and then, I find myself drawn
to weekend road hockey games
contested by the neighborhood boys
on the schoolyard's asphalt

standing on the sidelines, hockey stick in hand,

I watch the players shout and jostle

and there always seems to be that one guy

who asks me, politely,

if I'd like to join the game

and it comes as a kind of unexpected blessing

to see the door to that exclusive club

swing open

I never ask his name

but I imagine, sometimes,

what he'll be like, years from now —

how he'll drive his daughters to the rink

for their practices and games;

how he'll never let anyone tell them

they don't belong

Education. Education. Education.

Bryan Ripley Crandall
Abu Bility
Lossine Bility

We were new to the field, when we arrived – refugee youth & immigrants who fled with others from blowing, bloody sands of Sudan, Somalia, & Liberia. We carried intertwined histories with us, blistered, but ready to be written across national lines with stories often forgotten from the colonial and imperial games of yesterday. Childhoods uprooted...Family members lost...with a chance at life to compose our chapters in a global playbook, *Writing Our Lives* together.

Twins from Liberia, identical, living every breath with hope, while dreaming to gather our 15-year-old selves with *integrity* and a *responsibility* to speak out (aren't we all immigrants?) with this man asking questions. We answer, *Ndoh ah fuuhyenh dee.* "Soccer is life." A recreation that offered peace from Charles Taylor, Samuel Doe, the violent coups of Liberia. We ask him, "You ever hide from bullets? Step in blood? Run in fear from home?" The games are sometimes played without any rules. We wonder if he's seen dead bodies. And he writes...

captures our thoughts to page…helps us to heal memories…listens to every word we say by *writing,* understanding, and fighting with us to have our stories heard. We learn together. "Tell me more about the refugee camps," he prompts, and we recall soccer games played in dirt with footballs we made from taped rice bags, the displaced exercise of immigrants, and how *Makagbeh,* our mother, sold fish, kente cloth, and oranges in the markets of Liberia and Ivory Coast. The men in power wanted to kill, yet she fought to keep us alive.

Sometimes roots cut with a knife sever the blooms of poetry and the joy in life, yet he listens to our music, dances with our words, taps at the keyboard piano as he writes & questions everything that we share. *Sense of Humor. Self-awareness.* We're boys from Liberia who play varsity on a team of 12 nations with a *Focus* to set goals as we practice together. "Type this," we tell him. "The American kids cheat off us…refugee kids, the immigrants, because we do our homework. We stay up late, and study before and after our games."

We read books and teach him how suburban schools are the worst…how we hate those games. Stands full of red, white, & blue parents chanting loudly, "Go back to Africa!" This life didn't leave the struggles behind. Mom works three jobs now - a real hero, an immigrant. She can't watch us play, or she'll lose the money that we need. We tell him to write her story, too, to compose the universe, the stars, the Great Whatever. All of us together, *Ubuntu,* composing collectively beside dusty old books catalogued in a high school library.

And we ask more questions. Find additional sources. Become prouder of our Liberian-American history in the land of milk and honey...this country that lets us be part of the game. Mentors tell us there are three things we need to be successful and they go together: *Education. Education. & Education.* The greatest opportunity we have now in this life is to attend school...to learn...to illuminate darkness with a light for doing what's right. *Huddled masses yearning to breathe free.* Lady Liberty and her sunset gate for immigrants

welcomed us, twins from Liberia, opened her arms, gave us a chance for a better life....an opportunity to play the game of democracy, even as they want history rewritten with hatred upon their walls. *United we stand, divided we fall.* A land of refugees & immigrants.

Hope Wears Our Colors
Joe Bisicchia

Such a world of division.
Us and them.
But maybe both sides might know,
even in this universe seemingly of solitary selves,
all our flags run universal,
stitch by stitch to our fabric, embroidered close.

We are worldwide, and yet huddled here now
vast and vibrant to be seen, even in the narrow.

We may each tie our lace near the Achilles heel,
and be vulnerable to arrow.
But no matter our steel plate,
our fortunes simply rest in the tapestry of us as one.
Let it be this we might remember, amidst our games,
before our any war has begun.

First Heat
Margaret Simon

As sea creatures, we are born to begin
emerging from darkness, swimming toward light.

Emerging as swimmers, we're lighter,
afloat when buoyancy cancels gravity.

Buoyant bodies drag heat through cool water.
We pull backward to move forward.

Push back, move forward, be one with the glide.
Stroke, stroke, breathe, stroke, stroke,

breathe, stroke, stroke, beat a rhythmic groove.
Motion gathering speed, focus on the wall.

Flip at the wall, motion gathers speed.
Water forgets you are stirring it up.

Stirring up water mimics birth.
We begin again as sea creatures.

Seams
Sandra Marchetti

Grip this core
formed to your

hand. Your wrist
snaps elbow, arm,

whips chest and ribs
to pace the pitch's

spin and give,
to settle the grist

in the mitt's crib.

Flip the Script
Melissa Yolanda Bradley

Normal
was on the basketball court
not sitting here
pondering
what used to be.

The headlines
rang out my name
narrating
every game:

Belizean teen,
6' 4"
lightning speed.
No defense
could stop my agility.

Go Ebony
bellows the crowd
as the ball and my heart beat
in unison, stop,
revived by the winning throw.

Popular
what an understatement
every kid dreamt
about my accomplishment

though asking for my signature
is not a thing here.
Cyril Jones
autographed on hearts of
family
friends
and foes.

Imagine me
a Southside youth
daring to dream
would dare to be
DIFFERENT.

Am I destined
to fulfill the judgement
of a society?
Even a pandemic conspires
to limit continuity.

Where are the commendations?
How can I belong
when my identity
is found in the exclamations
of my fans?

Today it is not them but ME
who longs to live
in a world of normalcy.
I miss the praise, the acclamation.
This abduction is no misconception.

I am in this body
living with a stranger
longing for game to
calm my hunger.

A Runner's Impressions
Seana Hurd-Wright

16 years old

I'm not fast enough for

short distance competitions

and that's alright

being a roadrunner never appealed to me.

I was allowed to

join the cross country team,

so I find comfort here.

I stretch until my legs are

rubber bands then

run down Temescal Canyon until

the beach is in sight.

Running along the asphalt

peering at the

wonderful wavy water wondering

"How did I get so lucky

to be at a school where they trust

us to

return at the end of the period?"

Don't need an answer.

Just want time alone to breathe,

to feel the sandy salty air, to appreciate my muscular

calves, to forget about the silly boyfriend,

to process my Sunday School lessons, to figure out which
friends are significant and which aren't.

I daydream about the solo voyage I will take in a boat,

just to be alone in my thoughts.

I remind myself

I'm alright just as I am, as my parents kept telling me.

INTERNAL RHYME

The Girl Who Eats Baseball Cards

Karen J. Weyant

She never swallows the statistics:
the RBI's, the homeruns, the stolen bases.
She only wants to taste the tip
of the bat, the seams of the glove.

With every corner she tears with her teeth,
she imagines the perfect pitch,
or the great slide into home base.
Then, she remembers elbows bent

at bat, or a pop fly bouncing free.
You throw like a girl, her father says,
sounding angry. She wonders
if she has a choice. She rips Mickey Mantle
in two, chews and then spits.

Winning
Linda Mitchell

I've won the Spring Festival prize
A brand new all-road bike
electric blue and shiny all over
two perfect wheels ready to roll

A brand new all-road bike
I wrap the handle-bars with tape
learn to work hand breaks
test the quick-clicking glide
I wrap the handle-bars with tape
lean into everything ahead
test the quick-clicking glide
take off down the street for a ride

Lean into everything ahead
My world expands and speeds-up
past school and church and car wash
I peddle anywhere my legs can pump

My world expands and speeds-up

blocks become miles blurring

I can go anywhere my legs can pump

gear shifts soften the hills

Blocks become miles blurring

edges of town whiz past

I race in a *Tour de Self*

gear shifts soften the hills

I've won the Spring Festival prize

A brand new all-road bike

electric blue and shiny all over

two perfect wheels ready to roll

A Figure Skater's Triolet
Sarah Allen

My core is glacial. Grace and music spin my heart, my feet.

The time it takes to jump from knife to knife

is all my lifetimes, sentience in one beat.

My core is glacial grace. Music, spin my heart. My feet

accelerate to blurs, this one way street

of ice and crystal dreams that come to life

when cores are glacial grace and music. Spin, my heart, my feet.

This — time — it takes to jump from knife to knife.

St. Rita of the Baseball Fields
Karen J. Weyant

Long before you listened to a middle-aged man pray
for a young pitcher's arm, you were the saint

for abused wives, for those aching from illness,
even for the Texan nuns who wanted oil to spray

from a bone-dry, sick well. But now, fans
have christened you the Patron Saint of Baseball,

where you soothe bruised major league catchers
and sore baserunners, cheer for little boys who long

to be the next Mike Trout or Kris Bryant.
They say you guided Willie Mays to his famous

over-the-shoulder catch and that you helped a nun
catch Bobby Thomson's Polo Grounds homerun.

Now you wander through muddy little league fields
and World Series ball parks. They say you are present

for every lucky catch or slide or stolen home base.
In answer to pleas made with rally caps and to prayers

recited with fists pushed deep into worn palms
of gloves, you love every impossible cause.

The Perfect Ball
Dick Altman

Panchos, Gonzales and Segura hit it. So did Rosewall and Hoad. To-day's royalty, Federer and Nadal, rule *perfect's* kingdom. Nadal most of all. Imagine striking a ball with enough force to send it over the net at 3,600 RPM. A ball spinning sixty revolutions a second. Bone-shattering. Fool-making, as you run to retrieve it deep in a corner. Your line to the ball puts you exactly where you need to be to return it. Except it doesn't wait for you. It hits the court and sprints away faster than any human can run. But say you and ball intersect after all. As you and racquet fight to gain supremacy, the ball's momentum deflects your strings for an instant error. Today, though, you feel fast. Your feet have carried you into a five-set final with Nadal. You see with rare keenness. Your anticipation is a blade, cutting off the ball before it bul-lets away from you. The entire first set follows this pattern. Your speed nullifies Nadal's speed. He has thunder in his arm. You have lightning.

Nadal's scowling now, face in rictus, each point life and death. You swing freely, every ball on target, cleaving lines, wrong-footing the muscular Spaniard. So good is Nadal on his best days, and so crushing his strokes, he knows where you're going to hit the ball before you do. Not today. Not when you're playing out of your mind. And Nadal screaming at himself, "*Vamanos!*" after each lost point. Your elation, you realize, after running down hundreds of balls, leaves you rubber-legged. Nadal's string of imperfect balls slowly, inexorably reverses itself. The imperfect once again perfect. The cheetah in you less speedster than sloth. The perfect ball, like the perfect curve, can't miss the strike zone, the lines, the deep corners, the impossible angles. The perfect ball turns your hardest, most deceptive serves into untouchable returns. The perfect ball stuns hand, wrist and shoulder, as if hitting not a thing of air, rubber and felt, but an oversize, meteoric marble of granite that dissects the court with its beauty.

Athletic-Meta-Poetic
Stefani Boutelier

core

gutted letters

coupled in a call

of core-s

strengthen it

choreograph

positioned words

in a dance

sashaying together

perform it

core

stabilize, tempo-ed

lines into stanzas

the heart, hub

nourish it

choreograph

bolero of words

fluid, personal

put a pen on stage

to play with it

the *core* flows

to tell the story

choreographed body

athletic, poetic

art of movement

Depths
nikki fragala barnes

I.

skimming

at the surface you can barely feel

the pieces breaking off — shards and slices

sharp water piecing apart as you fly

holding tension right in between water

and air breathing in, diving under again, and the water pushes

you forward, your body powering in synch

when nothing feels right, nothing makes sense, the questions

sinking heavy, when you return to the water, you fly

II.

free, I close my eyes, counting everything, breaths

out, strokes, turns, laps, pulls, breaths in

I'm not fast, but

I am made for this, all rhythm

and systems in smooth mechanic symphony: breathe,

pull, stroke, roll, flip, breathe, pull, stroke, stroke, breathe

my kicks don't need anything from me, hips powerful and rolling

my feet flow without being told, and all the things I couldn't say and didn't

want to hear, all the times the words wouldn't come, dissolve

in pull, stroke, breathe until the rhythm is me and I save nothing,

hold nothing back, go hard into the wall, and hard out

III.

we return to the water, it bears us, receives us, holds us, carries us,

pushes and resists to make us stronger when we return to the water

uncountable centuries we begin in water, we move with water, surrender

within it, mourn and rise and we still return

to the water -- the way water returns to the earth traversing air and infinity

and we return

to the water breathing in uncountable centuries

A Golden Shovel Tribute to Athletes
Kim Johnson

keep mind, skin, and soul in the sport, even on

some days when the body resists – make

room to persist, cheering yourself through the hoops

in slumps, jump higher to tackle

your hurdles, to bat

heart-stopping grand slam home runs

for the love of the game, with

the grit of a true athlete – discover your

unimaginable power to accomplish the impossible

Note: this poem uses a line from "Evidence" by Mary Oliver as a vertical starter line: keep some room in your heart for the unimaginable

Dear Self-Love
Tanaya Winder

Dear Self-Love,

When I was little you were everything I strived for.
You, the type of love I stretched for with fingertips
gliding towards my toes and feet.
This type of grounding is what I ran for with each step,
each breath soul deep and every lunge forward.
I ran towards you with fists clenched at my sides in stride.
Thought I could be tougher than my anxious mind if I just held tight.

But, I did not know you would be so elusive,
that you'd slip through my fingers every time
I thought I got closer to my goals.
My mind filled with questions and doubt,
wondering why I didn't believe in myself.

So I kept moving. Breathe in. Breathe out.
Self-love is the hardest thing when battling self-doubt.
Keep moving. We do what we can.
Did you know in a day we take over 23,000 breaths?

Breathe in. Breathe out. No excuses, no procrastinating.
The closer I got to you I realized that the power
to change the way I see was always inside of me.
You taught me, "Our minds are a powerful thing,
when we reshape our minds we reshape our lives"

I uncovered you in my mindset.
I undressed myself from all the judgment
and doubt. I found myself covered in the beauty of the journey.
From each lunge, and run, and lift, and breath,
I stretched into everything.

If I work hard and don't judge myself or my progress,
I won't waste any of the breaths I take in a minute or a day,
a race, a game, or a lifetime.
Self-love is a journey and this is mine.

About the Contributors

J. M. Allen's two sons have played organized sports since 1st grade, and stories from both of them (and their friends) gave the author the inspiration for his poems. He is a long-time resident of Rochester, Minnesota.

Sarah Allen is the author of *What Stars Are Made Of* and *Breathing Underwater* (FSG/Macmillan). She is a poetry MFA student in Florida, and has work published in *Cicada, Caterpillar, The Evansville Review,* and more. She was a captain of her high school JV basketball team and was born with Turner syndrome. Find her online @sarahallenbooks.

Dick Altman is a life-long tennis player. His poems have been published widely in print and online, in the United States and abroad. He is a past poetry winner of the Santa Fe New Mexican's annual literary competition.

Kristin Bartley Lenz is a writer and social worker who has lived in Michigan, Georgia, and California. Growing up, her best friends were soccer stars, but she finally found her strength by scaling cliffs. She's climbed and hiked and traveled around the world. Her award-winning young adult novel, *The Art of Holding On and Letting Go*, is about rock climbing, love, and loss, and discovering that home can be far from where you started.

Erin Becker's work has appeared in *Barrelhouse Reviews, Lambda Literary, Ms. Magazine,* and other outlets. She holds her MFA in Writing for Children and Young Adults from Vermont College of Fine Arts and her BA in English from the University of North Carolina at Chapel Hill. Erin lived in Patagonia for many years before moving to Washington, DC, where she runs a communications consultancy and writes *The Storytelling Weekly* newsletter. In her free time, you can find her hiking and running.

Tamara Belko, a middle school English teacher with two left feet, has lived her sports life vicariously through her children. Her oldest daughter was a competitive gymnast. Her son was a fencer, and her youngest daughter dreamed of fencing, but recently decided the idea of fencing was more exciting than actually fencing and has moved on to other activities that don't involve swords. Tamara is the author of the forthcoming YA novel *Perchance to Dream.*

Abu Bility is an educator and Varsity Soccer Coach at Syracuse Academy of Science Charter School in upstate New York. His family fled civil war in Liberia in 1996, then again in 2002 from the Ivory Coast. They found safety at Camp Laine in Guinea. In 2005, his family relocated to Syracuse, where he began attending public schools and played both soccer and lacrosse.

Lossine Bility works as Teen Coordinator with RISE (Refugee Immigrant Self-Employment) and is an Assistant Coach with the Varsity Soccer team at Syracuse Academy of Science Charter School. Like his brother, he played soccer and lacrosse, and is now proud to put his social work degree into action.

Joe Bisicchia is a former television sportscaster who writes of our shared human dynamic. An Honorable Mention recipient for the Fernando Rielo XXXII World Prize for Mystical Poetry, his works have appeared in numerous publications with over 150 poems published. His website is www.JoeBisicchia.com.

Stefani Boutelier, Ph.D. is an educator in Grand Rapids, MI. She taught junior and high school English, Reading, Cultural Literature, and AVID in Southern California before moving to the Midwest. In high school she grew up fighting the stigma of cheerleaders not being athletes. As an adult, her athletic hobbies include running, yoga, and kickboxing. Stefani believes you should strive to move your body every day.

Beth Brody holds an MFA in Writing for Children from Vermont College of Fine Arts. She is currently working on picture books, a YA novel in verse, and children's poetry collections. She won the 2018 Writer's Digest Poetry Award and has poems published in literary journals as well as the middle school anthology *IMPERFECT*. In high school, Beth was not a math nerd but an art weirdo. Math was as scary as sports.

Bryan Ripley Crandall is an associate professor and Director of Connecticut Writing Project at Fairfield University. His 25+ years as an educator benefits from the National Writing Project and Hoops4Hope, an international nonprofit that supports youth communities through sport. With twins Abu and Lossine Bility, and several educators, Crandall initiated programs for young people, including Ubuntu Academy, a summer literacy lab for immigrant and refugee youth, and Let's Do It! A Sports-Writing Lab.

Mary E. Cronin's poetry has been published in the anthologies *Hashtag Queer Vol. 2; If You Can Hear This: Poems in Protest of an American Inauguration*; and in the picture book *Amazing Faces*. The apex of Mary's high school athletic career was playing intramural floor hockey, plus lots of cheering from the stands. A community college educator, Mary lives with her sporty wife on Cape Cod in Massachusetts. She can be reached at www.maryecronin.com.

In high school, **Chris Crowe** participated in football, basketball, and track. After high school, he played football at BYU for four years, graduated with a degree in English, and then became a high school English teacher who also coached football and track. He's now a university English professor who also writes fiction and nonfiction for young adults. His most recent novel is *Death Coming Up the Hill*.

Sarah J. Donovan, Ph.D., a former junior high school teacher of fifteen years, is an assistant professor of secondary English education at Oklahoma State University. Her novel in verse, *Alone Together* (2018), was nominated for a Cybil Award. She loves beach volleyball and always has her Wilson on hand for an impromptu pepper with whoever is willing to join.

Zetta Elliott is the award-winning author of over thirty books for young readers including *Dragons in a Bag* and *A Place Inside of Me*. Her poems have been published in several anthologies, including *We Rise, We Resist, We Raise Our Voices*. Her first collection of poetry, *Say Her Name*, was published in January 2020 by Little, Brown. She lives in Evanston, IL.

Nikki Fragala Barnes, MFA, PhD (*Texts and Technology*, in progress), is a poet-artist and curator. Also an editor (*Obra/Artifact, Journal of Interactive Technology and Pedagogy*), Barnes is an arts activist and community builder, with works exhibited/performed internationally. She began swimming competitively on the high school varsity team and served as an assistant coach before graduating. Later, she was part of the inaugural, award-winning coaching staff for Olympia High School in Orlando, FL.

Glenda Cowen-Funk has enjoyed sports from the stands throughout her life, and spent time competing with her brother to build the best "fantasy" sports teams with baseball, basketball, and football cards. Glenda taught secondary English and speech for 38 years and served twice as the Honorary Faculty Football Coach at Kofa High School, where she specialized in filling water bottles for the team, writing armchair coaching strategies, and composing sports-themed interpretations of Shakespeare titled "The Bard's Eye-View of Football." Glenda loved teaching student athletes and supporting them in the classroom.

New York Times bestselling poet **Nikki Grimes** received the 2020 ALAN Award for outstanding contributions to young adult literature. The author of over 75 books grew up playing handball, baseball, basketball, and running. Female athletes occasionally appear in her distinguished works for young adults including award-winning *Bronx Masquerade, Dark Sons, Between the Lines, Planet Middle School*, and memoir *Ordinary Hazards*, winner of the Printz Honor and Siebert Honor Awards. Ms. Grimes lives in Corona, California.

Valerie Hunter teaches high school English and has an MFA from Vermont College of Fine Arts in Writing for Children and Young Adults. Her stories and poems have appeared in magazines such as *Cricket, Cicada*, and *Paper Lanterns*, and anthologies including *(Re)Sisters, I Sing: The Body*, and *Brave New Girls*. While being spectacularly uncoordinated herself, she is in awe of all the student athletes who so admirably balance sports and academics.

Kim Johnson, EdD., is the District Literacy Specialist at Pike County Schools in Zebulon, Georgia. She is a former distance runner and played softball in her youth. In her free time, she enjoys walking with her dogs on her family farm and writing for her blog.

Stacey Joy, a National Board Certified Teacher, and L.A. County Teacher of the Year, teaches at Baldwin Hills Pilot and Gifted Magnet School in LAUSD. In addition to teaching for over 35 years, she is a teacher leader within her school community. Stacey first leaped into a pool at age 3 and loves swimming. Stacey misses her mom's backyard pool where she, her family, friends, and neighbors swam like Olympic champions for 40 years.

Sandra Marchetti is the author of *Confluence*, a collection of poetry from Sundress Publications. Her baseball poetry appears in various publications, including *Southwest Review, Hobart, Poet Lore, Blackbird*, and *FanGraphs*. Her sports essays can be found in *Pleiades, Baseball Prospectus, Mid-American Review, Barrelhouse,* and *Fansided*. Sandy is on the editorial staff at *River Styx Magazine* and is the Coordinator of Tutoring Services at College of DuPage.

Dennis McGonagle took up running as a way to build up his lung power and overcome asthma. He started with jogging in Whittier hills with his dog and progressed to competing in 5K races. His poem, "Finishing Kick" is based on his experience in the Uptown Whittier 5K. Dennis has competed in street races in Southern California, including the LA Marathon. He enjoys traveling to Ireland and Mexico, where he writes poetry and paints landscapes.

Linda Mitchell is a family girl and middle school Teacher-Librarian who writes when she gets a word in edgewise. Her favorite form to write is poetry. She's published in *Today's Little Ditty volumes 1 & 2* and college publications. Every day is new material for a poem.

Lisa Moore Ramée is the author of *A Good Kind of Trouble* and *Something to Say*. Because of the track theme in her debut, Lisa is often asked if she's an athlete. That's a hard no. Thankfully, her children took after their athletic father and both played varsity basketball and volleyball. It was at volleyball games that Lisa noticed the severe lack of BIPoC, and so she is determined to show Black girls setting it up and spiking it down in a future novel.

Heidi Mordhorst is a poet and PreK teacher working in Montgomery County, MD. Teased as a kid that she was chubby and slow, team sports were never her thing. But Heidi began dancing at an International Folk Dance Club in middle school and found her "sport." She grew up to be a bisexual married to a lesbian and warmly recalls leading the 1996 London Pride Parade with Salsa Rosada, an LGBTQ salsa demonstration team.

Gae Polisner is the award-winning author of several novels for young adults. She's an avid open water swimmer and hopes one day her wetsuit will help morph her into a superhero.

John G. Rodwan, Jr., is the author of *Fighters & Writers* (Mongrel Empire Press) and *Holidays & Other Disasters* (Humanist Press). He wrote the text (poetry and prose) for *Detroit Is: An Essay in Photographs* (KMW Studio). His writing has appeared in numerous anthologies, journals, magazines, and newspapers. He co-produced *No Neutral Corner*, a documentary about the business of boxing. He lives in Detroit.

Anna J. Small Roseboro, a National Board Certified Teacher has over four decades of experience in public, private schools and colleges, mentoring early career educators, and facilitating leadership institutes in five states. She was awarded the Distinguished Service Award by the California Association of Teachers of English and the National Council of Teachers of English. Her poetry appears in several issues of *Fine Lines* and her own publication *Experience Poems and Pictures: Poetry that Paints/Pictures that Speak* (2019). She is also featured in *Centered in Christ*, a devotional.

Pastel Schway resides in Las Vegas, Nevada. She has played tennis since the age of five and has been ranked as high as #63 nationally and #2 in Nevada. Pastel is a published author and has won national and international awards for her novel, *Empire of Embers*. When she is not playing tennis or writing, Pastel enjoys baking and playing with her dog Freddie.

Laura Shovan is a children's author, educator, and Pushcart Prize-nominated poet. Her chapbook, *Mountain, Log, Salt and Stone*, won the Harriss Poetry Prize. Her poetry appears in journals and anthologies for children and adults. Laura has written several award-winning middle grade novels, including *The Last Fifth Grade of Emerson Elementary, Takedown*, and the Sydney Taylor Notable *A Place at the Table*, co-written with Saadia Faruqi. Laura is a longtime poet-in-the-schools in her home state, Maryland.

Margaret Simon lives in New Iberia, Louisiana teaching elementary gifted students. Her first book of children's poetry is *Bayou Song: Creative Explorations of the South Louisiana Landscape*. Her poems have appeared in multiple anthologies for children. Her oldest daughter was a competitive swimmer throughout middle and high school. Six years of attending swim meets informed her poem, "First Heat." Margaret shares her writing on her blog: www.reflectionsontheteche.com.

A former high school English and creative writing teacher, **Kate Sjostrom** now teaches English education at the college level. In high school, she ran on the cross country and track teams and played violin in her school's orchestra. Unable to run since high school because of bone troubles, she now runs only in her dreams — but those are the best dreams ever.

Krista Surprenant has been a teacher for twenty years. Over the years, she has been inspired by her students' strength and perseverance. She has paired her love of poetry and writing as an MG/YA writer. Her relatable characters tackle tough topics such as friendship, poverty, and mental health, and finding beauty and hope in everyday life. She is a mom to three energetic children and spends most of her time in the stands and on the sidelines cheering them on in their games and life.

Natalia Sylvester is the author of the young adult novel *Running* (2020), and a forthcoming novel about an immigrant teen with hip dysplasia who auditions to become a theme park mermaid. Born in Lima, Peru, Natalia grew up in South Florida and the Rio Grande Valley in Texas. Inspired by the women in her family who played before her, she was on her schools' volleyball teams from seventh to twelfth grade.

Lisa Timpf's sports-related poetry has been published in *Aethlon, Third Wednesday, Eye to the Telescope*, and other places. In high school, Lisa was a member of basketball, volleyball, track and field, cross country running, and badminton teams. She has also participated in field hockey, fastball, ice hockey, and ball hockey. You can find out more about Lisa's writing at www.lisatimpf.blogspot.com.

Celeste Trimble was born in Los Angeles, California, and raised by her maternal grandparents on the traditional lands of the Tongva. She studied gymnastics for many years, and was also a gymnastics coach. As a young person she never got tired of reading books about gymnastics, but there were never enough of them! Now she is a professor of literacy and children's literature at Saint Martin's University in Washington State.

Padma Venkatraman is the award-winning author of *Climbing the Stairs, Island's End, The Bridge Home, Born Behind Bars* (2021) and *A Time to Dance* (the first South-Asian-American verse novel for young people). She's climbed Welsh mountains, ice-skated ungracefully, netted several tennis serves, and is in awe of her daughter's soccer skills. Her poems have appeared in *Poetry* magazine and elsewhere. Visit her at www.padmavenkatraman.com, @padmatv (twitter) and venkatraman.padma (ig,fb).

The author of two poetry chapbooks, **Karen J. Weyant**'s poems and essays have appeared in over 100 magazines and journals. As a fan of the Pittsburgh Pirates, she is always rooting for the underdog. She lives and writes in northern Pennsylvania.

Ismée Williams is the critically-acclaimed author of the YA contemporary #OwnVoices *Water in May* (2017) and *This Train Is Being Held* (2020), a Junior Library Guild selection and modern Latinx West Side Story retelling about a baseball prodigy poet and an aspiring ballerina. Ismée is a pediatric cardiologist in New York City and the daughter of a Cuban immigrant. Follow her on Twitter and IG @IsmeeWilliams and her website ismeewilliams.com.

Tanaya Winder is an author, singer/songwriter, and motivational speaker. She comes from an intertribal lineage of Southern Ute, Pyramid Lake Paiute, and Duckwater Shoshone Nations where she is an enrolled citizen. Her work emphasizes "heartwork" – the life path one is meant to follow by using their gifts and passions. She blends storytelling, singing, and spoken word to teach about different expressions of love. Her specialties include youth empowerment and healing trauma through art.

Seana Hurd-Wright teaches upper-elementary aged students and has been teaching for 30 years. She is a National Board Certified Teacher and focuses primarily on Literacy and Writing as an educator. She enjoys walking at the beach and spending time with her family.

Robin Yardi was a high school swimmer and varsity water polo player in Southern California. The rhythmic underwater quiet gave her the space to listen to her own thoughts and find out who she was under the water. Outside those lane lines, she's grown to be a parent, a teacher, and a writer for young people. And she still finds herself in the back and forth quiet of the pool.

Thanks

A very special thank you to high school teachers Katie Currie, Sarah Fleming, Jennifer Jowett, and Trista Owczarzak and their students (listed below) for being a part of the anthology review board. These students read over a hundred poems and shared very honest insights about "good" poetry.

Aaron E.	Blake B.	Dana D.	Joseph M.	Nick H.
Blake J.	Donnie B.	Joshua H.	Nick R.	Abi S.
Eden D.	Judah S.	Noah S.	Aidan N.	Bo J.
Justin R.	Payton R.	Aimee R.	Brad	Kade B.
AJ	Braden H.	Emerson B.	Kaden Z.	Rachel G.
Bria M.	Emilio M.	Kanye B.	RR	Alex C.
Emily F.	Kate A.	Ryan J.	Alex L.	Bryce B.
Katie C.	Rylee B.	Alex W.	Caleb W	Erica J.
Sam P.	Alexis J.	Cali A.	Erynn A.	Kevin E.
Alexis K.	Cam'ron B.	Zhone H.	Kieffer J.	Sam T.
Carla P.	Estefani M.	El R.	Sean O.	Amir S.
Ethan P.	Kya M.	Sean S.	Amirah D.	Carolyn H.

Lionel G.	Shawn M.	Andy G.	Carson H.	Grace A.
Tailon T.	Angel D.	Cesia H.	Grace M.	Maddisin F.
Angela G.	Chloe R.	Hailey G.	Madison D.	Taye
Christina U.	Hannah G.	Marcelly A.	Taylor	Angelo C.
Hannah G.	Marian W.	Tommy K.	Anna S.	Coby L.
Marleny C.	Tommy R.	Annalie C.	Colin W.	Hope J.
Tori S.	Anthony P.	Colten G.	Hoseah R.	Michael R.
Antonisha G.	Cooper B.	India F.	Michael S.	Tyler K.
Courtney K.	Jada D.	Miguel M.	Vada H.	Avery K.
Mike B.	Vanessa F.	Ayelet B.	Jalisha T.	Myshaun
Belle C.	Javaun M.	Nataly G.	Xavier W.	John Z.
Zane M.	Nick G.	Zoe Y.	Jaida W.	Abdullah A.
Ednie A.	Phaidra S.	Aleemah M.	Brigid N.	Eric H.
Sam S.	Amaya T.	Carley K.	Gigi M.	Lucas B.
Tara Q.	Angela M.	Claudia B.	Henry G.	Meighan B.
Travis K.	Ashtin C.	Daejin	Victina H.	Nate J.
Bo B.	Keegan W.			

Acknowledgements

I have spent a lifetime learning to ask for — and listening to — the stories of my students' lives. What I've learned is that the stories we tell in poetry are perhaps the closest to the truth. We hold in lines and stanzas the remembering and reimagining, and in the white space — dreaming and transforming. Every poem is at once partial and complete. I learned this from my students who trusted me with their notebooks, who read their poems during our Friday open mics, who asked me for my poems (it's only fair), and who showed me how the page always welcomes me without judgment, as long as I believed. Thank you, students, for showing me the power of a poetry community. And thank you, my beach volleyball ladies, for all the games in the sun and shadows of Chicago's skyline, for all the reasons you showed up and played hard, and for showing me the poetry of an athlete's life. Finally, my deepest gratitude to the team at Archer Publishing for welcoming a young adult poetry collection to their inclusive-affirming catalog of voices.

SJD